THE FICTION
WRITER'S
GUIDEBOOK

Books by Edwin Silberstang

Novels

Rapt in Glory
Nightmare of the Dark
Sweet Land of Liberty
Losers Weepers
Snake Eyes
Abandoned

Non-Fiction

Playboy's Book of Games
Las Vegas, An Insider's Guide
Smart Casino Play
Play Bridge Tonight
Play Pinochle Tonight
Play Chess Tonight
How to Gamble and Win
Playboy's Guide to Casino Gambling
Playboy's Guide to Craps
Playboy's Guide to Roulette
Playboy's Guide to Blackjack
Playboy's Guide to Baccarat
Playboy's Guide to Sports Betting
Playboy's Guide to Basketball Betting
Playboy's Guide to Baseball Betting
Playboy's Guide to Football Betting
Winning Poker Strategy
Winning Casino Craps
The Winner's Guide to Casino
   Gambling
Silberstang's Guide to Poker
New American Guide to Gambling
   and Games
The Winner's Guide to Sports
   Betting
Winning Blackjack for the Serious
   Player

Winning Poker for the Serious Player
Handbook of Winning Poker
Handbook of Winning Bridge
Silberstang's Encyclopedia of Games
   and Gambling

As J. Edward Allen
The Basics of Winning Poker
. The Basics of Winning Video Poker
The Basics of Winning Keno
The Basics of Winning Roulette
The Basics of Winning Craps
The Basics of Winning Blackjack
The Basics of Winning Slot
The Basics of Winning Caribbean
   Stud Poker and Let It Ride
How to Win at Sports Betting
Winning Craps for the Serious
   Player
Beat The Odds

As Montgomery Coe
The Basics of Winning Bridge

As Whitney Cobb
The Basics of Winning Horse Racing

As Jacob Cantrell
The Basics of Winning Chess

THE FICTION WRITER'S GUIDEBOOK

Edwin Silberstang

CARDOZA PUBLISHING

To Melissa and Stephanie

"The longest journey I ever took was through my own mind."
Henry Thoreau

———————————

First Edition

Library of Congress Catalogue Card No: 96-71753
ISBN: 0-940685-71-X

Cardoza Publishing
P.O. Box 1500 Cooper Station, New York, NY 10276
Phone (718)743-5229 • Fax (718)743-8284

TABLE OF CONTENTS

INTRODUCTION

Like any potential reader of this work, I had dreams of being published, of being a professional writer. Dreams are not fantasy; dreams are capable of coming truc. They did for me, and they certainly can for you. It was not an easy journey for me. Although I wrote short stories and took creative writing courses in college, for twelve years afterwards I did no writing. My typewriter lay on the bottom of a closet in my apartment, unused and gathering dust.

Thinking back on those barren years, I realize now that I was unwilling to test my dream. What if I tried to write and failed? What if my work was useless and would be rejected? Where would I be then, without my dream? Luckily for me, I met a friend who, though he knew nothing about creative writing or literature, knew about human aspirations. He was a psychiatrist, and I met him while practicing law.

He pushed me to write by asking me a question that no one had ever asked me before. "If I could do anything in this world, anything at all, what would I do?" I dismissed the question because I felt that it was an absurd one. After all, what did that have to do with life? But he insisted that it had everything to do with one's limited existence in this harsh world. So I told him I'd be a writer. He then asked me another pointed question. "Why didn't I write?" After all, if I didn't give writing a shot, I would always regret it, and would wake up one day, an old man living on regrets, a sad way to look back on one's life.

I went home that night, dusted off my typewriter and began a novel, a novel that was eventually published. Somehow his questions opened up a floodgate of energy in me; and from that moment on, I became a writer. I don't have to ask any reader of this book the same question he had asked me. I know your answer. The important thing is to confront your dream and write.

This book is divided into two, almost equal parts. The first deals with my life as a writer, and the second part with the art and craft of fiction. This book is a practical guide to writing fiction, whether it be a novel or short story. I wrote it carefully, remembering well all the pitfalls of my writing career, and all the triumphs as well. In the first part of the work, dealing with my life, I show that being an author is more than just putting words on paper. It is an attitude, a way of being, a way of looking at the world and at the human beings who inhabit that world.

I point out that the role of the writer is not to judge, but to understand, not to moralize, but to wonder. He or she must be open to all experience, and must open himself or herself so that no feelings are closed off. In this way, the writer is free to write of the full spectrum of human emotions because these emotions are truly understood and felt.

Henry Thoreau wrote that the longest journey he ever took was through his own mind. There is a sublime truth to that statement, and as writers, we all take that longest journey. It is a voyage of discovery, and as we go into our own minds to write creatively, we learn much about ourselves. It is the best therapy in the world.

When I took creative writing courses in college, none of this was dealt with, but what I have just discussed is more important than knowing what a point of view is, or whether to write in the first or third person. A writer must digest his or her experience and then present it to the world truthfully. You must write the truth no matter how painful it is, in order for others to be moved by what you write. All feelings are universal, whether they be sorrow or joy, loss or gain, heartbreak or happiness. A mother losing a child feels the same pain whether that mother lives in Borneo or in Hoboken, New Jersey.

If you, as a writer, touch this universal chord of feeling, then you will move others, and touching your readers in this way is one of the high points of writing fiction. In addition to the written words, there are other practical aspects to being a writer. In the story of my life, I try and show the self-confidence one needs. A writer is a unique individual, set apart from those who will never test themselves. Many of these individuals are jealous of someone who is creative and will subtly attack the writer's self-confidence.

I show the pitfalls of showing work to friends and amateurs, the dangers of losing faith in oneself, and the dedication necessary to be a writer. I deal with very practical matters, from submitting work to getting an agent to working with an editor. As a professional writer, I have been through everything you will encounter as an aspiring writer. The rejections and failures, as well as the joys and successes, are still fresh in my memory.

I have shared these high and low moments with you as truthfully as I can. I have shown how easy it is to blow an opportunity to get published, and how, if one gives in enough to an editor, a work one is proud of can turn into barren dust.

Before writing this book, I didn't look at other works on writing. I wanted to present what I have learned in thirty-five years, unencumbered by any previous conceptions or misconceptions. I believe my book is unique in several respects.

For one, I have discussed over one hundred writers, both strong and weak ones. I have put in numerous quotes from a number of these writers to illustrate various points. In addition, I have written a good number of illustrative scenes, showing how the first person narrative can be expanded, and how to avoid sentimentality, to give a couple of examples.

I have tried to cover every aspect of writing, from the beginning of the work to the book contract, from point of view to the genre novel, from language and imagery to how long a novel should be, from effective dialogue to the short story market. I believe that this book will be an invaluable tool for the aspiring and beginning writer. It will be a guide that he or she can rely on, and hopefully, an inspiration when his or her energy or self-confidence flags.

My goal is to make you a successful writer, to allow you to open up and touch others, to exalt yourself as a writer. To my mind, there is no finer profession, no other area of human endeavor that touches and moves others like writing fiction. To do this, to move generation after generation if you are fortunate enough to have your work endure, is to achieve immortality. What finer sense of accomplishment is there than this?

My Life As a Writer

I

HOW I BECAME A WRITER

Ever since I can remember, I wanted to become a professional writer. I wanted to see my name on the spine of a book, on the cover of a dustjacket. I wanted to see my stories published in leading literary magazines. I wanted to write, to exalt myself in what I considered the best of all possible professions.

I was an avid reader. When I was eligible for a library card at the age of eight, my mother took me to the local branch and procured one for me. I read everything I could, from boy's books of the time to the Reader's Digest, which my parents subscribed to. It was all the same to me. There were stories to read and I read them. By the time I was fourteen, I was able to travel to the main branch of the Brooklyn Public Library which was located on Grand Army Plaza. It took two trolley changes from where I lived near Kings Highway and East 2nd Street, but I endured the long tedious ride to be among all those books, books I could peruse and take home with me.

Not having any background in literature and not having a family that guided my reading, I was on my own. I still remember picking up a collection of Hemingway short stories and looking through them. There were stories of adolescent boys in the Michigan woods. They entranced me. I took his works home and read them in one fell swoop. A Farewell To Arms, The Sun Also Rises, even The Torrents of Spring.

Hemingway's style was simple. He used the appropriate words and never reached for a literary effect. I devoured his work, stories and novels full of adventure and tough guys, men who lived by a code. The only problem I had was with The Sun Also Rises. No matter how carefully I reread it, I just couldn't figure out what was wrong with Jake Barnes. Why couldn't he hold onto Lady Brett Ashley? In those days I didn't know anything about literary criticism, or where to find answers to the literary questions that puzzled me.

There was really no one I could ask about the novel. In high school, we were involved with Silas Marner and works like that, books that had no relevancy for me, not after Hemingway! In an introduction to one of his novels, there was a foreword by a literary critic who mentioned that Hemingway was a friend of F. Scott Fitzgerald, so I started to read Fitzgerald. This Side of Paradise was the first novel of his I read. Then The Great Gatsby.

Through Fitzgerald I came across John Dos Passos, and I read USA. Then The Three Soldiers. From Fitzgerald, I went to James T. Farrell. The Studs Lonigan trilogy I devoured the way a chocolate addict would run through a box of Swiss chocolates. Three novels about an adolescent and his growing up to young manhood and a tragic death. I loved Farrell's naturalistic style in those days. I read Ellen Rogers and discovered the philosophy of Nietzche, espoused by the main male character, whose name I can't now recall. Later on I used a line that he had used in the novel. When I was at a dance in college and asked a coed to dance with me, and got the reply "I'm not dancing with anyone," I told her "I'm not anyone." She didn't dance with me despite this retort, but she did give me a long questioning look which was worth the price of admission.

I lingered a long time with Farrell. I read the entire Danny O'Neill tetralogy, and was floored by My Days of Anger. Here was a book about someone like me, a loner, a boy lost in books, with literary aspirations. Today I collect the works of

Farrell, especially his first editions. He's difficult to read seriously now, and I see his flaws, especially the overwriting that came of his naturalistic style, but in those days he was my guardian angel.

So I kept reading, getting hints in prefaces and forewords of whom to read. Thomas Wolfe, John Steinbeck, even William Faulkner, who was tough to read for a boy of 14 or 15. But I kept at it. I read my way through modern American literature in the big library. When I graduated at sixteen from James Madison High School in Brooklyn, I enrolled in Brooklyn College. It was 1946, the year after the war ended, and it was tough getting into college with millions of veterans enrolling at the same time.

I majored in English at Brooklyn College, and spent a year there before transferring to the University of Michigan, drawn there by the Avery Hopwood writing awards. My family had little money in those days, having still been badly bruised by the Great Depression. But tuition was cheap and I held three jobs at once in school, and washed dishes and mopped floors at the local co-op so that I could eat a week's meals for $5.

What floored me about Michigan was the huge library. Not only was I entitled to a library card as a student, but I had stack priviliges, something I had never been aware of. I could roam the stacks without going through a librarian and pick up whatever books I wanted to read. And I read everything I could find. Michigan had a more varied student body than Brooklyn College. There were students from every state in the Union and practically every country in the world. I met geniuses who were studying Russian to read the great Russian writers in the original. I was turned on to Tolstoy and Dostoievski, Turgenev and Chekhov.

From Russian literature, I expanded my horizons. I read Proust and Balzac, Thomas Mann and Stendhal. I didn't read these books for class assignments, but for my own pleasure. I majored in English, and usually had read the entire required curriculum before classes began. I was bored with most of the classes. I started to realize that the instructors depended upon literary critics to fashion their opinions. Once the critics were quoted by the professors, the students were expected to write down their commentaries and regurgitate them back at exam time.

So I read the critics, and often disagreed with their opinions, and tried to show this disagreement in class. But the class would usually become bored and impatient if I interrupted the teacher's droning lectures. The students wanted to get on with it; they wanted to write notes to study later for the exams. It was at this time, when I was eighteen, that I discovered poetry. I picked up a copy of Oscar Williams' Anthology of Great Modern Poetry which served as my introduction to the great American, Irish and British poets of the Twentieth Century. From there I studied the older poets and especially Shakespeare.

I went to Michigan in great part because of the Hopwood Awards, which were open to the students. Having done all this reading, and having taken a couple of creative writing courses, I wrote a play and submitted it for the playwrighting award. I lost, with good reason. I also started to write short stories and sent them out to magazines like Esquire and The New Yorker. All were rejected. Looking back at this experience, I realize that there is a vast gulf between doing prodigious reading, even of the classics and fine literature, and writing. Writing is a craft and an art. Before it can be art, the craft must be mastered. I had not mastered the craft, and more importantly, I hadn't opened up myself to be a writer. I was young and impatient, but without any real experience of the world, especially the inner world of feelings. As Henry Thoreau wrote so succinctly– "How vain it is to sit down to write when you have not stood up to live."

The creative writing courses I took at Michigan were useless. Students read their work aloud and the work was criticized, but the pure essence of what it means to be a writer was never discussed. And this has nothing to do with the words on the paper, as I later found out.

In my senior year, my father, who was a struggling lawyer in New York, had a long discussion with me. What was I going to do with my English degree? I didn't want to be a teacher, just a writer. How was I going to make a living? He suggested that I have a profession, and since I had no interest in science, medicine was out of the question. Pushed by his meaningful intentions for my future, I took the law aptitude test one Saturday in my senior year, missing the Michigan-Indiana football game. I did very well, and told my father I would apply to only three law schools, Harvard, Yale and Columbia, the three finest in the land. If one accepted me, I'd go to law school, otherwise I would try and hack it somehow in the wide world, with my dream of becoming a writer intact.

I knew I had no chance of being accepted. I hadn't taken any pre-law courses. So I was shocked when Columbia Law School congratulated me on my acceptance. And following graduation from Michigan, and working a summer in an olive and marachino processing plant in Coney Island, I entered the hallowed halls of the law school.

The professors were brilliant and debonair, but I had no real interest in law. In those days I was under the illusion that overcoming difficulties was the road to success. Today I know better. Go with your talent; the road will then be paved with success. I staggered through a semester, bored and unable to get interested. After the semester I transferred to graduate school in English, but that bored me. I wanted to write, not get a Master's. It was now 1951 and the Korean War was raging.

I was 1-A and didn't ask for a student deferment. The army seemed a better choice than Columbia. I would test myself as a man in a war. I served my two years, not going overseas but spending my time as a special agent in the CIC, the Counter-Intelligence Corps. It was fascinating work, and I look back at my army days with thankfulness. I avoided combat in Korea only because of the cease-fire engineered by President Eisenhower. A lot of things happened to me during my time in the army. I married and when I was separated from service I had a son and another child soon was on the way. I didn't do anything for several months as a civilian except some work as a real estate salesman, then I started law school, this time enrolling in Brooklyn Law School.

The three years I spent there are but a blur in my memory. I had two, then three children; I worked full-time during the day and went to law school every evening the year around. I had an unhappy marriage. My dream of becoming a writer was now pretty well buried. After I passed the bar exam, I went into practice with my father, another in the long line of mistakes I was making in those days. I was admitted to the New York bar in 1958, and my practice at the beginning was a general one, since we had a streetfront office in Borough Park, Brooklyn. Because my father also had a real estate broker's license, I began to specialize in real estate law, handling contracts and closings, sometimes three or four a week. And other work came in.

In the course of a day, I would write a will, file complaints in auto injury cases, meet with a Mafioso to discuss an upcoming trial, dictate bills of particulars, and so forth. And of course there was the real estate work. I was buried in the practice of law. Years went by.

In 1959, after seven years of marriage, I moved out of our house in the Manhattan Beach section of Brooklyn, and moved into a small studio apartment about a mile away. It was a devastating time for me, leaving three children, but I managed to see them every weekend. When I was divorced, all I had from the marriage was a duffel bag full of clothing. I started fresh.

I moved from time to time, each time going downhill. Now I realize that the places I was living in reflected my attitude toward life. I began seeing a woman seriously, but she was just a mirror image of my wife. We broke up, at a time I was living in a basement room. I was touching bottom in my personal life. From there I moved into a newly built apartment house in the Flatbush section of Brooklyn. I now had a one-bedroom apartment, with some decent furniture. But still I was lost.

I continued to practice law, feeling more and more tension and pressure. Even though I was living alone, I didn't attempt to write. I didn't even want to think about writing. I saw myself as a failure, just another of the millions of New Yorkers buried in dead end work. I was earning more money now, but my days were filled with tension and despair. There was no purpose to my life.

The sixties came. In 1962 I was thirty-two, and then my life changed. A chance meeting resurrected my dream of writing, and turned my entire life around. I represented a speculator in real estate who owned some property in Crown Heights, an area of Brooklyn not far from the public library on Grand Army Plaza. At that time Afro-Americans were moving into the area and I arranged a contract at my office for the sale of one of his buildings.

The purchaser was a black man about my age. He came with an attorney, and we were introduced. His name was Albert Crum. Now, in New York, real estate is a complicated matter. In California, where I reside, the contracts are standard forms, money is deposited with an escrow company, and after a mortgage is arranged, the purchaser goes to the escrow company and gets the keys to the property.

But in New York in those days, each real estate transaction was a complex affair. The contract was prepared by the seller's attorney and given to the purchaser's attorney. Mistakes could cost a client hundreds and sometimes thousands of dollars. The purchaser's attorney in this matter didn't really know real estate. That was crystal clear to me. So I took him aside and asked him subtly if he was going to object to several clauses in the contract I had prepared. He stared at me blankly, then said he was.

We sat down again, and he objected, and we reached an agreement. All this time, his client watched the proceedings carefully, bent low in his chair and going, "mmm, mmm, mmm." The contract was signed by both parties, and the signature of the buyer was Albert Crum, M.D. We all shook hands cordially, and I wished Dr. Crum luck with his new home.

I went on to other matters, forgetting about this particular deal. A mortgage was the responsibility of the purchaser, and when one would be arranged, we'd have a closing, another meeting, this time with a representative of the bank and a title company. I had all kinds of deals in the pipeline like this. This was nothing extraordinary. But about two weeks after the contract, I received a call from Dr. Crum.

I got on the phone, and after he introduced himself, I explained to him that I couldn't really discuss the matter with him personally since he had an attorney, and that he should have his lawyer call me. But he didn't want to talk about the previous contract. He wanted me to represent him in the purchase of another piece of property. It was a bit surprising, but I agreed, and we arranged to meet at 120 Broadway in the Guaranty Trust Building to discuss the deal. We agreed to meet the evening of the contract, and go over the deal.

I would have preferred more time to discuss the matter, but he was a doctor and busy, so the next evening I entered the lobby of 120 Broadway, and there he was. The amazing thing to me was how he broke into a broad smile when he saw me. He shook my hand warmly, and asked where we could sit and talk. There was a restaurant in the basement of the building and we went down there to have a drink and talk about the deal.

He filled me in roughly about the property, but he was more anxious to talk about other things. He asked me all kinds of questions, how long I had practiced law, did I enjoy it, and so forth. And he told me a bit about himself. He was a graduate of Harvard Medical School, only one of two blacks in his class. The other was a Nigerian prince. He was now at the Psychiatric Institute connected with Columbia Presbyterian Hospital, finishing his residency in psychiatry.

We talked for about an hour, then went up to the attorney's

office and I handled the contract. This property was a block away from the other one he had bought, and now I realized he was purchasing property as an investment. After the contract, instead of saying goodbye, he insisted that we go down to the Village and have a late supper. We sat and ate at the Derby restaurant on McDougal Street and he asked me more questions about myself. Albert insisted that we meet again, just on a personal, friendly level.

He was an interesting guy, fascinating in his knowledge of psychology. He seemed more insightful than anyone I had ever met before. And he seemed to have an endless interest in my life. Here I was, in a life I hated, with no prospects for any kind of personal success, and this graduate of Harvard Medical School was treating me as if I was an interesting person. I just couldn't understand this. It turned out he was an only child, and that his mother whom he adored, had recently died, I guess he saw in me the brother he never had. I had no brother either, just a younger sister. And there we were.

He would call me every day at the office, and arrange for a dinner or a meeting over a drink or two. Even though I was swamped with work, and he was a busy man, we managed to meet.

He told me of his interest in paranoid leaders of the world and how he was going to do a book on them. He pointed out that Alexander the Great, Napoleon, Hitler and Stalin all had several things in common. For one thing, they all ruled countries they weren't natives of. Alexander ruled Greece, though he came from Macedonia. Napoleon was Corsican and ruled France. Hitler was Austrian and Stalin was Georgian. And all were men of short stature, whose fathers played no real role in their lives. Their mothers had been bigger influences.

He would also talk about feelings, and how to open oneself up to inner feelings. The easiest way to know if you were liked by someone was not to try and fathom the other person's feelings, but to study your own. If you liked someone, Albert explained to me, then that person liked you. Feelings were not in a vacuum. I argued that there were women I liked who didn't like me, but he told me I hadn't really opened myself up in those situations. If I was aware of my feelings, I would sense the lack of warmth on my part. I would be aware that nothing good was happening.

We would sit and talk for hours. It was if a window was opening in my soul, and for the first time I was becoming aware of things I had never known existed. I now tried to keep in touch with my feelings. I watched other people for reactions. I watched myself. I was getting to feel more confident, more aware of what was happening around me, and in my life.

One evening, sitting in a restaurant late at night in the West Village, Albert idly twirled his glass and then looked me in the eyes.

"Ed, I'd like to ask you a question."

"Sure."

"Now I know you're busy and everyone seems to think you're a successful lawyer, but I see something else. Forgive me for being personal, but there's a deep unhappiness in you. Am I correct?"

"You're right. I won't disagree."

"You told me once that you really didn't care that much about practicing law."

"It's a living. I have a family to support."

"Well, let me ask you a question. Ok?"

I nodded.

"If you could do anything in the world that you wanted, what would you do?"

"What do you mean?"

"Just what I said." He narrowed his eyes. "I mean, if it was in your power to do anything in this world, what would you do? What would exalt your life?"

"You mean, do anything I wanted to do?"

"Absolutely."

"Albert, what does that have to do with anything? You're talking about a dream world."

"No, I'm talking about what you would do with your life. That's what I'm talking about. Because if you avoid doing that, then one day you'll be old and you'll wake up and regret that you never took a chance. That you never gave life its' best shot. But it'll be too late then."

"You want to know the truth?"

"Yes," said Albert.

"I'd be a writer."

"A writer?"

"Yes, I'd write a novel."

"No shit. You know, we've known each other a couple of months now, and you never even mentioned writing."

"Well, you asked me a question, and that's my answer."

"Why don't you write?"

"Albert, I work fourteen hours a day as it is. I'll have to get up early tomorrow and get out a couple of contracts, then appear in court on some motion for summary judgment. I don't have the time. I'm buried with my work."

"I see. But, Ed, we see each other about five times a week. We've gone to a couple of parties together. Surely there's some time you could set aside for writing."

"There's time. But I'm exhausted mentally at night."

"Just a little time. If you wrote a page a day, that would be 365 pages a year. That would be a novel."

"It's not that simple."

"I'm not saying it's simple."

"I don't even have a ribbon on my typewriter at home."

"What?"

"I have this old Royal portable I bought in college. It's in a case in my closet. The ribbon is shot."

"The ribbon? How much can a ribbon cost?"

I shrugged.

"Jesus, Ed, I'll give you a buck for a ribbon."

"It's not that, it's everything."

"No...No. I know you lead a hard life, but if you wrote, if you had a dream to fall back on... that would make a difference. I know you would write a good novel. You're an interesting person. I just don't spend my time with anyone. Ed, there's more to you than you imagine."

No one had ever told me that, or asked me what my dream was in life, and encouraged me to fulfill that dream. No one, not my parents, my friends, my relatives, no one.

"I'll think about what you said, Albert."

"Think about it. Let's get going. I have to present a case at the hospital tomorrow."

We left the restaurant and got into our separate cars. I drove back to Brooklyn, to my apartment on East 8th Street. It was a little after eleven in the evening when I opened the door to my apartment. I went to the bedroom and hung away my jacket and coat, then went to the bathroom and washed my face. I was tired, and my face showed it. I dried myself and went to the kitchen and put on some hot water for coffee, then, when it was prepared, I sat down at a small table in the dining area.

I was thinking about the conversation with Albert. Yes, my dream was to write a novel. A novel about what? I must be just one of the thousands in New York who told themselves that someday they'd write a novel and get published and get famous. It was a joke, really. Write a novel...huh!

I got up abruptly and went to the hall closet, where my typewriter, unused for about ten years, lay quietly on the floor under a box holding my vacuum cleaner. I picked up the box and released the typewriter. It was in a yellow carrying case, whose top could be removed, leaving the typewriter intact on the bottom section of the case.

I dragged out the typewriter and put it on the table, and took off the case. There it was, this little Royal that I had typed my term papers on at Michigan. That I had written some inept short stories on. Everything creative from this typewriter had been doomed to failure. I looked around for some paper, in order to test the ribbon. I found a packet of yellow cap I had taken from the office for notes, and inserted a sheet of the yellow paper. But instead of typing "the quick brown fox," I typed this instead:

"Benny Katz stepped into his apartment and shut the door wearily. His wife, lying on the couch, smiled at him. Such a pale smile, he thought, she's so pale. He walked over and kissed her lightly on the lips. He bent and kissed her forehead, and sat down beside her, nestling her head in his lap. Without speaking to her, he patted her hair, smoothing it out with long strokes of his hand."

I stopped typing and looked over what I had written.

Where had this come from? Who was Benny Katz? It was all a mystery to me, but I kept typing. I typed on and on, single spaced. After a while I was finished. I had typed a full chapter. I got up and walked around, and then sat down again and read what I had just written. It seemed weak, inane. What did this couple have to do with anything that was going to happen? I took the pages and dropped them into a wastepaper basket, but I didn't go into the hallway of the building and drop them into the incinerator.

I went to sleep and the next morning, I showed up at my office at seven. I had some work to do, and then I headed for downtown Brooklyn, to Schermerhorn Street and the County Court building there, which was the criminal court in those days. Today, it is known as the Supreme Court. I had a motion to argue in a criminal case and had plenty of time to kill, since the judge was late and there were several cases before me on the court calendar.

I sat in the vacant jury box, and opened my briefcase, taking out a pad of lined yellow paper. I wrote this in longhand using a ballpoint pen:

"All the seats on the benches of the County Court, Part IV, courtroom were filled, mostly by women who looked apprehensively at each new arrival and sat stolidly, awaiting their man's turn before the judge."

I continued to write by myself. Near me several attorneys were talking in low voices, and an assistant district attorney came in and was conferring with two other lawyers. I kept going. I introduced a character named Roger Brunardo, appearing before the court on a charge of assault with intent to kill. The complainant doesn't show up and the case, which had been adjourned several times because of the complainant's no show, is dismissed. Brunardo, a big vicious man, leaves the courtroom, and goes to a bar nearby and meets James Fusari and they discuss a robbery of a drug store on Ocean Parkway in Brooklyn. I had based the character of Brunardo vaguely on a friend of mine, Pete Matarese. There were similarities in their toughness, but Pete was a good friend of mine.

I recalled a night when I was about fifteen and sitting with a couple of friends on a bench on Ocean Parkway. It was late at night and we had been goofing around, when suddenly we were surrounded by a bunch of toughs from Avenue U, a breeding ground of would-be Mafiosos. There they were with baseball bats, and my two friends and I just sat there, paralyzed with fear. We knew what those bats could do.

Then, as though Superman had descended from the sky, there was Pete Matarese. He had recognized one of the bat holders, a guy named Tony Balls, and had stopped his car. Then he spotted me.

"Hey, Tony, that's a friend of mine. Leave him alone."

Tony was a little slow on the uptake. Pete had gotten out of his car, and he grabbed Tony's bat and whacked Tony across the back of his knees. Tony went down like a shot.

Pete turned on the others. "Get the fuck out of here," he commanded, "and I find you bothering my friend again, I'll take your fucking eyes out." That was Pete at his angriest. He stood about five ten, but had shoulders that barely could fit through a doorway.

I wrote the whole chapter sitting in that empty jury box, and soon afterwards, my case was called. I stuck the pad back into my briefcase, argued my motion, and left the courtroom, driving back to my office. I worked through the day, left the office about seven that night, got something to eat in a local

Italian restaurant called Gragnano's on McDonald Avenue, and went home.

I washed up, and went to the typewriter on the table. The first thing I did was pull out the original chapter from the wastepaper basket and then I put the writing I had done in court underneath this. I had two full chapters involving three characters and I still didn't know what the story was about. I thought about my creative writing courses in Michigan and about articles I had read on occasion in writing magazines. An outline was necessary for a novel, with a chapter by chapter synopsis.

But I didn't know what this story was about or where it was leading. Instead of writing an outline, I sat down at the typewriter and typed this:

"Frank Sheehan ducked out of the rain and into Joe's Restaurant and, standing just inside the doorway, wiped his face and hair with a handkerchief. It was a hot Friday evening in May, and Joe's was already half filled with lawyers, politicians, and court officials from the nearby municipal buildings of downtown Brooklyn. They sat in groups at the large, white-covered tables, speaking in hushed tones. Cigar and cigarette smoke permeated the air, and the waiters, clad in long white aprons, moved about their tasks noiselessly."

Frank Sheehan is a detective and he is there to introduce his friend, Tom Fusari, to a commissioner for an appointment to the Brooklyn DA's office. Tom Fusari is the older brother of James Fusari. Again, I wrote a complete chapter, and then put it next to the other completed chapters. Where was this book going? What did this have to do with what happened before?

Up to now, the three characters were connected. Brunardo and Fusari were going to rob the drugstore and use Benny Katz as the getaway driver. But now the story was getting more complicated.

From then on, I found myself writing to find out what would happen next. I had no idea where the story was heading, or what the outcome would be. In order to find out what happened next, I wrote the scene. And I kept on and on, working late each night, going to the office more exhausted than ever.

I saw Albert rarely now, for the idea of writing had overwhelmed me. I worked away, and now, instead of feeling like a failure, I felt as if I was one of the few people in New York with some purpose, while everyone else was milling around, doing nothing. For the first time in my life, I had a purpose. I was exhilirated, and at the same time I was thinking, what am I writing? What if this is all drivel and nonsense. I happened to be reading Light in August, by Faulkner, and thought, what is my puny story set in Brooklyn worth, compared to his powerful writing?

I told Albert about my worries.

"I'm not familiar with literature," he said, "and I don't know who Faulkner is, but why is his voice more valid than your voice?"

I pondered his statement. It was true. My voice was as valid as Faulkner's or anyone elses' voice. I could trust my voice.

Then Albert said something else.

"Why are you reading Faulkner? It sounds destructive to me. First you're comparing yourself to him, and then you may be imitating him. Don't read another writer while writing."

These statements were words worth their weight in gold, told to me not by some creative writing instructor, but by someone unfamiliar with literature. But instinctively, Albert knew the truth.

Finally, I told him my fears about the novel I was writing. Who would be interested in it? Who would really care about these characters?

Albert immediately said, "Are you interested in these characters?"

"Yes."

"If you're interested and you put them truthfully on paper, others will have the same interest. You don't write in a vacuum; you're part of the human experience."

"Trust your vision, and your voice and your instincts. They won't fail you if you put down the truth."

More words of wisdom, words that freed me up to continue writing the novel and propelled me to finish the book. Albert knew something that no one else had ever articulated to me, nor had I read it anywhere in all the articles by so-called teachers of writing. Trust yourself as a writer.

What did he mean by the truth? Now I realize that we don't always know what the truth is, but we know when we're not writing the truth. When we put down feelings that aren't really true, but would please the reader, then we're not telling the truth. Later on, I started to see the difference between dramatic truth and the truth of life. We can use a dramatic truth, that is, an invented situation, when it makes the work stronger, when it adds to the narrative drive of the story or novel.

For example, if we merely follow a character's actions where nothing really happens, the story dies. But if we add a difficulty to overcome, or a danger, then the story takes on interest. That is a dramatic truth as opposed to the truth of life. Tension and unresolved conflicts are the heart of good writing.

I kept working on the novel, watching my characters take over the story. I learned that the best way to write is to create interesting characters and let them loose on the pages. They led me; I didn't lead them. I didn't really need an outline–it took away from the tension of the story. With an outline I would be bound by a plot that was formed in cement. Without an outline, I was free to have unexpected events occur, events that even astonished me. And so the novel marched on.

When I had completed about 100 pages, single-spaced, I called Albert and asked him to listen to the last chapter I had written. Up to that point, I hadn't shown or read the work to anyone. Now, I was dying to get a reaction. But he refused to listen to the work.

"I'm your friend," he said. "If I say it's good, it'll mean nothing. I want it to be good. And if I say it's bad, then you'll be crushed. My opinion is worthless. I think you ought to complete the novel without showing it to anyone. Just keep writing. What difference does it make what anyone thinks about it. The important thing is what you think of your work. Forget about showing it to anyone."

How wise those words were! In the course of teaching creative writing and working with aspiring novelists, how often I've seen them get discouraged by showing their ongoing work to others. A friend would criticize the story and they would lose interest. Showing work in progress to non-writers, to non-artists, is not only a waste of time, it is destructive.

The other side of the coin is the praise that non-writers might heap on the work. I've heard the same refrain over and over from would-be writers. "My friends loved the story (or novel). I can't understand why it keeps getting rejected."

Friends' criticisms are worthless. The writer must have the discipline not to show the work to outsiders. Of course, if he or she is in a workshop, the work can be read and criticized there. But too often the writer needs praise and shows the work around. What is a friend going to say but, "Yes, it's wonderful." What is that statement worth? Less than nothing.

Before I had begun the novel, I had made plans to go to Europe for the summer. It was my first trip there, and my travelling companion was Ray Reiman, a dear friend from the Army. So I put the novel away and took the trip, which formed the basis for my second novel.

When I came back, I continued to write. But the interruption had taken its toll. I couldn't write at the same pace. Days went by before I could put anything on paper. I was stuck with the novel, not knowing how to proceed. While writing, however, I felt more in touch with my feelings. I had become all the characters, and each possessed parts of me. I was open to my unconscious, and one night I had a vivid dream, involving a trial.

I awoke excited. Yes, that was it. The climax of the novel would be a criminal trial. It was crystal clear where the novel was going. So I perservered. Events led up to the capture of one of the three main characters, Roger Brunardo, and his trial for murder. Then there was the trial.

I was back at my original pace. And one night, a night I shall never forget as long as I live, I finished the novel. It had all been written single-spaced on that yellow cap. Now there was nothing more to write. My dream had come true. I had written a novel!

It was early in the morning. I paced around my apartment excited. Done. Finished. Edwin Silberstang, the author of a novel. A completed novel. I had separated myself from the thousands of would-be novelists, by actually writing and completing a novel. I have been a writer now for thirty-five years, but the thrill of that moment stays with me. I can honestly say it was the highlight of my life. I called Albert despite the hour. I told him the news.

He was excited as well. He asked me to read the final chapter to him over the phone. I read it, and then waited for his reaction.

"It's very strong," he said. "This book will be published."

I stayed awake the rest of the night, and showed up at the office haggard but full of joy. My father was worried about me, because the writing was all done at night, and I had few hours sleep weeks at a time. I hadn't told him or my mother or sister that I was writing a novel. It was a secret between Albert and me. So many aspiring writers tell the world about their novel in progress, to the point where the idea of writing becomes more important than the work itself. They want to be praised…"Oh, see that guy, he's writing a novel."

I didn't need praise. What I needed now was to get the novel in manuscript form suitable to send to an agent or publisher. In those days there were no Xerox machines and I hadn't made a carbon copy. The whole novel sat on a table in my bedroom. If it was lost or destroyed, it would be gone forever. I had no idea of which agent to send it to, or if I should send it directly to a publisher. That would wait, I figured, till it was retyped by a professional.

II

GETTING PUBLISHED

My cousin Leila was in the garment business with her sister, Ruth. Both were daughters of my mother's oldest brother, Jacob, who had died at the age of 46 of a heart attack, in my mother's arms. His death had been a crushing blow to her and to my grandmother, who mourned her eldest son the rest of her life.

Leila was sixteen years older than me and was also my godmother. I was handling a matter for her and asked if she knew of a typist that I could use. I told her I had written something and wanted to get it into usable manuscript form.

"I have just the person for you," she told me. "I have a friend who's a widow, who types from her home and could use the work. Here's her number."

I copied down the number and called the woman, whose name was Joan. I made an appointment with her for the following evening. She lived just north of Greenwich Village, in a fairly new apartment house. I brought up only twenty pages with me, since I was paranoid about giving up the entire manuscript to a stranger. We agreed on a price, by the page, and I left the work with her, telling her I'd call in a couple of days to see how it was going.

When I called, she told me she'd be finished by the next evening, so I trudged up to her place, bringing twenty more pages with me. She was a competent typist, and had bought twentyweight bond paper for the job, which I paid for as well. There were a few typos but otherwise the work looked good, so I left the additional twenty pages with her.

I brought the work with me to the office the next day, so that I could read it over carefully and correct it. That evening I had an appointment with an attorney named Alan Vuernick, who represented a woman seeking a divorce from one of my clients. My client, whom I'll call Tony, was a hairdresser who had come to me the week before. He was obviously gay, and I was surprised when he told me he wanted a divorce from his wife.

"What's the problem?" I had asked him.

"She refuses me."

"Refuses you what?"

"Oh, you know," he said coyly, waving one arm in the air. "You know what I'm talking about."

"Sex?"

"Yes."

"I see. Do you have any children?"

"No."

"Are you separated?"

"No, but she has a lawyer. Do you want his name?"

"Sure." That's how I called Alan Vuernick, who represented the wife. He told me he lived near my office and would drop in on his way home from work. His office was located in Harlem, where he rented space with a large legal firm.

He came in at six that evening. He was in his mid-twenties, and had just recently been admitted to practice. In New York, in those days anyway, the lawyer representing the wife held all the cards, and it was the attorney for the husband who went to his or her office. I figured he was inexperienced, and didn't know any better, but it was of small moment anyway. He was friendly, and explained to me that his client, the wife, was handicapped by an early bout with polio, and that she loved her husband and didn't really want to break up the marriage.

So we sat and talked about a way to bring them together again. We'd arrange a conference at my office for an evening and see what we could do about reconciliation. That done, we talked some small talk about the practice of law, and then his glance went to the manuscript on my desk, which I had been correcting.

"What's that? An appellate brief?"

"What?"

"Those papers."

"No. Actually it's something I wrote. You know, a novel."

"A novel?"

"Yes."

"You wrote a novel?" He was incredulous.

I nodded.

"What's it about?"

"Oh, Brooklyn, a crime committed by some men...It's hard to explain."

"Wow, you wrote a novel. That's something. What's it called?"

"Rapt In Glory."

"Wrapped in what?"

"No. Rapt In Glory. R-A-P-T in glory."

"What does that mean?"

"I got it from something carved in marble at the Cemetery for the American Dead outside of Florence. It stated that 'when these young men died, their eyes were not filled with fear, but rapt in glory.' It always stayed with me, and my main character is a veteran haunted by the war. The title came to me about halfway through the book."

"That's something. Listen, maybe we'll have dinner some night. I'd like to hear more about your book."

"Sure."

"I'm not far from here. I live in Bensonhurst."

"Great." We said goodbye, and I went back to correcting the manuscript.

We couldn't get the clients together that week, and had to

arrange for a meeting the following Thursday night. On Tuesday of that week, my secretary came in and told me there was a call for me. I was busy examining a real estate contract and asked who it was.

"Someone from Pocket Books."

"From where?"

"Pocket Books. The publishing company."

"Do we have a case with them?"

"Not that I know."

"Ok, I'll take it."

I said hello, and the man on the other end identified himself as Phil Fleyderman.

"Is this about a legal matter?" I asked.

"No. I'm an editor at Pocket Books."

"I see."

"I understand you wrote a novel."

I didn't know what to say. Had word spread throughout the publishing world that Edwin Silberstang, sitting in his apartment on East 8th Street in Brooklyn, had written a novel, a long awaited novel and now the publishing world was panting for it?

"How'd you know I wrote a novel?"

"Oh, I live near Alan Vuernick. We're neighbors and sometimes we play ball together. He mentioned that you wrote a novel. He said he read part of it and that it was very good. It's about a crime in Brooklyn?"

"I see."

"Well, if you wouldn't mind, I'd like to see what you've written."

At this point I had given Joan sixty pages of the novel and gotten back the original forty, which came to over fifty pages in manuscript form.

"Ok."

"We could have lunch. How about this Friday?"

"This Friday?"

"Isn't that ok?"

"Wait a second." I looked through my diary. I had nothing on. "That would be fine," I said. "Where?" "I'm over at 630 Fifth Avenue, you know, in Rockefeller Center. Could you come up; I'll show you around and we'll grab some lunch. And of course, bring the novel."

"I don't have it all typed yet."

"Bring what you have. Is noon ok?"

"Fine."

After I hung up, I sat and stared into space. First Albert had come into my life and inspired me to write a novel, and now Alan had come into my life, and he knew an editor at Pocket Books. I didn't need an agent just yet. I already had a publisher calling me, asking to see my novel. It was incredible.

And then another strange thing happened. In Brooklyn, near New Utrecht Avenue, three men robbed a storekeeper, and in the course of the holdup, a policeman was killed. The men who were charged were two Italians and a Jew. I happened to be in court the morning they were arraigned, and looking at them I couldn't believe my eyes. They were my characters! The Jewish guy looked just like Benny Katz, and his name was Jerry Rosenberg, who later had a television program made about his prison life. One of the other men was also later convicted, and only one of the three got off.

Watching them in court, with the walls lined with armed police officers, I realized that art doesn't always imitate life, that life often follows art. I sat mesmerized in court that day watching the proceedings, waiting for my client's case to come up. There were so many coincidences occurring with my first novel that I could only ascribe to fate.

When Alan came with his client on Thursday night, I told him about the call from Phil Fleyderman.

"Gee, I hope you don't mind me telling him I read part of the book. I wanted to tell him it was good."

"No problem. I forgive you." I laughed.

The meeting went well with our clients. By the end they agreed to reconcile and walked out of my office hand in hand.

I felt good about that.

The next day I took the subway uptown, getting off on the Sixth Avenue line at 47-50th Street, and walking through the labyrinth of corridors to 630 Fifth Avenue. I got to the office a few minutes before noon, and a secretary called Phil and told me he'd be out in a little while. He was a young man in his mid-twenties, about Alan's age, and he greeted me warmly. I was carrying the fifty typed pages in a clasp envelope, and gave it to him. He put it on his desk, as he showed me around the office.

I had never been at a publisher's, and looked around with interest. Pocket Books was a division of Simon and Schuster. People sat in individual offices looking at manuscripts. It was quite exciting for me. The publishing world of Manhattan, a million light years from my office in the Borough Park section of Brooklyn.

We went out to eat at a small luncheonette and took a booth by ourselves. Phil wanted to know about me, how I came to write the novel and roughly what it was about. I explained that I had written it in the last year, had not shown it to anyone (other than Alan) and that it was about a crime committed by three men in Brooklyn, a drugstore robbery that turns tragic after a police officer is killed in the course of the getaway.

He talked to me about the inner gossip of the publishing world, a world I was completely unfamiliar with. We had a cordial lunch, and he promised to read it as soon as possible, as we said goodbye out in the street. I returned to my office, but couldn't concentrate on the work at hand.

What would he think? I started to lose confidence as soon as I was back at my desk. He'd probably thank me for giving him the pages and mail them back. I had read that the chances of a first novel getting published were something like 30,000-1. I wasn't going to get my hopes up. I was going to prepare for failure. I told Albert what had happened that Saturday night as we had dinner in the Village.

"You did the best you could do, isn't that right?" he asked.

"Yes."

"Well, no one can fault you for that. Win or lose, you did the best you can do. If you didn't do the best, if you had cut corners, or didn't put down true feelings, that would be different."

I nodded. I didn't want to tell him I hadn't even reread the manuscript but had given it directly to Joan without any editing changes. Did that mean I had cut corners? My confidence was evaporating rapidly. I wanted to go directly to Joan's and get back the last twenty pages I had given her. I wanted to call Phil Fleyderman at home and tell him to return my work, not to read it. It wasn't ready. I could see how fragile the existence of a writer was, how his confidence was but a small candle with a flickering flame, ready to be blown out by any passing wind.

But I didn't go to Joan's, nor did I call Phil that evening. I sat tight. In my life, whenever I had been in difficult situations, and in the Army I was in some life and death encounters, I had not panicked. I sat tight, as it were, and held on. That's what I did now, held on.

In later years, in the company of writers waiting for a decision on their work, I saw the same thing going on that I experienced that night in the restaurant. Tension, confidence seeping away moment by moment, intimations of failure. A friend of mine, waiting for a decision from a magazine on a piece he had done, frantic with expectation, asked how I had been able to put up with this tension.

I told him I just held on; there was nothing else to do. I had long ago stopped surmising about decisions from editors. Was a delay good or bad? Should I call and see what was happening? No way. The delay could be positive or negative; there was no sense in trying to figure it out. Just hang in there. In the end, my friend's work was rejected. He was crushed, doubly so because by the time he got the decision he was drained out. I knew the writer's life was not for him. He'd be dead of a heart attack with a few more of these situations.

I went home that night, and had a sleepless evening. Since I was no longer working on a novel, I felt lost. All the work I had put into the book hadn't really drained me; there was still plenty of energy left in me, with no real outlet. Now I was part of the waiting game.

I had dinner with Vuernick that week, and I didn't bring up the manuscript over at Pocket Books. He told me that he had played some basketball with Phil, and Phil mentioned that he had the pages. But nothing else. A week passed, and I went back to Joan with twenty more pages, picking up the work she had done. I had another fifty pages for Phil, that is, if he cared to see anymore, which I doubted.

She was working slowly on the book, and I tried to rush her along.

"It's so interesting," Joan told me. "It's a great story. I can't stop reading." This was my first reaction from a stranger, a potential reader of my work.

"Don't read it, just type it," I said. "I need it in its entirety. I'd like to come here a few times a week, and get it done."

She promised to work faster. Well, she liked it. That was something. And Albert liked the ending. Something more. But was it publishable?

The next day, there was a small envelope with the Pocket Books logo on the front. And above it was typed "Fleyderman." It was on my desk when I came back from the Surrogate's Court, where I had filed a will.

I looked at the envelope, and then took a deep breath and opened it. A short note was typed.

"Dear Ed...I find the story really exciting. Call me, and let's meet again. Phil."

I stared at the note and reread it. "Really exciting."

Yes, I thought, yes! I called the Pocket Books number and waited for Phil to get on.

"Hey, Ed," he said, "I want to see more of the novel. Can we meet tomorrow?"

I told him I had fifty or so pages more to give him, and

that I was pushing the typist to work faster. The next day I was back at 630 Fifth Avenue. This time we went to a nearby Italian restaurant, a rather expensive one. I noted that this was a decided step up from the luncheonette we first had eaten at. Another good sign. Phil talked about the story, intrigued by several of the characters. Had I based them on anyone? Did I know people like this?

I was circumspect. I had met a lot of people on the fringes of society, both growing up in New York and in my law practice. I knew that world, I assured him. I gave him another clasp envelope with fifty two more pages. He put it under his arm, and promised again to read it as soon as he could.

I returned to the office, buried myself in work. I missed writing, but knew that it was senseless to start something else. I had to refresh myself, pause and take my time. It had taken me thirty-two years to write a novel; I could wait a bit for my next book.

Three days later, Phil called. He had read the pages I had given him, and wanted more. I was going to Joan every other night, picking up the typed material and giving her twenty pages at a time. She was working faster now, and by the next meeting with Phil, I gave him another seventy pages. We ate at another fancy restaurant. He was still excited by the book. And I still hadn't done any editing.

I had been reading the sections I was giving to Joan, and they flowed along. When I corrected the typed pages she returned to me, they held up. There was nothing to really revise.

I had heard about authors revising their works endlessly, spending more time on the revisions than on the original copy, but for me this seemed superfluous. When I wrote the first novel, I felt that it flowed out of some unconscious part of myself. I wasn't even aware of the words I was typing. After I finished the night's work, I'd reread what I had written and then place the pages on the previous pile of work. Now and then I corrected a typo, or made some very minor change, but I really wasn't doing any serious revisions.

Writers have different ways of writing. To many, it is important that their work be carefully revised. Some great writers of important classics wrote that way. All I can say is that for me, what I first put down on paper held up. Only one of my novels was heavily rewritten, but that was an unusual case, which I'll explain at the appropriate time.

What seemed to interest Phil about the novel was the narrative drive. He told me over and over again that he couldn't put the pages down, that he was being constantly surprised by the story. I didn't write it with unexpected twists and turns–I simply felt I was telling a story. The lack of an outline worked well for me. Nothing was foreordained in the story, because I didn't know what was going to happen next. I trusted implicitly in my characters and was willing, as a writer, to let them lead me down the path of the novel.

I've met writers since then who spent months working to refine an outline, rather than writing the novel. The plot was the important thing as far as they were concerned. This, I believe, is a great mistake. It is the characters that carry the story. What difference does a plot really make? No one reads or sees Hamlet for the plot. The plot is just a frame for the characters to operate within. The character of Hamlet makes the play great.

Too often, beginning writers concentrate on the plot or the storyline, and treat their characters in a secondary fashion. When they do this, the characters are dead on the page, without interest to the reader. If a reader can't be involved in the characters, he quickly loses interest in the work. By readers I mean the first people to look at a manuscript, the agents and the editors.

My best advice to beginning writers is this–begin with the character. If you bring the protagonist to life, and make him or her interesting, you're on the road to success as a writer.

This is not to say that the story isn't important. It is, of course, and the storyline becomes enhanced by the strength of the characters. A writer of a novel is basically telling a story, but no one will listen to a story with a main character that is essentially uninteresting. They will, however, be fascinated by an intriguing character, even if the story isn't that great. For example, if I were to describe a day spent with someone like Jack Nicholson, most people will be interested, even though the day was spent in a mundane way.

When you combine an intriguing character and a fascinating plot, then you have a winner. But don't worry too much about the plot. In looking back at my work, I realize that most of my main characters were in situations at the outset of the novel where they were on the outside of society, their backs to the wall of life. The plot just moved from there.

Think of all the books or movies that fascinated you. I'm sure you remember the characters rather than the plot. I've mentioned Hamlet. If we go on with Shakespeare, there's Othello, Falstaff, Lear and on and on, characters that spring to life on the pages of the play and on the stage. In novels, we have Raskolnikov of Crime and Punishment, Gatsby of The Great Gatsby, Joe Christmas of Light in August, Leopold Bloom and Stephen Dedalus of Ulysses. The list is endless, and if we go to another medium, the epic poem, we have Achilles of Homer's "The Iliad."

Even though Phil was excited by my novel, I was unsure it would be published. I had read of too many horror stories of writers whose work came close to being published, only to have some last-minute glitch or qualm by the editor jettison the novel. I felt I was on tenuous ground. I didn't know whether Phil had the strength in the publishing house to approve a book by himself. Surely there were others who would look at the work, and perhaps any of them might have a veto power over its' publication.

The main thing, however, was to give him the full manuscript. I pushed Joan to work harder, and was at her apartment every other night, picking up pages. When she finally finished the typing, I gave her the last check for her work, and called

Phil, telling him I had the rest of the novel for him.

He told me that the week was tough for him as far as lunches were concerned, so I volunteered to bring the remaining manuscript up to his office. Phil came out when I arrived and took the clasp envelope. We shook hands and I left. There were questions I had wanted to ask him, but I held by my credo of holding on, not saying anything that would portend weakness on my part. I wanted to know when he'd make a decision on the book, or if he was the only one to make the decision. I wanted to know who else would read the manuscript, and if they had veto power over its publication. But I said nothing. It was in his hands now and out of mine.

A week passed. Alan Vuernick arranged a dinner at his apartment, and I met his wife for the first time. We talked a bit about Phil, and I mentioned that he had the whole novel now. Alan was anxious to read the manuscript himself, but I told him I only had one copy, the original single-spaced work, and couldn't let it out of my hands just yet.

Another week passed. With each day's progress, I lost heart in the work. Fears of the inadequacy of the work came into my conscious mind again. Who was interested, really? Who could care about these characters, James Fusari, Roger Brunardo, Benny Katz, Frank Sheehan and Tom Fusari? And the others who populated the book. Who would care about a fictional story of a robbery on Ocean Parkway in Brooklyn, and its aftermath? I remembered what Albert had told me-that if I was interested, others would be. I didn't live in a vacuum.

I was seeing Albert rarely now. He was working at two hospitals, and I was spending late nights at the office on my cases. On a Wednesday morning, almost three weeks after I had given the final pages to Phil, he called. He asked if I could meet him on Friday for lunch. There would be some people with him, he mysteriously announced. Where?

We agreed to meet at noon at the English Grill in Rockefeller Center. At that time there were two restaurants, one on either side of the skating rink, which is a landmark in the Center. One was the French Grill, the other, the northern-most restaurant, was the English Grill. I marked it on my calendar.

I was a bit early for the lunch. The sun was shining brightly, and it was a warm Spring day. I sat on a bench and watched the passersby, young women in their summer dresses, men in shirtsleeves, tourists taking pictures. A lovely day, but I was full of anxiety. I had tried to fathom Phil's voice when he called, but couldn't. He had sounded rushed, and a little distant. What did this meeting mean? Who was he bringing along?

At five to twelve I went to the front entrance of the restaurant. Noon came and went, then it was five after, ten after, a quarter after. My heart sank. This wasn't a good omen. Maybe a messenger would come down and tell me the lunch was cancelled. I wiped the palms of my hand on a handkerchief.

I was about to ask for a phone to call Phil, when I saw him approaching, with three other men, all dressed in suits.

Phil apologized for the lateness, telling me they were delayed at a meeting. He introduced the men, all of whom were senior executives at Pocket Books, and whose names I can't now recall. They all shook hands with me, and we were greeted by the maitre d' who had a table waiting for us.

The five of us sat down, Phil sitting near me, the most senior of the executives opposite me. The men seemed glum as we ordered drinks. I had a Cinzano on the rocks, with ice, a mild drink. I wanted to keep my wits about me. From Albert I had learned to be aware of my feelings at all times, to keep myself as open as possible. The men said nothing. The drinks came. I sipped mine. We ordered lunch.

When the waiter had left, the man who had been introduced as the most senior executive of the company looked at me and told me he had read my novel. I nodded, not knowing what to say, and knowing enough not to ask what he thought of it. Hang in there, I told myself. He said nothing else for a moment, and I had this wild thought, that they had called me here for lunch to tell me they were rejecting my manuscript. But that was insane. A form letter would have done the trick, or a call from Phil telling me he was returning the novel.

Instead of saying anything else to me, he turned to Phil.

"Phil, why don't you tell him? You've been with him all this time."

Phil took a sip of his martini, and put it down.

"Ok," he said. Then he looked over at me. "Ed, to put it in a nutshell, we want to publish your novel."

The words floated in the air. I leaned back and took a deep breath. What had he said? Had I heard right?

"Now, you know," one of the other men said, "we're a paperback house, and so it would be a paperback original. We've all read the novel and feel it could be a hardcover book, but we aren't in a position to publish it in hardcover. You understand that?"

I nodded.

"We're in a position to print quite a few copies, well over a hundred thousand," the man continued. "Much more than if it were a hardcover work. You might only get a printing of five thousand or so for a first novel as a hardcover. You understand that?"

"Yes."

"Well, it's up to you. Do you want us to publish it?"

I thought fast. I could go to a hardcover house. But this house wanted it; it must have struck a chord with all these men. But if it was rejected by hardcover houses, where would I be? I'd have to come back to them defeated. They could have changed their minds by then. 30,000-1 against a first novel being published, and they were willing to publish it.

"I've enjoyed working with Phil," I said. "I would like Pocket Books to publish the novel."

Phil smiled. He looked relieved.

The same man continued. "Now, do you have an agent?"

"No."

"No agent?"

"No."

"Hmm. Well, do you want to talk about money now or wait to speak to an agent?"

"Now is ok."

"For an original first novel, we give a maximum of $3,000 as an advance. You understand, it's an advance against royalties."

"Yes."

"The book will probably sell for fifty cents. And our royalty basis is 6%. That's 6% of the cover price, or three cents a copy."

"Yes."

They waited for me to say something. On impulse I told them that $3,000 as an advance was alright with me.

"But," the man said, "that's the most we give as an advance on a paperback original."

"Yes, I know. But $3,000 seems right."

Another of the executives whispered something to him, and he nodded, then turned to me.

"All right, it's $3,000 then."

"You really ought to get an agent," the man said. "We're going to have the contracts prepared by the end of the week. Phil, can you recommend someone to Ed?"

"Yes, I have someone at Curtis Brown. A good man there. I'll discuss it after lunch with Ed."

We were served lunch, and there was no more talk about the novel by the other men at the table. Phil told me he was assigning an editor to me, that he wouldn't be handling the book himself. After lunch we all shook hands again, and I lingered behind with Phil.

"I'm glad you accepted the offer," he said. "I was afraid you'd opt for a hardcover house."

"I'm happy to be published by Pocket Books."

"Good. I'll be behind the book. They all were impressed with your writing."

"Thanks."

"Come on up to my office. I'll call Curtis Brown for you and make the arrangements. They're not far from here."

"Ok."

"I'll speak to the editor about the novel. I'll have him call you. It'll be in his hands from now on." The editor he selected I'll call Gene Galen.

I sat in his office while he called Curtis Brown. I was introduced by phone to an agent there, Del Jameson (not his real name) who told me he'd be representing me. Could I come over to the office sometime that week? I made arrangements for the next day.

And there it was. My novel had been accepted. I was to be a published writer. A major New York literary agency was representing me. It was like a dream. All during the long subway ride back to my office, I sat in a haze of joy.

I broke the news to my parents. My mother, so proud that I was a "professional," that is, a lawyer, was concerned that I'd give it up for writing. She told me she was pleased that I was to be published; but I knew she really didn't understand what had been accomplished. My father congratulated me, but I felt alone in a way. I wanted to share my joy but in the end it was just something that couldn't really be shared.

I called Albert and we went for a celebratory dinner. He was proud of what I had done and I told him that without his inspiration I couldn't have written the novel. He disagreed.

"It was all in you; it just had to come out sometime or other." He raised a glass of wine to my success. "What are you going to do now?"

"I'm thinking of another novel. But I haven't written anything yet."

"And what about law?"

"I'm tempted to leave, but this may all be a fluke. I want to have another book under my belt; then I'll make plans to be a writer, not a lawyer." I paused for a moment. "Albert, I'm going to dedicate the book to you."

Our eyes met. I could see he was touched by my gesture.

But without his inspiration I don't know if I could have become a writer. I've often thought about it; perhaps I'd have written a novel anyway, with or without Albert. But he was there for me at the critical moments, and I'll never forget his friendship.

Gene Galen called me the next day, and said he'd just gotten the manuscript. He'd call me in a week with his impressions. I met with Del Jameson, my new agent, and it was a perfunctory meeting. When he got the contract, which had been promised for the end of the week, he'd contact me. He expected no problems; he had worked with Pocket Books before. It would probably be all cut and dried. I was, in reality, paying an agent 10% for nothing; but I figured it would be a good investment for the future.

A few days later I had signed the contract, and received a check for $1,350, which was $1,500, or half the advance, minus the agent's 10%. The rest of the money was due when the manuscript was edited and ready for press.

A week later Gene called, and we met for the first time. He was a tall, angular man in his thirties, and had an Ivy League look about him. He had an upper class accent and had gone to Harvard, where he majored in English literature. He had copious notes. They ran for more than six pages. I read them with dismay. He wanted a multitude of changes, that would transform the novel into something that I hadn't intended it to be.

I read the notes carefully, and made a few of the changes, but I was getting depressed. The book was changing for the worse. At that point in my writing career I thought editors knew something; that they were wiser than writers. I quickly learned that editors are editors precisely because they can't be writers. They want to be part of the literary world, and so they fit in this way.

An editor, dealing with a newly published writer, will push the envelope as far as he can. He will ask for changes and see what the writer is willing to do. If the writer is compliant, then the editor will push more, till he or she transforms the work into something of their own. The writer must have confidence to stop this from happening. Or experience. I had the confidence, but not the experience, and after trying to make some changes, I got angry. I demanded a meeting with Gene after working on the changes for a couple of months. We met at a fancy French restaurant in the East 50s.

"Gene," I said, "I feel this novel is worthless now."

"What are you talking about?"

"Your changes. I can see a couple of them, getting rid of one of the subsidiary characters and tightening the story, but the other changes...that's not the novel I wrote. I'm sick of it now, and I want the book put back in its original form."

He shook his head. "My suggestions are valid. I've been editing books for ten years now."

"The novel is being destroyed."

I was livid. He sat there, so superior, and my work was being killed by his changes.

"You're overreacting. Look more closely at what I suggest. They'll improve the book."

"No...I made all the changes I'm going to make...and I want the others reinstated. I'll take out one of the minor characters and get rid of a couple of scenes that are tangental to the story, but that's it."

"Then you won't get the book published."

"Then I won't."

"It's up to you."

He was holding the pages of his suggestions along with the manuscript.

"Right. Give me back the manuscript. I won't have Pocket Books publish the novel, not the way you're changing it."

I held out my hands for the manuscript.

He turned white. "Give me the fucking manuscript," I said. "I don't want you handling it anymore."

"Ed, take it easy..."

"No, I'm serious. Give it back."

"Look, relax. We'll go back to my office and go over the

changes line by line. I'll listen to what you have to say."

"No. I've said what I had to say. I told you what I'd change. If you want more, give me back the fucking novel."

We went back to Gene's office, and I tore up his notes and threw them into a wastepaper basket. He didn't object.

The changes I agreed to shortened the manuscript by about six pages, and tightened the story line. There was some validity to these changes, but the rest was just an imposition of his ego. Write your own fucking novel, I wanted to scream. In the end, we shook hands. The editing was done with.

I had learned a valuable lesson, that I tried to transmit to my students when I taught or held workshops. The writer is the important person, not the agent or the editor. The writer is the creative one, and his or her work is to be dealt with respect. The writer must always be confident in his or her work, and not let it be tampered with or destroyed by those on the periphery of the literary world.

In September, 1964, Rapt In Glory was published. I received a call from Phil Fleyderman, and went up to his office and was given ten free copies. I took them back to my apartment, but restless that evening, I took the subway up to Manhattan, and got off the train at Times Square. In small bookstores, in drugstores and other places where paperback books were being sold, there was the novel. It was all over the place. In one store, I bought a copy on impulse and went to a local Chock Full O' Nuts coffee shop and ordered some coffee and sat and looked at the book. Next to me an attractive woman was sitting, also drinking coffee. It was close to ten in the evening.

"Is that book any good?" she asked.

"I guess so. I wrote it."

"No...you wrote it?"

I nodded.

"Can I see it?"

I passed it over to her. She was in her late twenties, slim, with long dark hair.

"Are you really Edwin Silberstang?"

"Yes."

"Wow. You know, I'm studying to be an actress. Is there a good part for me in the book?"

"A couple of good parts."

"You think it'll be made into a movie?"

"I don't know. It just came out today."

We talked some more. She lived in the East 60s, in a small studio apartment. I walked her home. On the way, she suggested I buy a bottle of champagne to celebrate the book's publication. I bought two bottles of Piper. At her place we started drinking the champagne. We both got drunk and wound up in bed. I stayed the night.

III

THE SECOND NOVEL

Now that my first novel was published, I turned my attention to another novel. It had to do with the breakup of a marriage, and the kidnapping by the mother of the one child of the marriage. I worked on it for awhile, but wasn't satisfied with the result. I tore up the fifty or so pages I had done, this time in doublespace, and began again. I wrote more than one hundred and fifty pages, and in rereading what I had put to paper, I was still dissatisfied. Finally I jettisoned the whole thing.

I was still practicing law, and still waiting for some kind of inspiration for my next novel. After all, I was a published writer, and all kinds of doors previously closed to me would now be open. Any agent would see me; publishers hearing that I had already been published, would be more likely to read what I had written.

I had spent a lot of time in Greenwich Village; in fact Albert and I ate most of our meals together there. Brooklyn was where I worked, and I remember going to a party in Manhattan years before, and meeting a woman at the party who asked me where I lived. This was before I had written Rapt In Glory.

"In Brooklyn," I told her, "near Cortelyou Road."

"How in the world can you live in Brooklyn," she asked me. "Nothings going on there."

"Well," I explained, "my law practice is there and it's more convenient for me."

But this explanation didn't seem to work. The woman lost interest in me right then and there. I had told Albert of this conversation, and he told me never to apologize for anything I did. Either don't do it, or don't apologize. Then, a year and a half later, having a book published by now, I had almost the same conversation with a different woman at a party in Manhattan, on East 53rd Street.

"Where do you live?" this woman asked me.

"In Brooklyn, near Cortelyou Road."

"How in the world can you live in Brooklyn?"

"That's where I live," I told her, "what difference should it make to you where I live."

"Well, it's the sticks."

"Really? What makes you so judgmental about where I live?"

She stared at me. Then she apologized. The tables had been turned. I was more confident of myself now. I had changed as a result of writing that book. I had proved something to myself, something no one could ever take away from me now.

But still I wasn't writing anything. But I did make one major change in my life. Walking in the Village one afternoon, I passed a rather new apartment building on Sheridan Square and saw a "For Rent" sign outside. I went in and asked to look at the apartment. It was an L shaped place, with the bedroom visible from the living room but set aside by the L shape of the apartment. I took it on the spot. It was time to move on. Albert told me I whipped my novel like a horse across the Brooklyn Bridge into Manahattan.

I loved the Village. There were tons of bookstores around, and Fourth Avenue below 14th Street was filled with quaint bookstores, row upon row of them. Then there was the Strand Bookstore, which advertised miles of books. I liked the small restaurants, the life of the Village. Now, instead of constantly taking my car or the subway there, all I had to do was step outside my building and I was in the middle of everything the Village offered. My social life improved dramatically. Women wanted to go to the Village; often they'd meet me at my apartment.

But I still wasn't writing that second novel. The work I had done before and thrown away, I didn't want to return to. I didn't want to be like those writers who worked for years and years, flogging the same dead horse. I trusted my instincts. That novel was now out of my system. I had to write something else.

I explained the dilemna to Albert one evening while we were sitting in a small French restaurant on West 4th Street in the Village, just down the street from where I lived. He listened soberly to what I said. Whenever we spoke of anything important, he listened seriously. I learned from him that when in doubt about being serious or not, always be serious. You can never go wrong, whereas levity could cause someone else to be angry. If you treat another person's serious concern lightheartedly, you can bring out terrific anger in that individual. As Albert said, "leave someone guilty, not angry. You don't need enemies in this world."

After I explained my frustration, Albert said nothing. He sat, as was his wont, his eyes half shut, going "hmm, hmm, hmm" nodding his head at the same time, the same way I had originally seen him at my law office when we first met.

Then he took a pen from his pocket, and handed it to me. I picked up the pen, and looked quizzically at him.

"You see this glass of water?" he asked. He pushed his tumbler of iced water towards where I was sitting.

"Yes, what about it?"

He ripped out a piece of paper from a small notebook he always carried around and handed it to me. "Draw the glass."

"This glass?"

"Yes."

I had no talent as an artist. I painstakingly drew the glass of water, then pushed the paper over to him. But he made no comment. Instead he asked what I thought of my own drawing.

"Well, it's crooked, I didn't catch the rim correctly. And the ice cubes look strange, and the water doesn't really look like water. I'm terrible at drawing. It just hangs there; there's no sense of the glass being on a table."

He nodded, and then was silent.

"That's why you're not writing," he said.

"What are you talking about?"

"Ed, what you should have said is 'this is the way I see the glass.' There's nothing wrong with the way you drew it. That's how you see it, that's how you visualize the glass. What are you apologizing about?"

I stared at him.

"Do you think, if you went to Picasso's studio, and told Picasso that he had put two eyes on one side of the head in one of his paintings, that he'd apologize to you for doing this? That's the way he sees that particular human face. It's his vision. You remember once I told you that your voice was as valid as some writer's..."

"Faulkner's."

"Yes, Faulkner's. Why is your vision less valid than Picasso's? This is not to say you're as great an artist as Picasso. That would be an absurd statement. But why not trust your vision? It is different than Picasso's, but there's no reason why it isn't as valid."

He paused, then spoke again. "Trust your vision and stop apologizing for it. You're too worried about your next book. Success came easily with the first novel; now you feel under pressure. Success is sometimes harder to handle than failure. We know how to deal with failure...both of us have had obstacles to overcome. But success...that's a different story. You'd be surprised at how some of my patients can't handle success. They're famous people, and it scares the shit out of them."

After dinner I walked him to his car and we hugged and I watched him drive off. I turned and went back to my apartment. It was a bitterly cold day, and I pushed the collar of my coat up around my neck. When I got back to the apartment, I went into the bathroom after taking off my coat and jacket, and washed my hands and face. My old ritual, the same one I had used for my first novel.

I sat down at the large walnut desk I had bought in New Hope, Pennsylvania from an artisan named Nakashima, one large piece of wood, seventy inches by thirty inches, without any metal holding the legs to the surface. On the desk sat my new SCM electric typewriter, a portable version much faster than the old Royal, which had once more been relegated to my closet.

I put in a sheet of white paper, and thought of what to write. I wanted to feel the way I had felt when starting Rapt in Glory, that glorious unconscious state of being.

I began to write:

"I was born in the late 1920's in a small village in the south of Austria. The exact date of my birth and the name of the village is not known to me, although several attempts have been made by the authorities to certify these two facts.

As I understand, from the stories and memories of my early childhood, my parents at the time of my birth were traveling from Vienna to Munich, where my father had been offered a position with a hospital. He took it, after some delay, and we moved to Munich when I was a small infant."

I continued to write till I had completed the chapter. Unlike my first novel, this was in the first person, and the narrator's name was Robert Lindner. After I finished the chapter, I sat in the darkened apartment, listening to Mozart, thinking of the story. Again, I wasn't going to outline it, but my feeling was that I would show the early childhood of the boy, his imprisonment in a concentration camp, and his release from the camp. Then his trip to America, where, like me, he served in the Army during the Korean War. I had met several survivors of the camps in service; they received instant citizenship after serving in the Armed Forces.

I would show, in this novel, the difference between the experiences of the main character, haunted by the camps, and the life of the average American he came across in the Army and in civilian life. At least, that was my plan. But as the story progressed night after night during January of 1966, the story changed. Robert Lindner took over, and once more I was content to follow my character.

I had lost a number of relatives in the camps, mainly my father's two oldest sisters and their families, people I had never met. Among my clients were several Orthrodox Jews who had survived the camps, but they never spoke about their experiences. I would see the numbers tattoed on their arms, and not ask questions. Men and women, whose lives, I knew, must have been nightmares. I wondered what their dreams were like.

In the summer of 1962, I had traveled to Europe for the first time with my friend, Ray Reiman. We met in Paris, and took the Orient Express to Munich, and while there, rented a Volkswagen bug. We drove around Munich, and I recalled the day when we were on Leopoldstrasse, one of the main avenues of Munich. We came to an intersection called Dachaustrasse.

We decided to follow it out of town. About ten or so kilometres out of Munich, we came across the town of Dachau, and soon after, a sign pointed to the concentration camp.

There we were. We parked outside the camp, and walked in through the main entrance, with the sign above us reading "Arbeit Macht Frei." "Work Makes You Free." The ultimate ironic statement of our time. I had put aside my first novel to take this trip and thought to myself, "keep your feelings open." But I couldn't help thinking of the dread I would have felt if I and my parents and sister had walked through that gate in 1938 or 1939, doomed to the gas chamber, to the awaiting ovens.

Ray was of German descent, and of course, unlike me, the Holocaust was not a large part of his psyche. He had heard of concentration camps, but what we saw that day shocked him into silence. We went throughout the camp, which I believe was being kept open by the Belgian War Commission as a memorial to the victims. We looked at everything; the SS barracks, the ovens, the blood ditches, the inmates' hovels. We took it all in, in silence. I noted the railway station nearby, the tracks, the gas chambers, everything.

When we left, we got into the VW and Ray turned to me.

"Jesus," he said softly. "Jesus Sweet Christ."

He stared straight ahead, shaking his head, then he turned to me and said, "Let's get the fuck out of Germany. Why stay in this fucking country? Let's get on the road; anyplace but this shithole."

When I started my novel, the Holocaust had receded in the national consciousness. It was old hat, people were tired of hearing about it. It was a dead subject, but I was still haunted by that day in Dachau. I remembered the camp vividly; in my mind's eye I could sketch out the entire place. So I continued writing. I wrote every evening, and during the night, I was haunted by nightmares. Reality and dreams merged; a few times I awoke in a panic, crying for my dead parents and sister. Dreams...they were still alive, thank God. And the work went on.

The story changed. I had expected to write a couple of chapters about the life in the camp, then switch to the Korean War, but this was not to be. Robert was in the camp, and he stayed in the camp, as horror after horror unfolded. The book took on a life of its own, and I felt just like a hired typist, writing a story someone else had made up.

I worked on the novel night after night. When I first returned from the office in the evening, I went up to my apartment and took the chapter from the night before, then left my place. I went to a small coffeehouse, the Cafe Peacock on West 4th Street, where the owner knew me. She always sat me at a table near a lamp, so that I could edit the work. Then she'd bring over an expresso, and leave me alone.

One evening, as I was working on the editing in the coffeehouse, some young men, dressed as hippies, were sitting at the next table, having a boisterous conversation. They were talking about novels they were going to write, "blowing the lid on the bullshit in society." They were intefering with my work, but I kept reading. Then, looking up for an instant, I could see one of them nodding in my direction, and telling the others, "look at that straight guy; Jesus, who the fuck wants to be like him." The others laughed, and then went back to the novels they were going to write.

I was dressed in a three-piece suit at the time, my standard wear for the court appearances I made during the day. Their talk was cheap; and I heard talk like that all through the years I was writing, whether it came from a table in the Cafe Med in Berkeley, or the Trieste in San Francisco, or small smoky restaurants wherever I was. Talk was cheap. Talk meant nothing. The thing to do, as Hemingway pointed out, was to go back to your room and do the work. I learned later on how important it was to put something on paper than let it float in the air, where it disappeared among the smoke and the stale air. Put it down, and it's a permanent record, something you can show to the right person. Talk about it, and it's nothing.

These guys were judging me, and yet the artist mustn't judge. It is the role of the writer to understand, not to judge. Let all the inadequate people who are never going to do anything, let them judge. Try and understand the human condition, the human struggle and you are on your way to becoming a serious writer.

I continued with the novel. I sweated out scenes, not knowing if my narrator was going to survive or die. It was possible, I knew, for a narrator to die in a novel. All Quiet On the Western Front by Erich Maria Remarque, was a good example. My character, along with two companions, was trying to escape from the camp. I couldn't figure out a way for them to get out. So I stopped trying, and turned it over to them. They found a way.

The novel was near completion a month after I started the

narration. Within a few days, it was complete. I was utterly drained by the book, not feeling the same exhilaration I had felt at the end of Rapt In Glory. This novel haunted me. Now that it was complete, I called my agent at Curtis Brown and made an appointment to see him. I brought along the manuscript and left it with him, then waited for his opinion. I expected him to be moved by it, but instead, he sent me a short note stating that he didn't feel he could handle the work. It wasn't commercial, and he saw no future in it.

Now I needed a new agent. I looked up several in the Manhattan yellow pages, and called one of the well-known agencies, telling the secretary who answered the phone that I was a published writer looking for a new agent. In a few minutes a woman came on, whom I'll call Carol Johnson. She asked me to bring over the manuscript.

Her response took two weeks. She asked to see me about the novel, and in her office she explained that it really was two books, one a horror story of the camp, and the other an adventure story where the three inmates escape through Germany towards Switzerland. Carol felt that the adventure story was the better story, and that I should rewrite the novel using only that part of the book.

I took back the manuscript and told her I'd think about it. Then I contacted another top agency, and once more went up to an office and left my manuscript. The head of the agency promised to read it. I waited and waited. I called him a month later, and asked what the status of the novel was. He told me he hadn't gotten around to it yet. "Did I think that was all he had to do?" I went up that morning and took back my novel.

The third agent did read it within two weeks, and asked to see me. He explained that the novel was really in two parts, and that I should eliminate the escape and concentrate instead on the camp, ending the book with either the boy's death in the camp or his liberation after the war.

I thanked him for his opinion, and took back the novel. It was amazing to me that these agents, who weren't writers themselves, were willing to tamper with a serious work. Why didn't they just submit it to a publisher and see what happened? What made them think that they knew how a novel should be structured?

I now sat in my rooms with my manuscript, with no agent and no representation. How different this was from the first novel, where things moved rapidly and without any agent, I had gotten it published. Phil Fleyderman was no longer at Pocket Books, and wasn't, as far as I knew, in the publishing world anymore. I wanted a hardcover house to look at this novel, but I couldn't just call up an editor. I needed an agent.

A month passed. Another agent turned down the novel, telling me it was a distasteful book. Then I received a postcard in the mail. It was from an agent whom I'll call Robert Marks, who had originally been with Curtis Brown, and now was forming his own one-man agency. Basically it was a notice that Robert Marks was now an agent on his own. A simple announcement. What the hell, I thought, I'd call him up. I vaguely remembered being introduced to him a year or so back.

He was happy that I responded, and I went to his office in the East 50s. It was a small office, with a bathroom that was a little bigger than the room he worked in. The building had been an apartment house once, converted to small offices. Robert greeted me warmly and I sat at his desk, my manuscript on my lap.

We talked a bit about the publishing business, and then I told him about my experiences with other agents.

"What I'd like you to do," I explained, "is not even read the novel. Take my word that it's strong enough to be published. Just submit it. I trust the work as it stands. I don't want to alter it." I told him that some agents wanted the first part thrown out and others the second part, but they were integral to the whole of the work. "Is that agreeable with you?"

"I liked your other novel," he said. "I'll trust your opinion of this book." This said, we shook hands and I left the novel with him. I hadn't yet picked out a title, and so the front page simply said "Unitled Novel." I was leaning towards "Ashes," but he felt it was a weak title, and one that was rather depressing.

That done, I went back to my office. I would see what happened. At least the novel would go to publishers. Within a week, Robert called me and said it had been rejected by a major publisher. Did I want to see the rejection?

"Sure."

He sent it to me. The editor thought the book was disgusting and vile. Another rejection followed. This editor said the book made him feel like vomiting. A third rejection followed in much the same vein. Robert was getting discouraged.

"These are good rejections," I told him. "Obviously I'm touching a chord with these editors. They're reacting. The worst rejection would be 'it's a nice book, but unfortunately we can't add it to our list.' That's the kiss of death."

"Don't worry," he said, "I'll keep sending it out."

I felt I was right about the rejections. I knew a couple of writers who had showed me their rejections, bland dismissals of their work. But at least I was getting a strong reaction. I felt secure despite words like "vomit" and "disgusting" and "distasteful."

Months passed. The rejections piled up. Then I received a three page rejection from James Silverstein, the editor-in-chief of Random House, with a long critique of the novel, and a statement from him that it was the closest he had ever come to publishing a book that he finally had to reject. He wrote that the work had moved him immensely. At last a bit of encouragement after months of rejections.

In early October I was sitting in my office, dictating a bill of particulars, when Robert called.

"Are you free this Friday at 11AM?" he asked.

"What's up?"

"The novel went to Knopf a few weeks ago, and I got a call from Harding LeMay. He's editor-in-chief, and he'd like to meet you."

"This Friday?"

"Yes."

"Ok. Where we will meet?"

"At his office. 510 Madison Avenue."

"I'll be there."

This was Wednesday. Two days to think about what this meant. I didn't try and surmise. I would go there and see what happened. On Friday morning, I arrived at the building at a quarter to eleven. I rang for the elevator, and when I got in, there was a chimpanzee in there, dressed in a green suit, on roller skates. The most amazing sight. Was this an omen of things to come? I hesitated but the chimp seemed friendly enough and didn't want to leave the elevator. I pushed the button for Knopf's floor, and watched the chimp roller skate around me.

I got off, and pressed the button for the first floor, leaving the chimp in the elevator. He seemed to be having a good time. I paused and looked at my watch. It was ten minutes to the hour. I composed myself. I realized I was entering the office of the most prestigious publisher in America, whose editor-in-chief wanted to see me personally.

If I was close to getting published by Knopf, I wouldn't blow it. Little did I know the questions that would be asked me, putting me on the razor's edge. At five minutes to, I opened the door, and spoke to the receptionist sitting in the outer office. I told her my name and that I had an appointment with Harding LeMay.

"Oh, yes, he's expecting you. Just go to the door at the end over there."

I followed her directions and knocked at a closed door.

"Come in."

I opened the door and saw LeMay sitting behind a desk, with my agent sitting in a chair nearby. Both men stood up and we all shook hands. LeMay was in his forties, I guessed, a good-looking trim man.

"Good to finally meet you," he said. "I read your book with

great interest."

"Thank you," I said. I could see that my manuscript was on his desk, divided into several parts.

"Would you like some coffee?" he said.

"That would be great," I answered. "I'll drink it black."

He stared at me, his brow furrowing. "You seem to have no accent," he said, "you sound like a New Yorker."

"I am a New Yorker."

"Isn't this a true story?"

"No, it's a novel."

"Yes, I noticed that you called it that, but I thought it was a fictional account of your own life."

"No."

"I could have sworn these experiences happened to you. Well, I am impressed. This is just a made-up story?"

"Yes, I guess you could call it that."

"Hmm." The fact that I wasn't really the boy in the story threw him.

He rang for the coffee and he and my agent engaged in small talk while we waited for it to arrive. A secretary brought in a small tray with a silver pot and three cups on it. We helped ourselves, and then LeMay looked piercingly at me.

"Let me ask you something?" he said.

"Yes?"

"What weaknesses do you see in your novel?"

I hadn't expected that question. I leaned back, and then spoke as truthfully as I could. "If there were weaknesses, I wouldn't have submitted it. This is the best I can do."

"So you see no weaknesses?"

It was an anxiety provoking question. There was my manuscript laid out in front of him. And he had the power to accept or reject the novel. I wasn't dealing with lieutenants or junior editors, I was dealing with the general, the editor-in-chief. And I felt what I said now would determine the acceptance or rejection of the work.

"No. That's the best I can do," I repeated.

"Well, let me ask you something else. If you see no weaknesses in your work, would you object to any editing of the novel?"

Another curveball. I leaned back and took a deep breath. "No, I wouldn't object to editing. If an editor could show me how to make the novel stronger, I'd certainly listen seriously to him."

I hadn't said I would accept his findings. I simply said I would listen seriously.

LeMay looked at me, and was deep in thought. My agent sat next to me, saying nothing. If this book was accepted it would be a big plum for him. We waited silently. Then LeMay spoke.

"Ed, if you wouldn't mind, if you could step out of the office, I'd like to talk to Robert for a moment."

"No problem." I stood up, went out and closed the door behind me. I had no idea what would happen. I knew that I had answered his questions to the best of my ability. It was out of my hands now.

The door opened after about five minutes. LeMay had opened it and was standing there, his hand extended. "Let me welcome the newest author to the house of Knopf," he said.

Robert was all smiles.

A few minutes later, Alfred Knopf himself came into the room. He shook my hand warmly then told me he wanted to show me something. He took me into another room, filled with bookshelves loaded down with books, all the books that Knopf had published in its illustrious history. He pointed out Nobel Prize winners like Ivan Bunin, the works of Thomas Mann and others. I was in their company now. I can't describe my feelings at that moment. I felt a surge of excitement, a feeling of pride. I had stuck with my novel, through better or worse, not listening to the rantings of agents who wanted me to chop it up. I had perservered.

After we left the office, Robert told me he had another appointment for lunch, and apologized for not having a celebratory lunch with me. "But we will," he said, "next week. The best restaurant, the finest wines. Just you and me. This is the first book I've represented that's been accepted, Ed. And by Knopf! I know you feel great but I'm floating on air."

We said goodbye. I went into a nearby luncheonette and had a tuna fish sandwich with a side of cole slaw. I really had little appetite. It was a great day for me, and I thought back to the questions that LeMay had asked me. If I was uncertain of the book, and told him about weaknesses, he'd probably give me back the manuscript.

Then I would have probably rewritten the "weak" sections and given it back to LeMay. But by then, who knew what would have happened to his enthusiasm? That's why it's so important to do your best, and at some point, feeling you've done your best, let go of the manuscript. Later on in life, I've seen writers and artists talk about weaknesses in their work, at the point where they were about to be published or have their art exhibited in a gallery. And by not having confidence in their work, their anxiety was catching. The publisher or dealer caught that anxiety, that the work was weak in the writer or artist's eyes, and they themselves lost confidence in the work. So it's worth repeating:

If a writer hasn't done his or her best work, it shouldn't be sent out for publication. Only when nothing more can be done to improve the work should it be submitted.

Years later, when I taught creative writing or had workshops, I'd tell students who confessed that they hadn't done their best work that they had no right submitting it for possible publication in a magazine or with a publisher. They were competing with the best writers in America, and here they were, not even doing their best. What did they expect but failure?

After lunch, I returned to the office. But I knew my days as a lawyer were numbered. I had proven myself, with two novels written and two that would be published. It was time to think of a different future for myself. But it was difficult to broach this subject with my father. He was proud of my work as a writer, and my mother, who had read the manuscript of this second novel, told me she began weeping halfway through it, and that it moved and pained her immensely.

By this time in my legal career I was a full partner of my father in the firm of Silberstang & Silberstang. My father was now sixty-five and didn't have the energy he had had as a young man. Still, I had to think of my future. Perhaps it is being selfish to be a writer, because you're so involved with yourself, with your unconscious, your feelings, your outlook and vision of the world. And writing is a solitary pursuit. No one else can do it for you.

When the Metropolitan Museum of Art purchased "Aristotle Contemplating the Bust of Homer," by Rembrandt, I went up to see it. The painting floored me. Rembrandt seemed to be speaking to me directly, as I looked at a pensive Aristotle staring into the distance with one hand on Homer's head. What he was saying was this–that although Aristotle was the most learned man of his time, all his wisdom would one day be supplanted, but no one could have written a word of Homer's other than the great epic poet. Art reigned supreme over wisdom and science.

The writer has that burden. He creates something original, something that was not there before, and but for his efforts would never be reproduced again. Anything the writer didn't put on paper would be lost forever. Shakespeare gave us thirty-seven plays, but what about all those he didn't write? What about that sublime language of the bard that we would never be able to read or see on a stage?

With these feelings, I held back and didn't yet make the move to leave the law. I now was interested in the editing of the manuscript and the naming of the new novel. I had quoted a poem about W.B.Yeats by Auden as the epigraph of the novel. It contained the words "...nightmare of the dark."

Harding and I finally agreed upon the title, Nightmare of the Dark for this novel. Despite his sharp questioning of me concerning my feeling about the editing of the work, this wasn't a problem. I worked directly with Harding, meeting him for dinner a couple of times at his spacious and comfortable apartment at 170 Second Avenue, near East 10th Street, in Manhattan, a building my uncle also resided in.

In the end, only one small scene was removed from the novel. The work remained intact, as it moved towards publication. In April, 1967, it was published. When my first novel came out in paperback, there were very few reviews of the book. That was one of the drawbacks of having a novel come out as a paperback original. I gave up the possibility of extensive reviews in order to get published. Now I awaited them. The most important was from the New York Times, especially the Sunday Book Review section.

To my surprise, the review covered six columns of the paper, and the reviewer wrote that "In its own way, this is a perfect book...it is required reading." I couldn't have written a more laudatory review myself. Then came other newspapers and magazines, all praising the work. The Book of the Month Club News called it "a genuine novel... Unforgettable."

James Michie, senior editor at Bodley Head in London, asked for the UK rights. It came out in hardcover in the UK and then in paperback, published by Corgi Press. The reviews in England were also full of praise for the book.

The people at Knopf were happy with these reviews, and Harding felt that his judgment was upheld in taking the book in the first place. But still the Holocaust was not in the public consciousness, and the sales were just average, but many libraries bought the novel. As weeks went by after its' publication, I began to receive letters from people who had read the novel. Some were concentration camp survivors, others were fortunate enough to have fled from Europe before being imprisoned.

The letters stunned me. A writer from England told me he had been treated by my father in Vienna, and remembered him well. Others told me that they had seen my mother in the camps, had seen my brother and father. Although the book was a complete work of fiction, somehow the family I had written about had a life of their own, and people responded to them.

A couple of students wrote that they used the book in their classrooms, and had written term papers discussing the novel. They enclosed the papers. More letters poured in. The novel had struck some kind of chord both in Europe and the USA. I had gotten letters from Australia and several from Israel as well. Although the sales weren't that strong, people were buying it all over the world and reading it carefully. And they were moved by the story.

It was at this point that I sat down with my father and told him I was going to leave the practice and devote myself to writing on a full-scale basis. To my suprise, he didn't argue or seem disappointed. He told me he understood and from this time on, our relationship changed. He became my biggest fan, looking forward to anything I would write in the future. And from that moment on, whenever I finished a novel, I sent him the manuscript to read first.

A reception was held by PEN, an author and editor organization, in which both myself and Elia Kazan, who had just published The Arrangement, were the honored guests. Most of the people there had read my novel, and I was honored myself to meet Maxwell Geismar and Malcolm Crowley, names that I had constantly come across in literary criticism. It was a high point in my career.

After the reception, I took some time off, and met a woman who was to become my second wife. Lynn and I traveled to New England, to Virginia and then to Tucson. Then we came back East and were married at my apartment in the Village. By this time I had a larger apartment on Charles Street. We sublet the place and bought a home in Woodstock, New York, in 1969, the same year we were married.

During that year, I tried to write a sequel to Nightmare of the Dark. I wanted to tell the story of Robert Lindner's experiences in the United States, but no matter how I struggled with the novel it didn't work out. I submitted part of it to Harding, but he didn't like it at all, feeling that it was a real comedown after the novel he had accepted.

So I put it aside, and moved to Woodstock. While there I struggled to write another novel.

IV

THE THIRD NOVEL AND PLAYBOY'S BOOK OF GAMES

I moved to Woodstock in 1969, purchasing a house on three acres of land for $25,000. It had only two bedrooms, and since my wife, Lynn, was a painter, I remodelled the garage so that it became a painting studio. I replaced the wooden roof with plastic panels to let in natural northern light. She also used the house, putting up an easel in the living room. Meanwhile, in order to find some privacy for writing, I strung together two extension cords and put my typewriter on a redwood picnic table in an adjoining screened in porch area, that had no heat and was open to the elements on three sides, covered only by large screened walls.

I guess I submerged my ambitions to my wife. She thought of herself as an artist, and I supported her work, but my own work suffered. Woodstock was basically an artist's colony, and the Arts Student League had their summer classes there. Artists came to our house, looked at Lynn's work, and we traveled to their studios to examine their work. I sort of moved to the background. Although my wife had never exhibited any work in a gallery, and I had two books under my belt, she was jealous of her time and space. When she painted, I had to be out of the house. My presence interfered with her work. I had no room to write in the house, and realized, after a while, that I had made a mistake buying it in the first place. It was my money that purchased the property, and I should have gotten space that I could use as well. But it was too late. So I was exiled to the screened-in space to the east side of the house. It was an unhospitable site for writing, but I perserved, trying to get something started.

I kept writing and discarding work. Nothing came easy this time. I began to envision plots instead of characters, and I no longer had the constant support and wisdom of Albert, who now lived 90 miles away and was busy with his private practice of psychiatry. Since my marriage, we had drifted apart.

The marriage itself was rocky. I had lived alone while writing my two novels, but now, there was a lack of privacy. Although I couldn't even speak when Lynn was painting, if I was sitting quietly, thinking, she would interrupt and ask me to do something, a chore around the house, take the car somewhere, something intrusive.

"As long as you're doing nothing," she'd begin, and I'd try and explain that I was doing something, I was thinking. She didn't see this as a viable answer. I became more and more annoyed as my privacy vanished. I'd go out to the screened-in porch and try to write, but nothing happened. I'd take long walks with my dog Sam.

In January of 1970, a week before my birthday, I knew I had to get out of there, even for a short while. I told Lynn I had a trip to take.

"Where?"

"I don't know where. Just a trip."

She was angry as usual, but I took the bus from Kingston into New York City. I didn't want to stay in New York, and thought longingly of the days I had spent in Baltimore, when I had attended Counter Intelligence School in Dundalk, a suburb of the city. I was twenty-one then, and every day in that school was an adventure. So I went down to the Port Authority Bus Terminal, and boarded a bus for Baltimore.

This wasn't the old Baltimore of twenty years before. While we went through the streets, some kids started throwing bricks at the windows of the bus, splattering them and injuring some passengers. Luckily I wasn't hit by flying glass. We stopped near the downtown section, and I went to the Y near the Enoch Pratt Free Library and stayed the night. The next day I arranged to drive a new Chevy to Sarasota, Florida. My expenses and gas would be paid. At least this transportation would be free.

I got as far as South Carolina, then the car began to have problems. By the time I hit Manning, I could only get it in second gear. I went to a Chevrolet dealer and then called the driveaway company that had hired me, telling them there were problems. They told me to wait it out and keep driving when the car was ready. It took three days to fix it, and meanwhile I enjoyed the hospitality of the small Southern town. As a northerner, I dreaded getting stuck in the South, subject to prejudice. Of course, I wasn't black, but I was Jewish. Instead of prejudice, the people in the town helped me out. They let me take out library books and provided a car for me to use.

When the car was ready, the manager of the dealership told me there'd be no charge. He wished me good luck, and now I drove a little faster, heading for the west coast of Florida, to the city of Sarasota. I delivered the car to an older lady, a retiree, and she took me to the local Greyhound station.

The trip back was dreary. I bought Arthur Hailey's Airport to read at a rest stop, but after getting through fifteen pages, I gave it to a fellow passenger. Someplace in Georgia, at three in the morning, I wandered around the rest stop and found a book that seemed interesting. I read the first couple of pages, then bought the book. It was Frederick Exley's A Fan's Notes. I read it with great interest as the bus crawled north. On my birthday, January 11, 1970, the day I turned 40, I ate alone at a Kentucky Fried Chicken outside of Alexandria, Virginia. When I got back to Woodstock, Lynn was pissed at me, but I didn't care. I was excited about writing again. Exley had put down the truth, I felt, in his book. His long slow decline into madness must have been difficult to write.

I thought about what he had done. Here I was thinking

about plots, and all I had to do was put down the truth. I reattached the extension cords to the screened-in porch, and put my typewriter out there. It was cold, but I dressed warmly, and sat and thought about a character to center the novel around.

I began to write a novel on that porch, working only at night, surrounded by the night noises of this rural area, and the smell of the pine trees which stretched on all sides. There was also hickory, sugar maple and birch trees in abundance on the property. It was also damp and cold. I went into the secluded area I had chosen, bringing paper with me, and carrying the portable SCM electric typewriter. My cat, Kitzy, accompanied me and lay on the table.

On the one wall that was a common wall with the house itself was a huge map of the United States. I stared at it and wrote:

"He used to sit in his room on the farm near Lamoni, Iowa, staring up at the wall map of the United States of America, the states outlined in five colors, noting that there were twelve yellow states and only eight green ones, noting that the breadth of America consisted of twelve states from California to New York, noting that in the Midwest from north to south there were only five states, Minnesota to Louisiana or Michigan to Mississippi, while in the crowded East there were as many as thirteen, if you counted from Maine to Florida, noticing most of all the hugeness, the immensity of the country.

And sitting there, feeling that he wanted to wander over all of it, wanted to embrace America, to see past the flat farmland country of youth, his youth, past the Rockies, to see the Pacific, feel the bulge of that enormous waterfront that faced Asia."

I felt that I was writing the story in a certain cadence, a certain rhythm. I had been to Lamoni, Iowa, with Lynn. Her grandfather lived there. Like Dachau, it had stayed in my mind, of course, for different reasons. I seemed to have the ability to remember places, though I was terrible at remembering names. But like the camp at Dachau, I had the small Iowa town in my mind's eye,

I kept writing at night. I started to realize that this book was vastly different than the others. The first novel had been a voyage of discovery for me, the second had been as taut as I could make it. In Nightmare of the Dark, with all its darkness and horror, I had simplified my prose dramatically. Now, this new book was expansive. My language was more involved with images and fantasy.

I was excited by it, and worked on through the nights. Writing at night, surrounded by the night smells and sounds, gave me a new outlook on my work. It was a book conceived in darkness. While working, my savings were rapidly running out. My money from the books and my law work were almost gone, and soon after I finished the novel, I was reaching a point of financial desperation. My parents lent me some money to continue on, but I needed a steady income.

A few months after beginning the novel, I wrote the last paragraph of the work.

"And spring came to America, and the seeds were sown in the great belt of prairie extending through the heart of the USA, and buds pushed through the ground breaking the soil, and children watching, wondered, and the mountains looked down on those plains and the rivers flowed through and time hung heavy on the nation."

The novel was finished. It still had the same cadence of the beginning. It was a big book, close to 800 pages long in manuscript form, and contained many characters and many stories, though at the heart of the book was the story of Dean Curtis Stillman, and his group's kidnapping of the daughter of the President of the United States.

I no longer had an agent. I had a disagreement with Robert after I found that he had disregarded publications such as L'Express in Paris which wanted to serialize Nightmare of the Dark. All sorts of subsidiary rights to the novel had been lost because of inaction. To find another agent, I took my manuscript on the bus down to New York, which was about eighty miles away, and decided to call agents in the city, staying temporarily at my parents' home. I started with the As and the Zs, going from the top of the alphabet to the bottom.

When I reached Y, I spoke to Mary Yost, who was interested in the novel, so I went to meet her at her office. We got along well, and she was enthusiastic about reading the new novel. She asked if I had anything else to give her.

"The only other thing is a few pages on games," I told Mary.

"What games?"

"Well, my friend Roy Friedman and his wife had wanted to go to Puerto Rico and gamble, and asked me to write something for them."

"Do you have it with you?"

"No, it's back in Woodstock, but I could mail it to you."

I had met Roy Friedman though my editor at Pocket Books, and we used to play tennis regularly on the courts at Central Park. Roy had published a novel at the same time that Rapt In Glory came out. It was called The Insurrection of Hippolycus Brandenberg and had been published by Stein and Day, and been selected by a couple of book clubs. Roy and I hit it off, and I spent a great deal of time with him and his wife, Louise.

Having grown up in Brooklyn, I knew a lot about gambling, and especially blackjack and craps, as well as poker. I had always been good with numbers, and remembered a time in Seth Low Junior High School in Brooklyn, when I was fourteen and sitting in the last class of the day, a study class. Everyone was restless, because it was late June and the sun was shining, and we were all hot and anxious to get out in the fresh air. In those days school ran almost to the end of June.

The teacher, desperate to create some order, told us that the first one to add up all the numbers from one to 100 could leave. So everyone got busy. I sat there, thinking. I always liked to fool around with numbers and this was a challenge. How much did the numbers 1 to 10 add up to? 55. That was easy. But why did they add up to 55? I wrote them out and realized that there was a pattern to these numbers. 1 and 10 added up to 11, and so did 2 and 9 and 3 and 8. In other words, there were 5 sets of 11. Well, the numbers between one and 100 meant that there were 50 sets of 101. I multipled these numbers; something I could do in my head. The answer was 5050. After a couple of minutes I raised my hand with the answer. The poor teacher was working away like everyone else, adding up columns of numbers to find the correct answer.

I told her how I found the answer and she looked at me in amazement, but I was out of there. But what good would arithmetic do me in life? This was not mathematics after all, and I never had any interest in science.

Roy had purchased a couple of books on games, and found he didn't understand them, for good reason. The writers were egotists, who tried to show off their knowledge with complicated and incorrect formulae, instead of patiently guiding the reader through the games. I wrote a couple of pages on each game and gave it to him.

He never did take the trip, but instead, without me knowing about it, he gave the pages to Stein and Day, to his editor. Roy was like that, helpful to a fellow writer. I never knew a sweeter guy. The editor he gave the pages to almost commissioned me to write a book on games, but in the end, decided against it. Gambling wasn't the big business it was today, and he felt the sales would be negligible.

Roy gave me back the pages, and when I got to Woodstock I mailed them to Mary. She read the new novel and liked it, and said she'd start submitting it. And in the meanwhile, out of money, I saw an ad for legal editors in The Law Journal, which I read from time to time. The company was Lawyer's Cooperative, and it was a publisher of legal books located in Rochester, New York. I figured with my writing background as well as legal background, I'd have no trouble getting a job there, and I was right.

Rochester was 270 miles north of Woodstock, and I took the long drive up there in April of 1970, found an apartment and became a long range commuter. Lynn stayed in Woodstock. Every other week, in good weather, I'd drive down and stay for the weekend. I had never really worked in a corporate structure before, but I needed money. At that time, the company was working on a definitive study of various legal topics, for its American Law Review series. They were up to the Rs, when I arrived, and I wrote three articles for them, "Rape," "Receiving Stolen Property," and "Replevin."

I had problems with my supervisor from the beginning. Before I worked on these articles, he gave me short assignments which I'd complete in two days. Since the average time to write these was two weeks, he thought I was being sloppy in my research. But I was used to writing at a fast pace. So, to conform, I followed the crowd, and wrote a few lines a day instead of three pages. Now I pleased him. The drive back and forth to Woodstock was wearying, and I was exhausted every Monday morning. But that paycheck was coming in on a regular basis. I could buy some new shirts, and pay the mortgage and put food on the table for Lynn, my two cats and my dog, Sam.

The summer dragged into fall, and it got cold in Rochester. I always hated overcoats, so instead I bought a blue lined raincoat, which I wore every day. I also wore an old checkered jacket inside the raincoat, and when I got to the office, I took off the coat, with the jacket inside intact, and worked in my office uniform of white shirt and tie.

Meanwhile my novel kept getting rejected. Then, in one conversation on the phone with Mary, she told me she thought the reason for the rejections was that the novel was too long, and she suggested I eliminate a couple of the subplots to shorten it. I reread what I had written, and saw that I could easily do this and still keep the main story intact. So I sent her a letter, with instructions to cut down the novel. The next publisher she sent the work to was Putnam, in its shortened version.

In early September I got a call from Mary. She told me that she had submitted the few pages on gambling to Playboy Press,

which had just been formed by Hugh Hefner. They were looking for men's books, and after reading the pages, an editor
wanted me to submit a couple of sample chapters to him. I
quickly wrote a chapter on poker and one on blackjack and
mailed them off to Mary. A couple of weeks later she called
me at the office.

"I have some good news," she said. "Playboy liked your
work and their people in New York want to meet you. I think a
contract to do a games book for them is in the works."

"Great. By the way, how's the novel going?"

"Oh," said Mary, "I guess you didn't get my last letter yet.
Putnam's taking it."

And there it was. Two acceptances in one day. We arranged for me to fly to New York to meet with both Playboy
and Putnam on the following Monday, to tie up all the strings.
I told my supervisor I had to go for some medical treatment to
a doctor in New York, and he readily agreed to give me some
time off from my article on Receiving Stolen Property.

In New York the following Monday, a warm beautiful fall
day in New York, with the air crisp and clear, I met Mary at her
office. She told me we were meeting Walter Betkowski, the
managing editor of Putnam, at the Italian Pavilion for lunch.
Off we went. The restaurant was spacious and expensive, and
when I went to check my raincoat, it was difficult to get the
jacket out of the sleeves of the coat. For months now I had
worn them as one unit. Now they were stuck together. When I
finally, with the help of the hatcheck girl, extricated the jacket,
I saw to my horror that the garment was wrinkled and looked
horrible. But I was already at the restaurant. Too late to go and
get another jacket.

Betkowski came in. He was a tall man, with blond hair, of
Polish descent, dressed immaculately, with a foulard tie and
matching handkerchief for his breast pocket. He looked like a
young god, and here I was in this old fashioned wrinkled
jacket, looking like a bum.

We were quickly seated, though the maitre d' looked

askance at my outfit. Betkowski had a packet of notes that he put on the table, and told me he wanted to discuss various aspects of the novel with me. I agreed. I knew I was two inches, as some baseball wit once said, from the big show, and there was no way I was going to blow it.

We ordered drinks first. I had my usual publishing drink, Cinzano on the rocks with a twist of lemon, thinking back to my meeting with the executives of Pocket Books. They both had stronger drinks. We ordered lunch, and Mary and Walter discussed some inside gossip about the publishing world. I tuned out. Then Walter turned towards me.

"Ed, I found your novel fascinating. And not only me. The novel was handed around the shop, and even the president of the company read it. It's a real counter-culture book. Very witty and very poignant at the same time."

I thanked him for his comments.

"What I want to talk about is the symbolism. The lief motifs that run through this work. I've made notes on several of them."

Now, I knew I never wrote anything to be symbolic. I just told my story, and let my characters loose on the page. Walter discussed the American flag, the highways, certain scenes as symbolic of the malaise of the American soul. He kept talking and I listened, nodding my head sagely. If he wanted to discuss symbolism in Hemingway's Farewell To Arms, for example, the diving into the water by Frederick Henry after the retreat at Caporetto, which might symbolize a baptism, a farewell from that time on to arms, I could relate to that. But I frankly didn't know what he was talking about. I listened soberly however, occasionally taking a bite of food and sipping iced water.

The meal went well. Mary thought it was a great success. We left the restaurant and walked over to Putnam's offices and there I signed a contract for the novel. Walter had a list of prospective titles for the new book. One of them, Sweet Land of Liberty, was finally selected.

From there I walked Mary back to her office, then went on

to the Playboy offices. After a short meeting, it was agreed that I would do a book of games for them, of about 80,000 to 100,000 words, or from 325 to 400 manuscript pages. The advance I was to receive was my biggest ever. I promised the book by March 1st of 1971.

I returned to Rochester to begin work on the games book. Although Rochester had a couple of fine libraries, there was very little on gambling or games to be found. I didn't know about places like the Gambler's Book Club in Las Vegas, Nevada, run by John and Edna Luckman, who would eventually be of enormous help to me, and turn out to be two of my closest friends.

I was residing in a small studio apartment with a couch that opened up into a bed. The place was spare and depressing, and the halls outside were simply cinder blocks painted over. I went to a local stationery store, purchased a couple of dozen file folders and wrote on each folder the game that it was going to contain. In all I used 26 of the folders. There were to be chapters on gin rummy, craps, bridge, poker, strip poker (the editors at Playboy wanted something like this to spice the book up) horse racing, sports betting, the psychology of winning (my choice) and others.

As with the novels, I followed a basic routine each evening. I came home from the office, washed up, and did some writing, then ate something, wrote some more and went to bed. A Spartan existence keeping me out of mischief. My goal was three pages a night and ten on the weekends. In this way I was sure I could finish the book by March. It was already the middle of September.

I told no one at the office about my contract for the games book, though I told a couple of friends I had made in Rochester about the acceptance of my novel. Both books were to be published the next year, in 1972.

As I wrote the games book, a strange thing occurred. I became mesmerized by the work, and felt as if I was in a trance most of the time. The folders filled up, and I was doing more than three pages a night. For a while, I commuted to Woodstock, but then told Lynn it was too draining, and that the book came first. This work, with the final payment due upon submission of a satisfactory manuscript, was my ticket out of Rochester. I wasn't going to blow it.

I had never done a non-fiction work before, so it was all new to me. First, I thought about my luck in getting the assignment in the first place. I had to thank my friend Roy Friedman for his interest in those pages. I also realized that by putting something down on paper, I had a shot at getting published. Words, as I have mentioned before, when spoken,float meaninglessly in the air. Words on paper are concrete. From that time on, whenever I had a meeting with an editor or publisher scheduled, I brought something in writing to leave with them. As a result, I frequently got small assignments where none would have been forthcoming if I had just spoken about a possible project. The editor or publisher would say, "ok, can you give us a few thousand words on this subject?" and I'd be off and running. I gave the same advice to my students when I held workshops...write it down!!

To me, one of the most pathetic and boring things is listening to would-be writers talking about the novels or books they were going to write. And they end up without anything but talk. Often I'd tune out of these conversations, knowing full well I had to return to the typewriter and put something on paper, either on spec or because I had a contract to write an article or book. I was never late with any deadline I ever had, and I wrote quickly. By writing fast I was able to get some lucrative assignments, because the people hiring me knew my work, and knew, even though I wrote at a rapid pace, it wasn't shoddy work. I always tried to do the best I could. It just so happened that I could get away with writing fast, doing little editing or rewriting. It was my style and my strength, a personal matter.

I know that writers operate in different ways. No one way is better than the other, but what any writer must do is his best work, and not submit anything that he can improve on. Handing in second-rate work is the earmark of the amateur and loser.

I worked on and on through the grim Rochester winter, where snow constantly fell, where the city prided itself on using more salt on its roads than any other community in America. During the day I kept on the Rs, finishing "Receiving Stolen Property" and beginning "Replevin." I could afford to work at a slow pace in the office, because that was what was expected of me. I had frightened my supervisor with my speed; now I settled into a leisurely crawl and that made him happy.

Thus most of the time in the office was wasted. I thought of doing my games book there as well, but decided against it. Even though I had a private office, I would feel pressure, worrying about someone coming in and noticing that I was doing personal work on company time. I left the games book writing for the evenings.

Even though my contract called for between 325 and 400 manuscript pages, by late November I already had reached this page mark, and was nowhere near the end. The book was getting bigger and bigger. I still had the original twenty-six folders, but in addition to the rules of play of various games, I added personal stories and anecdotes. I had never really written serious short stories, and I made up for this by putting all these anecdotes in the work. The games book was not going to be some dry exposition on games, nor was it going to be the ego trip of some games writers I had read, showing how clever they were.

In January I was near completion and went to find a typist in Rochester to put the work in final manuscript form. It took three tries before I could find the right one. The first was incompetent; and the second, everytime she made a mistake, would tear up the page and start anew. In one week she had four pages ready for me. Finally, I met a legal secretary who did the work evenings. She was efficient and fast.

When the final pages came back to me, I found myself with a manuscript of 922 pages! This was insane. I called the editors at Playboy and told them I would be coming in with the final manuscript. This was now January, 1972, and my novel was about to come out. I arranged for a flight to New York City, to pick up my novel and to turn in the completed manuscript of the book eventually called Playboy's Book of Games.

I carried in the manuscript to the Playboy offices in an empty box that originally held peaches and placed it on the table of the woman who would be editing the manuscript. She riffled through the pages and shook her head, and called in the editor-in-chief. He congratulated me on completing the book ahead of schedule, and liked the idea of this monster work. It could sell for more money and could be advertised as a definitive work on games and gambling. The subtext of the cover read "A Modern Day Hoyle for the Sophisticated On-The-Go Gambler." In its' original oversized trade size, the book ran 489 pages.

After taking care of this bit of business, I went over to Putnam and picked up ten copies of Sweet Land of Liberty. I liked the cover, which showed a crumpled map of America, with bloodstains over the state of Arizona. I shook hands with Betkowski, who was pleased with the way the book turned out, and then called Lynn in Woodstock to come into New York and meet me there. I was going to spend a couple of extra days over the weekend in the city. She drove down the next day, and we met at the Museum of Modern Art's bookstore. My plan was to go to the Brasserie Restaurant on Fifth Avenue, the restaurant we had eaten at on our first date, and make it a special occasion.

I had brought along the ten copies of Sweet Land of Liberty to show her, and planned to drive back with Lynn to Woodstock that night. But while we were in the bookstore, she ran into a playwright both of us knew from Woodstock. He was a neurotic guy, a manic-depressive. This day, he was full of energy, and insisted that we join him for lunch at the private dining club in the museum. I tried to beg off, but Lynn, who was in a sour mood, suggested that I was cheap, and wanted to get away with a meal in some hamburger joint.

I tried to explain to her that I wanted a private lunch, that I wanted to show her the new novel. She wasn't interested. She insisted on the lunch. I stood there like a fool, holding the bag of books. My own wife had no interest in looking at them. After all, I thought, how many novels does one get published in a lifetime? She was turning a big occasion into ashes. But she stood firm, and the playwright, hopping from one foot to another as though he needed to take a leak, insisted we go right up to the dining room.

I told Lynn to have lunch with him, and turned my back and walked out of the bookstore and the museum.

"What are you doing?" she said. "Where are you going?"

"I don't know."

"We have to drive to Woodstock tonight. Where will you be?"

"I'm not driving back with you," I said, and walked away.

It has been my experience as a writer that angry people have a simple way of venting their anger on artists. They simply refuse to look at the work they've done. Whenever I've given a novel or book of mine to someone to read and discover that they haven't gotten around to it after a week I know that unconscious anger is the cause, no matter what excuse they give. Whenever anyone asks me to read something they've written, I read it immediately. If I don't have the time, I tell them. I'm always anxious to look at someone's art or writing.

I think this is because I'm a writer myself. I'm not intimidated by excellent work. I'm always anxious to meet a fine artist. But inadequate people, who are never going to do anything important or serious in their life, get even with those who do. If they're given a book or manuscript, they don't read it, or worse still, they lose it. I had a good friend who met a woman he was attracted to, and like a fool, gave her an only copy of his manuscript, which she promptly lost by leaving it on the subway. What is this but unconscious anger?

I never give my work while it is in manuscript form or unfinished to anyone to read. I don't need opinions. The only opinions I care about are those of an agent or editor. And I'm always loath to give someone I've recently met any of my books. I'm tired of hearing from inadequate persons that they didn't get around to reading it. Or hearing some criticism that is vicious and would make a beginning writer lose all faith in his or her work. In this I take heart from Vladimir Nabokov, the author of Lolita, who wrote:

"Only ambitious nonentities and hearty mediocrities exhibit their rough drafts. It is like passing around samples of one's sputum."

When I walked away from the museum that afternoon, I knew that my marriage was over. I had supported Lynn in her art, going to galleries and agents with her, displaying her work, trying to be supportive of her work. At this point, she still hadn't a one-woman or group show in any gallery, though a couple of her paintings were exhibited before performances of Shakespeare in the Park in a temporary gallery set up there. This came through the auspices of Gail Merrifield, a friend of ours, who had married Joseph Papp, the director of the Public Theatre, which put on Shakespeare in the Park.

Well, I thought, she'd be on her own from now on. I returned directly to Rochester, and now that I had completed my work on the games book, I went in to see my supervisor to tell him I was leaving the job in two weeks. He was a soft and overweight man, and he looked at me in wonder as I told him I was going to quit.

"What do you mean, quit? You have security here. After five years you get three weeks vacation. And we have all these benefits. You can get a nice pension after thirty five years here."

As though any of this meant squat to me. I reiterated my desire to leave.

"What are you going to do once you leave?" he wanted to

know.

"I'm going to write."

"But you're writing here."

"A different kind of writing. Not about the law."

"You mean you want to write a novel or something like that?"

"Something like that," I repeated.

"You know, maybe you want to speak to my wife. She had a couple of articles published in "True Confessions." She could give you some advice."

"No thanks."

In March of 1972, after 11 months on the job in Rochester, I drove back to Woodstock. Lynn and I knew the marriage was over. She was anxious herself to get to New York and be in the art scene there. We sold the house and split the money and everything else down the line. I drove west in my Karmann-Ghia and left her the Volvo. I was heading for San Francisco. I would try my luck out there, and see what happened. I was finished with the East.

I loaded up my car and on a summer morning in 1972, I drove onto the highway, and was on my way.

V

THE WEST
AND LOSERS WEEPERS

I had always found it exhilirating to drive long distances, and going across the country this time was no exception. To wake up in strange places, to see cornfields and deserts, mountain ranges and the deathly eerie silence of the night sky across New Mexico; these were welcome sights to me, trapped so long in the East.

After six days of driving, I landed in San Francisco, a city I had visited many years before. I didn't know my way around, but by luck I met a stewardess while having breakfast, and she suggested that I try the Marina. It was an easy drive down Van Ness to Chestnut Street into that section of the city.

There were only a couple of "for rent" signs showing, and the first two apartments I examined were unfurnished. I needed a small furnished place, and one of the landlords suggested that something was available on Lombard. I went over and rented a small studio, much like the one I had in Rochester, with a couch that opened up into a bed. The rent was cheap and I liked the area. I unpacked the car, leaving a few things in it like blankets.

Then I explored the area. I walked down to the Marina Green, which abutted the bay, and then walked along the water to Fort Mason. Near to my apartment was a park with a public library and tennis courts. Everything was immaculate and shining and fresh. I had a good feeling about San Francisco. That night I opened the couch and went to bed, putting a light sheet over me. After all, it was August. In the middle of the night I woke up freezing, and went down to my car and brought up a couple of blankets, remembering wryly Mark Twain's remark that "the coldest winter I ever spent was August in San Francisco."

I had taken my tennis racket with me, and bright and early the next day I went down to the park and got into a game of doubles. After playing for about an hour, I returned to my place, then drove to the Marina Safeway and bought some food. I made breakfast, dragged my typewriter out and placed it on the kitchen table, and started work on a novel that had been in my head for a while. I was once more back in New York, back in the world of the courts and the Mafia.

I began the novel as follows:

"The assistant district attorney, Joseph F. Iola, had an oval face, which, in repose, reminded some of his friends and associates of Shakespeare's. When they told him about the resemblance, he was surprised, for he thought he had a typical Italian face; not that of southern Italy or Sicily, but of the northern region, near Padua, where his father and mother's family had resided."

Iola wasn't going to be a main character; he was there to begin the novel and introduce by conversation Carmine Abatto, a vicious tough guy who becomes a Mafioso. In a later chapter, I have a father and brother speak of Jacob Kaplowitz, a tough gambler, and they introduce him also in conversation. Thus my main characters make their appearances later on, after being spoken about by others.

I became immersed in the novel, typing every morning from about ten to noon, and sometimes at night. But after a couple of weeks every time I started to type, the tenant underneath me would bang on his ceiling. Thud, thud, thud. I'd stop typing and try a different time. Then would come the same pounding. After a few days of this, I went down to see whoever was doing this pounding. I knocked on the door, then heard a man ask who it was.

"I'm the guy who lives above you."

"Go away," he screamed.

"Look, if I'm bothering you with the typing, tell me what hours I should type."

"Just go away," he screamed even louder. The nut case underneath me was making it impossible for me to write. So I went to the manager of the building and told her I was typing at reasonable hours, but still this guy was pounding on the ceiling.

She shook her head. "He's been with us for five years now, and how long have you been here? A couple of weeks? If you don't like it, why don't you just leave?"

I had paid for one month, and given one month's security, and asked if I could get my security back.

"Are you giving notice now?"

"Yes."

"All right, come to me the morning you're about to leave and you'll get your security."

There was still a week to go in August. I started looking for another place in the Marina, but couldn't find anything. Rentals were tight. Then I got a letter forwarded to me from Playboy Press. It was from Jim Seagreaves, the public relations director of the Flamingo Hotel in Las Vegas. He told me that he had gotten an advance copy of Playboy's Book of Games and he and Burton Cohen, the president of the Flamingo had looked it over. If I ever wanted to examine the inner workings of a casino, they'd welcome me. I called Jim that afternoon, and told him I was thinking of visiting Las Vegas soon. He told me to look him up whenever I was in town.

After a few more days of looking for a new place to stay, I thought, why not go to Las Vegas? So, the last day of the month, I went to see the manager and got my security deposit back, loaded everything back in the car, and took off. It was about 580 miles from San Francisco to Las Vegas, and I spent the night in a motel near Gustines. The next day was a Saturday, the beginning of the Labor Day weekend, and that evening, after a leisurely drive, I found myself in Baker, about 90 miles from Las Vegas.

Other than Jim Seagreaves, the only one I knew in Las Vegas was a first cousin of my mother's, who had lived there since 1945. I had met him a couple of times, and figured, what the hell, I'd call him and find out where I should stay. I dialed his number, and he got on. I told him I was Fay's son, and he heartily asked how I was and where I was. I told him I was in Baker, on the way in to Las Vegas.

"Gee," he said, "the town is as tight as a drum. You can't find a room this weekend."

"I see."

"Stay in Baker for the weekend. Then things will open up."

Not once did he offer to put me up, even though he had a spacious house. I said goodbye and looked around the town, which wasn't hard to do. It was a stretch of dingy motels and gas stations, with a population of about 500, priding itself on being the gateway to Death Valley. That's where it stood, in an inhospitable desert with the sun blazing down, and the temperature close to 100 even in the early evening.

I got back in my car, and kept driving to Las Vegas. At the present time there are plenty of hotels at Stateline and all the way into Las Vegas, but then there was nothing but desert. I went past Stateline, with another 40 miles to go. I drove on I-15 and straight to downtown, where I knew there were a bunch of cheaper hotels and motels. I parked in the Mint parking lot, under a lamp, since I had everything I owned in the car, and I figured the lamplight would discourage a breakin.

I got out, carefully locked the Karmann-Ghia, and started looking for a room. My mother's cousin was right. The whole town was already taken by tourists. I traipsed around for about an hour, then got into the car and drove out of the city to North Las Vegas, where there were even cheaper hotels and motels. Nothing was available. I drove back to the Mint, and went to my old parking spot. In the casino I got a bunch of dimes and started phoning ads from the Las Vegas Sun. No luck. I walked to the coffee shop in the Mint and had something to eat. Then I went to the Keno lounge and sat and closed my eyes. I was beat. It was now close to midnight. Within a few minutes, I felt a rap on my shoulder. A security guard told me to get up and move on; this wasn't a bedroom.

I got up, and walked around, then spotted a lowball draw game of poker. One of the employees of the casino asked if I wanted to play. Why not? After all, I had written the book of games. I sat down among a bunch of drunken cowboys. By the time I quit I had won over $300. I got up, cashed in and walked to the men's room. Then I stepped outside for a minute. It was light out, and it was eight in the morning. I went to the gift shop and bought the Sunday Review-Journal, which I saw was much thicker than the Sun. There were plenty of classified ads in there.

Flush with the winnings, and feeling that Vegas might be lucky for me, instead of calling for motel rooms, I looked under "Apartments Furnished." One ad caught my eye. It announced it was halfway between the University and the Strip. Perfect. I called the number. A sleepy-voiced young woman answered, and I apologized for calling so early on a Sunday morning, but I explained I hadn't slept and was very interested in the apartment.

The place was out on Royal Crest, off Twain. I had no trouble finding it. It was a small one-bedroom apartment completely furnished, that rented for $140 a month. I took it immediately. I went back to my car, and brought up some sheets and blankets, and then lay down to sleep. Blissful sleep. When I awoke a few hours later I felt refreshed. I had made a decision. I'd explore Vegas for awhile.

The next day I went to the Flamingo and met Jim Seagreaves, who introduced me to Burton Cohen. Cohen and I got along well, and he told me to look around and explore any part of the casino I wanted to, and to use his name to gain entry to anything I cared to see.

Thus began my eleven months in Las Vegas. I'd go to the Flamingo every day, and look around. This experience eventually led to my fifth novel, Snake Eyes. Each evening I'd continue writing. Although people told me that Vegas would be a cold place, other than my cousin, everyone was helpful. I called the English Department at UNLV and spoke to the chairman, Arlen Collier. He invited me over that Wednesday afternoon, and when I arrived at his office, he had several professors there who were interested in writing, and it was like a small literary reception. One of the men I met there, John Unrue, eventually became chairman of the department and later vice-president of the University. He and his wife, Darlene have stayed my friends all these years. Both were extremely helpful and supportive to me, and I dedicated my next novel, Losers Weepers, to John Unrue and Roy Friedman.

Las Vegas was a twenty-four hour city. No longer did I have a nut job pounding at his ceiling whenever I typed. I typed at all hours, and the book moved along. I ran into my mother's cousin a week later at the Desert Inn, and he was all smiles and hellos. Why hadn't I contacted him now that I was living in town? He'd open up some doors for me. Yeah, I thought, like he opened his home to me.

I became friendly with his son, Steven, and the two of us hung around together some evenings. I saw all aspects of Vegas, from the chip hustlers who operated in the casinos; the crossroaders who would steal anytime, anyplace; the small-time gamblers; the petty scam artists; the hookers; the card counters; the whole spectrum of the city including the English department at the University. It was a wide canvas indeed and I soaked it all in. It was all grist for the mill.

After I had been in Vegas a couple of months, a big package arrived from Playboy Press. In it were my ten copies of Playboy's Book of Game. Then Steven showed me ads for the book in Playboy magazine. The ads stated that the book was a top choice of Playboy Book Club. Then a friend of mine from Rochester, Irwin Schiffres, mailed me a copy of the Book of the Month Club News. The games book was featured in the magazine, taking up two full pages in the center of the magazine, with my picture there as well. Other book clubs picked it up. The book started to sell briskly.

I continued to go to the Flamingo. At that time it had not been remodeled, and was the same place that Bugsy Seigel had built, with ornate chandeliers and carved statues, a sort of desert Monte Carlo. This was the first of three times I lived in Las Vegas. I returned again in 1976, and finally in 1980, and each time stayed a little less than a year.

While in Las Vegas, I encountered a number of people who had read the book on games, and wanted advice from me on how to gamble. Several wanted to back me at the casinos. One of those men, John Mechigian, asked me to write a travel guide to Las Vegas and vicinity, which he would publish privately. I went around to the casinos, interviewing executives and looking over the facilities at all the hotels and casinos. The next year, 1973, Las Vegas, An Insider's Guide, was published.

By the time I left Las Vegas, I had divorced my second wife. I handled the divorce myself. The time I spent on the travel guide hampered my efforts at finishing my novel, and when I moved back to San Francisco, I was still working on it. I found another studio apartment right off Chestnut Street, in the Marina and moved in. This was in July of 1973.

I knew only a couple of people in San Francisco. One of them, my wife's cousin, was Ron von der Porten, a world-class bridge player. We'd get together for tennis a couple of mornings a week, and afterwards go out for breakfast. I began to realize that most of the people I knew led unstructured lives. They were independent and worked for themselves, living, as I did, by their wits and talent. But I hadn't met any serious writers in the city, and in an attempt to meet some, I went to a workshop held at the main branch of the San Francisco Library.

I was pretty naive to think that this was the way to meet writers. I brought along the first few chapters of my novel to read, and sat at a long oblong table in one of the rooms, with about fifteen others, men and women, most of them younger than me. The leader of the workshop had published some stories, and when he read from a couple of them and mentioned the magazines they had been published in, I began to realize that these were cowboy stories.

The first man to read read a section of a novel, which took place in 16th Century Spain, was embarassingly bad, but when he finished, the comments around the table ran from "great" to "brilliant." I thought, maybe this guy needs some support from the group. They can't all write like this. The next reader was a woman describing some mawkish moment in the life of her characters, with tears running down the cheeks of the characters. It was sickening in its sentimentality. Again, the comments were of the same tenor. "Moving, absorbing, great, brilliant, remarkable stuff." The leader of the group told her to send it off immediately to Knopf and Viking Press.

The reading continued. One was worse than the other. Then some fellow in a leather jacket read a chapter from his novel about bikers on Highway 1, the Pacific Coast Highway. One of the bikers zoomed off the road and flew three hundred feet into the ocean. The other biker parked at the spot and drank a beer and when some tourists came by and asked what happened, he said "you wouldn't understand."

There was a long silence after he finished. Then a woman in the group asked if he had submitted the novel.

"Yeah, but it keeps getting rejected."

"Anytime they see a California postmark," the leader explained, "they automatically reject it. This is fine work. Keep pushing."

"It's the best thing that was read today," someone else said. "It's awesome. It's profound."

And on and on. Now it was my turn. The leader turned to me. "What's your name?" he asked.

"Ed."

"Would you like to read?" I had foolishly put a file folder

containing pages from my novel on table in front of me.

"No...no thanks...I don't think I'm ready."

"Well," he said,"don't be intimidated by the work read here...after all, they've been at it a long time."

A couple of minutes later, I got up and left. So much for meeting writers in San Francisco. If I was to meet them, it wasn't going to be at these places.

I now concentrated on the new novel. It was a complicated plot, the story of one character moving back and forth, from childhood to manhood, and back again, while the other character's story was told in a straightforward fashion. I was living off the money I had from Vegas, and of course, the royalties from Playboy's Book of Games, which continued to sell at a rapid pace.

I lived frugally, and felt that money meant only one thing to me, freedom to write. I still had the Kharmann Ghia, and would have it for several more years. My needs were simple, but two of my kids were now in college and that ate into my funds.

I visited the coffeehouses in the area. In one I met a poet, whom I'll call Betty James. She was sitting at the next table, looking over pages of poetry, and I was correcting the last chapter of my novel. Our eyes met and we began to talk. She had the open face of someone from the heartland of America, and she had come from Illinois a couple of years before. She asked me if I'd like to look at her poetry.

I read several of her poems, and then handed them back to her. "What did you think?" Betty asked.

I have a policy in reading that I've always adhered to since I became a writer. If someone wants me to look at his or her work, I do it as soon as I can. And I never critique the work unless asked. I'll simply hand it back and say, "thanks for sharing it with me."

If I'm asked what I think of the work, and I find it isn't really good, I'll say "I see your writing is serious. Keep at it." If the work is better, then I'll give my honest opinion. But I will never comment unless asked, and I never will savage a work. I refuse, as I often told my classes and workshops, to tread on anyone's dream.

When Betty asked me what I thought, I answered as truthfully as I could. I felt that the poetry and the images were strong and moving, but there were a number of extraneous lines in each of the poems.

"I'd do some cutting," I said.

"Such as..."

"Can I write on these pages?"

"Ok. I have copies."

I cut various lines from each of the poems. Betty watched me silently, then when I was finished, she said that I was mistaken; the poems didn't need any cutting. And she got a bit peeved.

"I guess I better get going," she said, and summarily picked up her work. I'd seen this reaction before by writers and would see it again over the years. We had exchanged numbers before I did the cutting, and I never expected to hear from her again.

About two weeks later, I finally finished my novel. I called it Losers Weepers, without hesitation, the only novel since Rapt in Glory that I had an immediate title for. Having completed it, I sent it off to my agent, with a simple letter, stating that here was the completed novel, and making no comment about its quality. I knew anything I said positively wouldn't sway her or an editor, and I was certainly not going to say anything negatively.

I've often been asked by students and beginning writers about the cover letter for a submission. I tell them the simplest is best.

"Enclosed please find a short story (novel) entitled X, and running X number of words and pages. I would be interested in your feelings concerning the same."

Always ask the editor or agent for his or her feelings. Usually this will give you a good idea of just how the reader feels about the work. And never comment favorably or unfavorably about your work. The kiss of death is to write "I think this is the best work I've done," or, "I think you'll find this to be a solid novel," or anything in that vein.

Well, I thought, that novel is out of the way. I didn't know what to write next and I felt I needed a break from writing. I explored the city, and took a couple of short trips to Big Sur and up to Lake Tahoe. When I returned from northern California, I was surprised to hear from Betty James. She told me she'd like to have dinner with me one night, and so we met in the Marina at a small restaurant on Union Street.

She greeted me with a cheery wave when I saw her. We sat down, and she pushed over a letter to me. It was from a literary magazine. They had accepted four of her poems.

"That's great," I said.

"The thing is," Betty said, "I sent them off with your cuts. They've been rejected a bunch of times, but boom, right away, they've been accepted. I want you to look at my other poems. And I have a friend I told about you, and she wants to show you her short stories."

Betty asked if I would be interested in holding a regular workshop. I told her I didn't know anyone in town, and she suggested that I put an ad in the Bay Guardian for possible members. We went out later and bought a copy of the newspaper, published weekly. That week I put an ad in, mentioning that a published writer was going to hold a weekly workshop, and poets, short story writers and novelists could apply. I listed my phone number and the calls started to come in when the new edition was published.

The first workshop I held was on a Tuesday night in my small apartment. Ten people came. Of these, about six were serious writers. Others were of the caliber that I had seen at the library workshop. I set strict rules. The work had to be serious, and this wasn't going to be a handholding kind of therapy where everyone said "great" or "wonderful" just so they would be greeted with the same kudos. In fact, I told them, it was unimportant what they thought about the work being read. What was important was what I thought. So, we wouldn't be going around the room for comments after work was read aloud. I would first comment, and then others could say what they wanted.

I told them I was going to be tough, but I wouldn't be vicious. I wanted them to do serious work and get published; that was the goal of the workshop. Of the ten who came the first week, six came back the next week, with two new students. The workshop held. Gradually, it expanded to about fifteen writers, with ten or eleven coming on any Tuesday night. The workshop lasted for two and a half years, and a lot of work was done there. Eight full novels were written. The group was like a family. We'd hold parties and friendships and even romances developed. One couple got married as a result of the workshop.

Among my students was Ray Riegert, who started writing science fiction, then switched to travel writing. I encouraged him to buy back Hidden Hawaii, his first published travel book, and he expanded his little publishing venture into Ulysses Press, one of the premier travel publishing companies in the world. He and his wife, Leslie Henriques, have stayed my lifelong friends. Henry Toledano, who runs Books, Etc. in San Francisco, is another lifelong friend.

A friend of mine in New York wrote to me and told me that someone from the old neighborhood I had grown up in in Brooklyn was living in San Francisco. His name was Herb Wilner, and he was a writer. I called him up, and he told me to come right over. He didn't remember me, though I remembered him well. At the time I knew him I was about fourteen and he was sixteen, and two years at that stage of life is a big difference. Whereas I was a clumsy athlete, Herb was the captain and president of the Aces, a social-athletic club in the neighborhood. He was their top athlete, and excelled in all sports.

He greeted me warmly, and introduced me to his wife and children. His wife had been his childhood sweetheart and he wanted to know if I stayed in touch with any of the old gang I knew. I still had a couple of friends from that time, but their names meant nothing to him. He rattled off the names of the athletes I had remembered from the Aces, and told me what they were doing at this time. He had stayed in touch with everyone.

At that time, Herb had already published a novel, All The Young Heroes, about the old neighborhood. All the main characters in that novel were teenage boys. He filled me in on his life. After college, he had gone for a Master's and PhD in English, had been an instructor, then professor, and finally, at this time, he headed the creative writing program at San Francisco State University. He had spent his entire adult life in academia.

As we spoke, I began to ascertain that the glory years of his life were the teenage years, when he had been a star athlete and leader of his club. He asked me if I recalled how great those years were. I told him they were dismal years for me, growing up as an adolescent in Brooklyn. Then I told him what I had been doing as an adult. I basically was still living by my wits and talent, while he had this ordered life, tenure and security, two things I wanted no part of.

The shoes had been reversed. He was anxious to hear about my travels and adventures, and the books I had written. I told him about my workshop, and how well it was working out. At that time, unfortunately, Herb had a bad heart, though he looked in the same fine physical condition I had remembered. Several years later, he died an untimely death on the operating table, and Esquire later published three short stories of his posthumously.

Another writer I met was Jerry Kamstra. At the time he was working out of a small studio on the second floor of the City Lights Bookstore. We had been introduced, and he asked me which writers I liked. When I told him about Frederick Exley, he got up and shook my hand warmly. He also admired A Fan's Notes. Jerry had published Weed, a book about his adventures as a dealer of marijuana, and was to soon publish The Frisco Kid, a novel about the early days of the beats in San Francisco.

My novel had been rejected by Putnam, but it had soon gone to Doubleday, where a senior editor of the house, Tom Congdon, had read it. I was going to New York, and called Mary, who told me that Congdon wanted a meeting with me at Doubleday to discuss the work. So I flew to New York, and then wound up at 245 Park Avenue on the 38th Floor for a meeting with Congdon.

He had the manuscript in front of him when we met. He told me he liked the writing, but there was one problem. He felt this should be strictly a Mafia book, and that I should eliminate the character of Jackie Crews, the name the character Jacob Kaplowitz used when gambling. If I could do that, he said, then they'd publish the novel.

I had been through this kind of thing before with editors. My feeling remained the same. I trusted my judgment in writing over theirs. I sat and thought about it, and then told Congdon to return the manuscript to me. He was surprised by my reaction.

"I said we'll publish the book if you make these changes. We want to publish this novel."

"I can't decimate the book," I told him. "There's a reason for both characters. This is not a Mafia book; this is a book about fathers and sons, about manhood and self-destruction as a result of pride of manhood."

"Well, I'll look it over again and let you know my decision."

"If you hold onto the novel, I'd like some option money."

"What?"

"Why don't I call Mary and let her know what is happening." I called her from my office and explained my position. She got on the phone with Congdon. They had a brief talk, and he hung up the phone.

"She's agreed to let me hold it, and I'll give you my answer within two weeks."

"Ok."

The meeting was over. I left the office, not knowing what was going to happen. I spent a week in New York, and during that time we didn't hear from Congdon. Then I returned to San Francisco, where a letter from him was waiting for me. It was just a brief note.

"Not bad news is coming," it said. What the hell did that mean? A double negative. Well, the two weeks would soon be up. Then, a week later, there was another envelope from Doubleday in my mailbox. I brought it upstairs to my apartment and put it on the coffeetable. I prepared a cup of coffee and sat and calmed myself. I told myself that I would feel the same, rejection or acceptance.

I had learned an important lesson as a writer. When a book was accepted, I didn't get that high, because I knew I'd go that low if it was rejected. I tried to keep at a steady temperament, win or lose. Otherwise, it's practically impossible to be a writer, with rejection always staring you in the face.

I sat there for fifteen minutes, the envelope on my table. Win or lose, it would all be the same. I'd go up a little, of course, if the novel was accepted. But I'd drop a bit only if it was rejected. I had been rejected many times before. My best novel to date, Nightmare of the Dark, had been rejected with words like "distasteful" and "disgusting."

Finally I opened the letter. The novel had been accepted, and Congdon informed me that Lisa Drew and Betty Heller would now be handling the book. I had never met either woman, but in the years ahead, I grew to like both of them. They were competent and goodhearted, enthusiastic editors.

Losers Weepers would be my fourth published novel. A booksigning would later be arranged at Minerva's Owl Bookstore on Union Street. With the workshop and the acceptance of the novel, I felt fulfilled in San Francisco. The years I spent there at this time, from 1973 to 1976, were the happiest years of my life.

My girlfriend during that period of time was Molly Pratt, a

lovely Southern woman from Charleston, South Carolina. She had originally been brought to my workshop by Judy Askew, one of the members, and afterwards, she gave me her phone number. From the first time we got together, we hit it off. Whenever my mother and father would visit San Francisco, we'd all go out together. My parents loved Molly, and although they usually stayed out of my private life, they nudged me constantly, asking me why I didn't marry her. Why didn't I? Again, it was my work. I needed the privacy to do the writing. As Goethe wrote "a talent is born in stillness," and the only way I could find that stillness was by myself. Certainly, I traded certain pleasures in life for the pleasure of writing. Was the tradeoff worth it? I don't know.

At the party at Minerva's Owl bookstore, I was introduced to Floyd Salas, the author of a fine prison novel, Tattoo the Wicked Cross. We were both a little high from too much wine, and he took me aside and told me something that I've never forgotten.

"The only kind of novel to write," he said, "is one, if you don't write it, you're going to die." Those words made a tremendous impact on me, for he was right. Not that I'd die for a novel, but one should write something important, something that must come out. Some novels have to be written; they have to come out of you, or you'll be sorry for the rest of your life that you didn't write them.

Writing that way separates the hacks from the serious writers; separates those who are looking for big bucks out of their fiction from those whose words bleed on the page. It's why I could be inspired by Frederick Exley's book, A Fan's Notes, and something like Airport, with all its crafted plots and subplots, could safely be given away after the first fifteen pages.

It's hard to define the difference between serious work and garbage, but for me, it often boils down to how I feel from the work, whether it moves me, whether it touches a raw nerve of the soul. That's why Chekhov remains my favorite writer, that's why a novella like Death In Venice is great. Thomas Mann, as well as any writer, knew the torments of the artist, and to read Tonio Kroger should be required of any aspiring writer.

Instead, many beginning or would-be writers are looking to strike it rich with a bestseller. And in order to write that bestseller, they read bestsellers. I've always maintained and still do, if you read junk you write junk. I believe it was Mark Twain who wrote that it is "better not to read than to read trash."

When I taught my creative writing classes at UCLA and USC I always went around the room at the first session, asking the students whom they read. And I insisted that they stop reading the popular authors of the day, and read the classics. For many, reading Mann or Chekhov or James Joyce were real eyeopeners. Great writing is inspiring to the serious writer. If only money is inspiring, then the writer should go into business.

There are those who get million dollar advances and wind up on the bestseller lists and are courted by Hollywood. A good example is a writer as mediocre as John Grisham, whose novels read like plot lines to movies. When people recommend books for me to read, I know the quality of their taste in an instant. I had a producer recommend Rage of Angels, by Sidney Sheldon. How could I take him seriously after that?

Of course, this is not to say that I am among the great writers of the time. Far from it. But I have attempted, in my fiction, to write seriously. Whether or not I have succeeded is not my judgment call. I tried my best, and as I've often written, to do one's best is all that can be asked of anyone.

After the party at Minerva's Owl, Molly and I walked down Lombard Street, away from Union Street. We ran into someone she knew, Ken Uston, who had read a couple of my novels and Playboy's Book of Games. He asked me to give him a call at the Pacific Stock Exchange, where he was a vice-president. I called a few days later and met him there. He had completed a book and wanted to know if I was interested in editing and collaborating on it in final form. We never did agree, and the book, The Big Player, came out a year later and never went anywhere. It was about big time blackjack by teams of cardcounters in casinos.

Later Ken and I stayed in touch, and he went on to be the best known of the blackjack counters, appearing on shows like "60 Minutes." He loved the notoriety and danger of beating the casinos in disguises of all kinds, and courted publicity, but died rather young in Paris, supposedly of a heart attack.

In 1976, my workshop had been going for over two and a half years. Novels had been completed, and I was getting restless myself. I received a note from Tony Bill, who had produced "The Sting," a wildly successful film starring Robert Redford and Paul Newman, telling me that he had enjoyed reading Losers Weepers, and asking me to give him a call anytime I was in Los Angeles.

It was the second time I had heard from movie people. When Rapt In Glory came out, and I was living on Sheridan Square in the Village, I was surprised to get a call one afternoon from Richard Conte, who had read the novel. He was calling from the Beverly Hills Tennis Club, and had gotten my number through my agent at Curtis Brown. Although he was interested in starring in the film version, nothing came of it.

But now, in 1976, I was ready for a change. I packed all my goods in the Karmann-Ghia and headed for Los Angeles on the spur of the moment. I took a furnished apartment on Larabee Street in West Hollywood, right off Sunset Boulevard. Then, after settling down, I called Tony Bill. He invited me down to his office in Venice, and I went there one afternoon. With him was Ulu Grossbard, a director of both films and plays. We talked about Losers Weepers, and, though he liked the book, he didn't think it would play as a film. But he told me to try my hand at a screenplay, for he felt that writing dialogue was natural for me.

I wrote a screenplay and brought it to him. He gave it to Ulu Grossbard, who called me up one day and invited me to his house in the hills near Bel Air. I went up there and we discussed screenplays. I had written the screenplay like a novel, and it had several long scenes. He put on a movie for me and showed me that the average scene in a film lasted about twenty seconds, before another camera angle was inserted.

"If you write a 120 page screenplay, which is the average length," said Grossbard, "then you should have that many or more scenes in the script." We spent a couple of hours talking about film and screenplays, and I learned more in that session than I ever did reading any material about the art of the screenplay. I started to realize that the best way to write a screenplay was to have the camera as the narrator, and to let the actors breathe with action, not dialogue.

Later on, I used this knowledge in fiction, often imagining an imaginary camera stationed above the scene I was writing, taking in everything, but unable to go to the interior of the characters' minds. In a screenplay, the actors' skills reveal their interior feelings. In prose, the dialogue and the movements of the characters in narration can accomplish the same thing.

I spent six months in West Hollywood. During that time I met a lot of young people on the fringes of the movie business, desperately trying to break in. Some of them worked in theatre as directors and actors. I attended a number of plays, some put on by people I had met, usually in small theatres around the city. I also met several agents and showed them my novels, but nothing really happened. But the experience was invaluable, more grist for my writing mill. Later, in Abandoned, I made good use of all these experiences.

On a trip to New York, Mary told me that Tom Congdon was now with Dutton and wanted to see me. I went over and he asked me what I was working on. I told him I was thinking of doing a novel about Las Vegas, based on my experiences there. He asked me to submit an outline to him, which I did, and then a few sample chapters, a big mistake. I signed a contract with Dutton to do a novel about gambling, the first time I had a contract in advance to do a novel.

Back in Los Angeles, I worked on it, writing and rewriting the material. For the first time since I had become a novelist, I found it difficult going. I believe one of the difficulties was having to send finished material to the editor, and then getting critiqued. I would rewrite and rewrite, till the pages fell at my feet like crumpled leaves.

I wrote and abandoned a good six hundred pages before I got the story and the characters straight, much of this complicated by adhering to the outline. Finally it was done. I worked closely with Congdon on the book, and it came out in 1977 as Snake Eyes, my fifth published novel. Before it was published, but after it was done, I took a trip to Las Vegas, where I dropped in on John Luckman at the Gambler's Book Club. He wanted me to do a series of small books for him and suggested that I return to Las Vegas, as nothing was really happening for me in LA. I left my car in his parking lot, and he gave me a van to drive back with to Los Angeles. Once there, I loaded it up and headed back to Vegas.

In Vegas I wrote Smart Casino Play, Play Pinochle Tonight, Play Chess Tonight and Play Bridge Tonight. These came out in 1976, the year I returned to Las Vegas for the second time. I still get royalties on these books, small sums, but they still come in.

While in Vegas, I met Alan Goldberg at John Luckman's office. He wanted me to organize a book he was doing with Doyle Brunson,a two-time poker world champion. The book was originally called How I Made $1 Million Playing Poker, and is still in print today as Doyle Brunson's Super System. In the course of working on the book, I spent many long hours with Doyle, who is one of the most brilliant men to ever play poker. I sat and listened to his wisdom. It was invaluable. While in Vegas I met A.D. Hopkins, an editor at the Las Vegas Review-Journal, who also worked on Doyle's book. I've stayed close friends with him and his wife, Pat, ever since, sharing an interest in writing and literature.

Again, Las Vegas could only hold me for a short time. I left after eleven months and returned to San Francisco in 1977. I seemed to be traveling in triangles, San Francisco to Las Vegas to Los Angeles, or any combination of the three.

San Francisco was not the same for me the third time around. I missed the workshop but didn't have the energy to start a new one. I found an apartment in the Marina again, this time on Chestnut Street. The year was 1977. I started to get assignments to do gambling books, which now took up most of my time.

Roy Friedman had introduced me to Carolyn Trager, a senior editor at Franklin Watts, and I wrote How to Gamble and Win for that house. For David McKay Publishing, I did Winning Casino Craps, which came out in 1979 and is still in print after all these years. I also did Winning Poker Strategy for the same publisher. Playboy's Book of Games had established me as a writer of games; now I was an authority on games, soon to be called the leading authority on gambling in America.

After doing a few of the gambling books, I turned back to fiction. In early 1979 I started another novel, which I wrote within two months. I was back to my old rhythm in writing fiction, and felt good, especially after the difficulties I had had with Snake Eyes. This book dealt with a failed writer in Hollywood who is offered a chance to relive the Robinson Crusoe story, that is, go to a desert island by himself, and then write his story. After I completed the book, I sent it off to Mary Yost.

She liked it, and told me to fly into New York so that I could have a couple of meetings with editors. My first was with Lisa Drew, who had been my editor at Doubleday when Losers Weepers was published. She hadn't seen the manuscript but wanted to have lunch with me. I told her over coffee what the story was about. In the course of the novel, my character is allowed to have five books on the island, any five he wanted to select.

Lisa was intrigued by this, and told me the five she would select for a two year stint on a desert island. By the time we finished our coffee, she called Mary to messenger the manuscript over. I returned to San Francisco, and a short time after, the book was accepted by Doubleday. But as I basked in the acceptance, Mary called me a few weeks later. Although it had been accepted by a senior editor, the sales department had vetoed the acceptance. I was nowhere. I couldn't believe this.

But it was so. It's bad enough being rejected, but to have a book accepted and then have a publisher reject it was a brutal experience. I stewed in my apartment. Then fate intervened, as it had so often in my writing career. I had a close friend in San Francisco named John Capman. He owned the Writer's Bookstore off Union Street. John drove an old Jaguar and had a great love of books. His bookstore sold both new and used books, the new ones being review copies for the most part. It was visited by all kinds of people, and one time I had a short chat with Daniel Ellsberg in there, who had been the instigator of The Pentagon Papers.

I'd usually show up at the bookstore near closing time at about eight, and John and I would then hang out together. One evening, after the catastrophic news from Doubleday, I was introduced to Maria Theresa Caen, the wife of Herb Caen, the well-known columnist for the San Francisco Chronicle. Everyone in the city read Herb Caen. He was to San Francisco what Walter Winchell had been to New York journalism.

John mentioned to Maria that I was a published writer and had written a new novel. She was a literary agent and John suggested that she read it. Maria Theresa was lukewarm about the idea but told me she lived on Broadway a few blocks away,and told me to bring the manuscript up the next day at noon. When I arrived at the big Caen house a maid showed me in. Maria Theresa was in the kitchen, on the phone, and told me to leave the manuscript; she'd get back to me in a few weeks. She had other material to read. I told her I understood, and left the manuscript on the parlor table.

My feeling was that nothing was going to happen. She had been a little hesitant about reading it when I met her at John's store; only his insistence had caused her to ask me over. I could wait a few weeks. Nothing was happening with the novel right then. And I doubted whether she could do anything with it.

I always felt the best agents operated out of New York City, and I knew nothing about Maria Theresa, other than that she was Herb Caen's wife. So I was surprised when two nights later, my phone rang. She was on the phone and asked if I could meet her at her house the next morning at ten.

"Sure," I said.

She said nothing more. At the house the next morning, she asked about the history of the manuscript. Where had it gone? I told her about the acceptance at Doubleday, and the rejection afterwards.

"They're out of their minds," she said. "This novel must be published. It knocked me out. Where did you ever come up with a story like this?"

It was really a rhetorical question. She told me she had contacts at Doubleday, that she knew the publisher, Sam Vaughn, personally, and was going to get the work published there.

"You think it's possible?" I asked.

"Look, the reason I wanted to meet you now...I want you to sign something showing I'm your agent." I told her that Mary Yost was my agent, but I'd be happy to pay each a full commission, and signed a note to that effect. Maria Theresa told me she was flying to New York the next week to meet with some people, and would see Sam Vaughn then.

I didn't think she could pull it off; it had sounded like a dead issue, but I didn't want to dampen her enthusiasm. It's always good to have someone champion your work. John Capman told me she was tight with people at the highest level of society, and it might just work out.

This was in November of 1978, in a couple of weeks my parents were coming out to see me. When they arrived, we went out on the town, along with Molly, who I still saw. One night we went out to Adolph's in North Beach, a favorite restaurant of my father's. We all had a big meal. At about two in the morning, my mother came into the living room where I was sleeping on a couch and woke me.

"What is it?" I asked sleepily.

She told me my father was thrashing about, couldn't sleep and didn't look good. I called the local hospital and asked to speak to a nurse. I had seen my father; he was sweating profusely and said his left arm was in pain. The nurse told me to bring him in right away. I helped him down the stairs and to the car and drove like a madman to the hospital. He was immediately wheeled in, and a little while later, a doctor came out and told me my father had suffered a massive heart attack. He was alive, but the attack had done a lot of damage.

He was resting comfortably when we saw him. It was agreed that he would stay with me after his release from the hospital, while my mother would return to New York. I could take care of him easily. He stayed in the hospital for about a week, then in my apartment for several weeks. When I returned with him to New York his cheeks were rosy; he looked good.

In New York, he insisted on returning to the practice of law; he didn't want to become an "invalid." I tried to talk him out of it, insisting that he retire, but it was to no avail. When I left him a week later, his complexion was ashen, and his hands were shaking badly. My heart sank.

While in New York, I saw my agent and some publishers. Carolyn Trager, who had been at Franklin Watts, and for whom I had done *How to Gamble and Win*, had moved to Holt, Rinehart and Winston. She wanted a big gambling book, and I signed a contract to do *The Winner's Guide to Casino Gambling*. When I returned to San Francisco, I began work on that book.

I was tremendously worried about my father's health, and from December, 1978 to March, 1979, I flew into New York three times at my mother's request, each time praying that my father was ok; that he hadn't died. I would go right from JFK to the hospital, where he'd be in the Intensive Care Unit, recovering from yet another heart attack.

By March of 1979, I was about halfway through the book, which was turning into a big project, almost as big as the original games book I had written for Playboy. I wanted this to be a work that would be the reference work for gamesters and carefully crafted it.

In March, my father called me. He was at home, resting, and we had a long talk. He told me he missed me, and wondered if I could fly into New York and spend a little time with him. I agreed. What was unsaid was that he was dying and knew it, and wanted to spend time with his only son before he passed on. That night I was on a plane to New York.

When I got to my parents' home, my father was resting comfortably, but still involved in the practice of law. Because of his illness, everything was disorganized. I had freed myself of that practice a decade before, but I couldn't allow my father to be under pressure. So I became a lawyer again, handling contracts and motions and whatever else had to be done. I discouraged new business, and would sit in my father's law office going over files, trying to close out legal matters. It was chaotic.

At the same time I continued writing the book for Holt, Rinehart. The pattern of my life was now set for awhile. I practiced law most of the day, and wrote most of the night. When I hear writers complain that they don't have the time to work, I can't be that sympathetic to them. With my very first novel, I was a full-time professional, and since that time I've been under enormous pressure to work and write at the same time. If that's the only way to do it, then it must be done that way.

My parents had been married for fifty years that February 24th, but at that time my father was in a hospital. My sister Phyllis and I wanted to give them a Golden Wedding Anniversary party, and we arranged it for April 1, 1979. The weather would be warmer and better for my father, and we'd have a couple of weeks to set it up and invite guests. The party went off as planned, a festive occasion, with many of my parents' friends and relatives there.

But within a couple of days, while sitting at home, my father had another heart attack. I rushed him to the hospital, and on the way his heart stopped. But by some miracle, it was started again and he survived. He stayed for about ten days and was released.

And so it went. Periods of resting, then a sudden heart attack, and once more I would be driving at 80 miles an hour to the hospital in the early morning. I knew the end was near; still I desperately hoped he could last. But on the evening of April 20, 1979, my father suffered a massive heart attack in the ICU of Coney Island Hospital and died. No matter how I had tried to be ready for his demise, it hit me hard.

I had lost my biggest fan. When *The Winner's Guide to Casino Gambling* was published, I dedicated the book to my father.

> *"In memory of Louis Silberstang.*
> *He was a gentle man, but a tough player."*

A few days later I returned to San Francisco. I had a book tour to go on on behalf of *How to Gamble and Win*. It took me around the country, from Oakland to Philadelphia. Then I returned again to San Francisco. I thought hard about my future. I felt I couldn't leave my mother alone in New York, and there was the question of my father's law practice. That had to be closed, and his estate taken care of and what about my mother? She would have to live somewhere else. So, in June of 1979, I closed up my apartment in San Francisco and headed to New York in my Kharmann Ghia.

VI

BACK IN NEW YORK

Driving back to New York City gave me plenty of time to think. I followed I-80 across the country, going up to Reno and past Winnemuca in Nevada, then heading east. I thought a lot about my father. After finishing my last novel, I had given the manuscript to him, and he read it quickly. Then we had a long talk about the work. He couldn't understand how I had conceived of this story. Of all my novels, this was the only one he couldn't imagine me writing. He was proud that I had written it, and proud of me.

During our years together, we had our disagreements, and there were a number of things I resented about my father, especially when growing up as a young boy. But in his later years, I made peace with him. I knew how much he loved me, and I loved him. Father and son. Simple. As I thought about his passing, once more the finality of death had come to my consciousness. My first friend to die had been Ray Reiman, who had a massive heart attack at the age of 41, in 1970. His mother called me to tell me that he had gone to take a hot bath after a drinking bout, and when he was in the bathroom for over an hour, and didn't respond to her knocks on the door, she went in and found him dead.

Ray had gone to Korea, to the front lines, and the war had a hard effect upon him. He came back with the memories of the war haunting him, and became a heavy drinker. I went to the funeral, run by the American Legion. When I saw him in the coffin, I wanted to shake him and say, "hey, Ray, get out of there, let's go take a drive and get out of here." And later, as taps sounded over his flag shrouded coffin, I stood stony-eyed, my lips pursed. The memories flooded in, of our time in basic training in Fort Dix, both of us young men and strong, and now he was gone. The notes of the bugle faded away, and I stood there for a while, but what could I do? I hugged his mother and grandfather, and made my way slowly to my car.

And I thought of Peter Matarese, another friend from my youth. He was a powerful man, and I always figured Pete could empty any bar in Brooklyn by himself. I first met him when I was fourteen, and we stayed friends throughout our lives. I based the character of Brunardo in Rapt in Glory on Pete. And as tough as Brunardo was, Pete was tougher. He landed in jail at an early age, got out, went to college and returned to New York, where he made a reputation for himself as a tough guy. He too went from a heart attack, dead at 43. His wife wrote me a long sad letter, and sitting in my apartment in San Francisco, I read it carefully.

She wrote that Pete always considered me as one of his best friends, and that he felt I had changed his life by my support at a critical time in his life. It was hard losing friends like Ray and Pete, strong powerful men, friends who would walk through walls for me.

As I closed in on New York, I became more and more weary. I was returning to a place I had spent a lifetime running away from, and I was returning, not in triumph, but in sorrow. I remember parking the Karmann-Ghia in front of my mother's house on West 10th Street in Brooklyn and stepping out, feeling completely down. As an adolescent I had lived a couple of blocks away, a hard time for me.

My mother was happy to see me. There was much to be done, she told me. I had to pull together the pieces of my father's law practice and handle his estate. My father kept few records and his files were in disorder. And I still had to finish the book for Holt Rinehart. Once more I was working day and night, starting at seven in the morning and often writing till midnight. I finally finished the games book, and then Mary told me that Playboy wanted me to do a series of books on games.

So from the Holt book, I started writing what eventually became Playboy's Guide to Casino Gambling, as well as individual books on Craps, Roulette, Blackjack and Baccarat. I was exhausted by it all; the law practice, the estate and the writing. I stayed with my mother for awhile, then took a dreary apartment in Bay Ridge on 95th Street. In the midst of all this, Jack Anderson, the columnist, was introduced to me. We were going to do an espionage book together. But that eventually fell through after many meetings. I've had several offers to collaborate in my lifetime but nothing ever panned out. I guess I was fated to write my books alone.

I became more and more worn out. One night I awoke, just as my father had done in San Francisco, my heart racing, sweating and scared. I called a good friend, David Swift and he rushed me to Victory Memorial Hospital. My heart was still racing a mile a minute and I was immediately hooked up on a machine. The resident asked me if I was a smoker. I told him no. He wanted to know if I was a heavy drinker. I told him I hardly ever drank. Then he told me to relax; it sounded more like a panic attack brought on by exhaustion than a heart attack.

Immediately I calmed down. I was put in a bed in the dark in a side room as a temporary measure. Once I felt relaxed, I got up and told the nurse I was leaving the hospital. I took a cab home.

After that episode I knew I couldn't go on like this. But I didn't seem to have any alternatives. I had to finish the games book for Playboy; I had a bunch of real estate closings to handle, and somehow I had to watch over my mother. I felt trapped, but I toughed it out as best I could.

The Playboy Guide to Casino Gambling eventually ran over

600 pages. I didn't have the energy to rewrite or even edit it. I submitted it cold to my editor and hoped for the best. This was the first time I didn't reread a games book and I felt negligent in not doing so. But I simply had run out of energy. I tried to look at the pages a few times, but my head drooped and my eyes closed.

I had written a number of games books, and trusted my instincts. When I write rapidly, I do my best work. The work flows. When I spend my time rewriting then I know I have problems with the work. And this book had flowed right along. So I trusted that it was ok.

Meanwhile I stayed in touch with Maria Theresa Caen concerning the last novel. After meeting with Sam Vaughn, there were delays in him reading the work. 1979 dragged into 1980 and still nothing was happening. There were always delays and reasons for the delays. I despaired of anything really happening.

After I gave my editor at Playboy the games book, she contacted me a few weeks later and asked me to come up to the Playboy office at 747 Third Avenue. I went up there with great trepidation, wondering about the mistakes I had made in the book. I went into her office, and she sent for coffee. She leafed through the manuscript, then told me what a pleasure it was to work with a pro. There were only two or three minor changes to be made. Somehow I had pulled it off. This was in September, 1980.

That same month, Maria Theresa came to New York, and I had drinks with her and Ann Getty at the Hotel Pierre. She told me that Sam Vaughn had finally read the novel and was going to give it back to the committee. This was a good sign, she told me, but it was no guarantee that Doubleday would publish the novel. It was in the committee's hands.

Mary Yost told me the committee met every Wednesday, and then, on October 3, 1980, she called in the morning and told me this was the day they'd decide. I'd know by three o'clock in the afternoon, when Lisa Drew, my original editor at

Doubleday, would give her the news. I had a couple of matters on that day, and around two in the afternoon, I left the office and took a long walk, walking down to Kings Highway, to the streets where I had spent my adolescence. I had no control over the decision; all I could do was sweat it out. I didn't know what to think; once more I tried to put myself in the frame of mind where, win or lose, it would all be the same. However, it wasn't working this time. I felt drained out, and a rejection, a defeat at a time like this would crush me. I was worn out.

I returned to the office at a quarter to three. Three o'clock came and went, and the wall clock's minute hand slowly moved on. At ten after the phone rang. It was Mary.

"They've accepted it," she said.

I thanked her and hung up. My mother, who had been sitting in the office watching me, asked me for the news.

"It's accepted."

She began to cry. Up to that moment I hadn't realized that she was going through the same tense hours as I was.

Now that I had finished the games book, now that the sixth novel I had written was about to be published, I sat down and had a long talk with my mother. I told her I was going to leave New York as soon as I finished working with the editors on both the games book and the novel. To do this, I started closing up cases, returning files to clients and giving some to other attorneys. I finished my father's estate, and discussed the possibility of my mother moving to Florida.

We took a plane ride to Fort Lauderdale, and she checked out Century Village in Deerfield Beach, where a few of her old friends lived. We went down again, and eventually she bought a condo there, in a retirement community.

At Doubleday, Betty Heller was assigned as my editor. She was a pleasure to work with and we hit it off at once. One day, at lunch, I told her a little bit about my life.

"You know what my dream was," I told her, "when I was in college?"

"What?"

"That I'd send out a novel, and I'd get a letter back from the publisher, telling me how moved they were and how proud they were to publish the novel. It's never happened. Either Mary sends me a short note or calls me, or in the other cases, I'd find out my work was accepted at lunch or whatever. But I never got that letter."

"I'll write a letter like that to you," Betty said.

"I appreciate it, but it wouldn't be the same. The book's already taken."

"Well," she said, "the offer's open. Anytime you want that letter you tell me."

A couple of weeks later, Betty told me she had finished editing the manuscript and invited me up to look over the changes she suggested. I went into her office, and she told me that although she had made a few minor changes, if I wanted, I could veto them all. It was up to me. I picked up the manuscript to go to a private room, and turning to leave the office I bumped into someone, knocking the person off her feet.

To my dismay, I was helping Jackie Onassis up off the floor.

"I'm so sorry," I stammered. "I was clumsy."

"Oh, that's all right," she said in that girlish voice.

Betty introduced us.

"I've read your novel," Jackie Onassis said. "I liked it very much. A real work of the imagination."

"Thanks."

I had only seen her in pictures and on television. She was slim, dressed beautifully but simply in a sweater and skirt, and had very wide spaced eyes.

We just stood there. If it was anyone else, I'd have been tempted to ask her out for a drink to discuss the book further, or just to talk. She was an editor at Doubleday; I was a published author there. But I guess I lost my nerve, and the opportunity passed.

I went into a private room and looked at the changes Betty had flagged. They were very minor, and I decided, for once I'd have a novel that was my own words throughout. I vetoed the changes.

We then had to think of a title. I wanted to call the novel DeWinter's Island, for the main character's name was Tom DeWinter, but Betty said readers might think it had to do with the DeWinter of Daphne Du Maurier's novel. In the end we agreed on Abandoned. The book came out in 1981, and I dedicated it to John Capman, my friend in San Francisco who had introduced me to Maria Theresa Caen, and salvaged the novel.

My days in New York were numbered. I was finished with the Playboy editing, and they wanted me to do a series of books for them, this time on sports betting. I signed a contract for the series, and decided that the best place to write them would be in Las Vegas. That's where all the action was; that's where the big bettors and handicappers hung out.

In March of 1981, a week before my mother was to move to Florida, I bought an old car from a client in the used car business, a 1969 Plymouth Fury. My Karmann-Ghia had finally given out. I just wanted transportation to Las Vegas, and he assured me that it would get me there. I paid $125 for the junker, loaded it up, and headed west once again. My work was over in New York. The law practice was closed, the estate of my father was complete, my mother had sold her house, the books I had written were all edited. I was off once more.

VII

ONCE MORE WESTWARD BOUND

John Luckman had once told me that Las Vegas was a flaming candle and I was the moth, always attracted to the flame. Whether I'd get burned or not, that was another story. I knew the temptations of Vegas, and had made up my mind that it was much easier and more lucrative to write about gambling than to gamble. I had seen a number of people destroyed by gambling, and therefore knew I had to live there on an even keel. Occasionally I'd play some poker, but for the most part I was involved in research and writing.

I was fortunate at this point to have written a number of games books, so that my name was rather well known in the gaming world. I already had published twelve books on games in addition to my six novels. When I'd call someone in the sports betting world, my name always rang a bell with them. They had read at least one of my books, and everyone knew about Playboy's Book of Games.

I was fortunate to meet Lem Banker, who at that time wrote a syndicated column on football betting and handicapping. He was a gracious man, and immediately shared his knowledge and contacts with me. Through him I met Bob Martin, who at one time made the line for all football games, both college and pro, throughout the country. He was another open and friendly person.

I went to Los Angeles to talk to Mort Olshan, who published the Gold Sheet, the authorative and popular weekly on sports handicapping. Like Lem and Bob, he was gracious and helpful. Most people think of gamblers and people associated with them as hard and ruthless, but they were just the opposite. I was grateful for their help, and could never have written the books on sports betting without them.

Lem and Debbie Banker became friends of mine, and I spent a great deal of time at their spacious house off Charleston Road. I watched Lem in action, handicapping football games and getting the line on the games. He was brilliant in his specialty. Bob Martin explained how he made his line, and told me that the key to football betting was to understand the point spread.

This was but one of the gems I learned. I went around interviewing people in sports betting and wrote the book at the same time. In the end I covered in separate volumes betting on football, basketball and baseball, as well as a big book called Playboy's Guide to Sports Betting. Counting all the individual volumes, I eventually published ten books with Playboy Press.

Another of my previously written books, The Winner's Guide to Casino Gambling, had come out and was selling very well. I had a special interest in that book, since it was dedicated to the memory of my father. The paperback rights were sold by Holt, Rinehart to New American Library, which put out both trade and mass market paperback editions. Originally published in hardcover in 1980, the paperback editions are still in print, revised several times, and having gone through many editions. During those years, I've worked with Hugh Rawson, whom I consider both a friend and a terrific editor. In 1995, a Japanese publishing house brought out a trade edition of the work.

I spent eleven months in Las Vegas, and completed the work on the sports betting books. My task finished, I now thought of where I would go next. My youngest son, Allan, who was visiting me, now lived in Santa Cruz, California, and suggested I go there and stay with him a while. He came to Vegas, and still driving the 1969 Plymouth Fury, which had somehow held up, we headed for Santa Cruz.

I stayed with Allan for a couple of months. Santa Cruz was a lovely town, though a bit slow for my tastes after Vegas. While thinking about getting an apartment there, I got a call from Playboy Enterprises in Los Angeles. They had tracked me down, and asked if I could come to Los Angeles to do a program on casino gambling. I agreed, and that same day I got another call, this time from Sheldon Renan, a producer, who wanted to know if I could be a consultant on a video about casino blackjack.

Faced with two offers of work, I left Santa Cruz and headed for the second time to Los Angeles. I took an apartment in West Hollywood, on Norton Street near Fairfax Avenue. Like most of my temporary apartments, this was furnished and dreary, on property containing a big house and two garages in the rear. My apartment was over one of the garages.

The work for Playboy was a rush job, but they knew I could write fast. It was to be about Atlantic City gambling, and I did it in eleven days. Eventually it was recorded by the Smothers Brothers, though I never saw the finished product. A cousin of mine did a couple of years later and wrote me to tell me he was surprised to see my name in the credits as the writer.

Sheldon Renan was going to do an interactive video for VHD Productions. This was to be done on a laser disc, new technology at the time. When he met me he hadn't yet written it, and was interviewing actors and actresses for various parts. He invited me to his place in Santa Monica and showed me previous work he had done, which was very impressive. He had spent a great deal of time in Japan, and was well known there for his documentaries.

As a consultant, my first job was teaching him blackjack. Sheldon was a brilliant filmaker, but he had a bit of trouble grasping the game. Writing the script, in addition to all the other work he had to do, would be burdensome and overwhelming, considering that he was not that familiar with the fine points of the game.

So, in the end, I wrote the script and helped him interview actors for the key position of host. We selected Avery Schreiber, a very funny man, and we were off. I attended all the filming of the work, and within a few months my work was finished.

Abandoned had come out in 1981, and then the rights to publish the book in Sweden were sold. I received several copies of the Swedish version, called Overgiven. Then one of the Swedish editors wrote to me, enclosing a magazine that was similar to Book of the Month Club News. The novel had been selected for the leading book club in Sweden, known as Bra Bocker. He invited me, if I had the opportunity, to visit the publishing house in Hoganas, Sweden. Having completed my work on the blackjack project, I decided that summer, in 1982, to travel to Europe again.

I flew to London, then to Amsterdam, and rented an Opel there, and drove through the Low Countries and Denmark, then took a ferry across to Sweden. I wondered how I'd find the publishing house in Hoganas, but when I got there, a building the size of an automobile factory proclaimed the name of the publishing company, Bra Spanning.

I met my editors, and they put me up in a lovely modern hotel in town. That evening, several editors came over and we had a long dinner, washing down bottles of wine in the process. Everyone became gloriously drunk. I stayed a few days in the town, then drove a bit through Sweden and back to Amsterdam. In Sweden, I'd go into bookstores to check on the novel. It was a big seller there, and every bookseller seemed to know about it.

"Ah yes," they'd tell me in English, "a modern day Robinson Crusoe." They told me the Swedes liked the book because by nature they were loners, and could understand a man going away by himself, testing himself in the process.

I returned to Los Angeles and the dreary apartment. While

in L.A. I had met a woman whom I'll call Karen, and we became rather serious, or at least, I was seriously in love with her. She couldn't stand the place I lived in, and pressed me to buy a house away from West Hollywood. Up to that point, I had no real intention of staying in Los Angeles, but Karen arranged for a broker to call me and show me property in Studio City, in the southern part of the San Fernando Valley.

The second house I saw was on Bloomfield Street, near Coldwater Canyon. I liked the area. Nearby was a tennis club and Ventura Boulevard, the main drag, was filled with good restaurants and small shops. The area had a smalltown feel to it. Sitting in the house, I wondered if I should buy it. I had owned a house during my first marriage, which I had signed over to my ex-wife, and I had owned property in Woodstock.

I got up and looked around the place for the third time. It had two bedrooms and a den, with wall-to-wall bookcases. It had two fireplaces, one in the living room and one in the den. There was an oldfashioned kitchen, one and a half baths, a small dining area. The backyard was spacious, dominated by a big apricot tree, with rosebushes lining one side. A gardenia bush grew at one side of the house, and its fragrant blossoms filled the house with exquisite odors.

I thought, "what else did I really want in a house." I could see myself working in the den, with a door leading to a backyard, with a fire going in cold weather. I asked the realtor for the price of the house.

"It's been on the market only a week. The owner lives in Santa Barbara, but his mother occupied the house. Now she's in a nursing home. She's 93. They're asking $155,000, and that's a real bargain in Studio City."

This was May of 1982. Interest rates were at 18%, the whole real estate market was depressed. I told the realtor that I would offer $120,000 if the owner would take back a mortgage at 12%. I'd put one-third down in cash, and the mortgage could run for five years with a thirty-year payout.

She was surprised by my offer. I guess she didn't figure I

would know so much about mortgage payouts, but my old law experience kicked in.

She had no problem with the mortgage, but told me the price I offered was out of line.

"You can't buy a house in Studio City for that price," she said.

"But I can make an offer, right?"

"Yes, I have to give the owner any offer."

"That's what I'll offer."

"But you won't get it."

"Do you know what I do for a living?" I asked her.

"No."

"I'm a writer."

"So?"

"I'm used to rejection. All they can do is reject my offer, right?"

"That's right."

I wrote her a check for $4,000 to go with the offer, and went back to my apartment. The next morning at nine the phone rang. It was the realtor.

"They accpeted your offer and all your terms. Congratulations."

And there it was. I told Karen what had happened, figuring she'd be pleased. I felt we had something serious going on, but she almost panicked.

"You actually bought a house?"

"Well, you sent the realtor. You wanted me to buy it, didn't you? You've always been hinting about us living together."

"But so soon. I didn't expect this."

I knew right then and there she wasn't going to live with me, and in fact, about six months later we broke up. But I owned a house that was comfortable for me to work in, unlike the Woodstock place. I bought furniture, my daughter sent me my Nakashima desk from New York, and I was in business.

I wrote other games books there. Silberstang's Guide to Poker was published, then the New American Guide to Gambling and Games, followed by The Winner's Guide to Sports Betting.

In 1984, a friend of mine was set to teach a writing course at the UCLA Extension and had to back out the last minute. He asked if I could take over the class. I called the director, explained my credentials, and found myself teaching a class called "Getting Started." It was the beginning of a long association with UCLA.

I also was approached by James Ragan, head of the Professional Writer's Program at USC, and he asked if I'd teach a novel workshop there. So soon I was teaching at both universities. At UCLA my classes prospered, and some semesters I taught three different courses. These were classes that held from fifteen to thirty students. In contrast, my class at USC was a limited one, with from six to eight students.

In late August of 1986, I was working at my desk at home, when the phone rang. The man on the phone said that Harold Becker would like to speak to me. Whenever I got calls like that, I knew they were from a studio. It was always the secretary or assistant calling first. I waited, and Becker got on the phone.

"I've had a hell of a time tracking you down," he said, "and it turns out you're in Studio City."

"Yes."

"You wrote Winning Casino Craps, right?"

"Yes."

"Well, I sent one of my people to a few bookstores, and they bought some books on craps, but yours was by far the best. Here's the situation. I'm going to direct a movie about a professional craps player, and wondered if you'd like to be a technical adviser on the film."

I knew the ways of Hollywood by then. Unlike the Bible's advice, "ask and thou shalt not receive," was the guiding light of tinseltown. So I asked a few questions about the film before committing myself.

"I'll tell you what," said Becker. "Why don't you come over

to the studio tomorrow, say about eleven in the morning. I'll show you the novel the screenplay is based on. And we'll talk."

I agreed.

Harold Becker was a well-known and respected director. His last movie had been "Taps." Later, he would do "Sea of Love" and other films. We got along well, and I took back a xeroxed copy of the novel, The Arm, by Clark Howard.

I called Becker two days later.

"What did you think?" he asked.

I told him the main character was shrewd like the one that Steve McQueen had played in "The Cincinatti Kid," but he also had the weakness of Fast Eddie Felson in "The Hustler."

"That's how I feel about him. That's good. Look, next weekend we're going to Vegas. Why don't you come along?"

"Who's we?"

"Matt Dillon is going to play the lead." Becker gave me the name of the line producer, who was in Toronto. I called and spoke to Don Carmody and we arranged a daily consultant's fee for my work, which would begin with the trip to Las Vegas.

That Friday I met Becker at the Burbank Airport and we flew to Vegas. We were to meet Matt Dillon at the Desert Inn, a place I knew well from the old days in Vegas. Matt was late, but came on a midnight flight, and the first thing he wanted to see was the craps tables there.

The weekend went well. Matt learned how to play casino craps, and I was to fly to Toronto in October for the early work on the film. I spent a few days in Toronto, met some of the cast, which included Tommie Lee Jones and David Marshall Grant.

By the second trip there, I was introduced to a new director, Ben Bolt. Harold Becker had some kind of disagreement with the producers and left the film. As it turned out, this meant a great deal more work for me, which was ok with me, since the more I worked, the more I made. Ben Bolt was English and knew nothing about craps, and the book, taking place in the Midwest, was really a slice of Americana. Bolt just wasn't familiar with this subject.

I ended up working for several months, flying back and forth from Toronto to Los Angeles. In the course of filming, I spent a lot of time with Matt Dillon, and for some reason, he'd call me every evening to hit the town with him, usually accompanied by David Grant, and sometimes by Del Close or Diane Lane, who was the female lead in the film. In the course of filming, I became good friends with two of the actors, Robert Morelli and Sam Malkin, who have remained close friends with me to this day.

One of the best things about being a writer, and getting published, is that you never know who is reading your work. People are out there buying the book or taking it out of a library. You touch lives, and even with a book like Winning Casino Craps, which is not a work of fiction, it opened doors for me that I never expected to be opened.

After my work on the film was over, in early December of 1986, I returned to LA and teaching. During that period I embarked on a series of beginning games books published by Cardoza Publishing. In all I wrote thirteen small books, all with titles starting with The Basics of Winning... They included books on craps, roulette, poker, video poker, horse racing, slots, keno and so forth. These were written under pen names, the most common being J. Edward Allen. Eventually I wrote more advanced books on games for Cardoza Publishing, such as Winning Poker for the Serious Player and Winning Blackjack for the Serious Player. They've been extremely successful and well over a million have been sold in the various series.

But a great deal of my time was spent teaching. I not only taught at both universities, but held private workshops in my home, and worked with individual writers. I taught from 1984 to 1989, when I sold my house. I lived in Florida for about a year, returned in 1991, and taught again at UCLA for another two years.

Eventually I gave up teaching at a university. I now limit

myself to one or two students, who are working on novels. I look back now, in 1997, at a career in writing that has spanned thirty-four years, and produced forty-eight published works.

While writing fiction, I never thought of the principles that make up the craft and art of creative writing. I was more concerned with keeping my feelings true and open, with putting down the truth, with bringing characters to life by making them human. And of course, as I have shown in this narrative, I was very involved with those aspects of being a writer and artist, such as self-confidence and a belief in one's work.

No matter what situation I was involved in, or what hardships I faced in my career, I tried to be true to myself. I felt that a writer must understand, not judge, that all of us have within ourselves the ability to be a saint or a murderer, and every aspect of human conduct in-between. I listen closely to what would-be writers say, and when I hear someone telling me "I don't want to know about that," or "I'm not interested in that," or "I'm not into that," whatever "that" represents, whether it's violence or a different way of looking at the world, I feel that the person saying this will never be a good writer.

When we write, we touch our own feelings, and in turn, touch the feelings of our readers. The more we won't examine in ourselves or in the world around us, the more narrow our work will be. Instead of a full spectrum of feelings, the characters will end up pallid, robbed of their humanity. It was only by being in touch with my feelings that I was able to write in the first place, and I try to stay open in that regard. It is almost a sacred mission for me.

As I have stated, I didn't examine the principles of the craft. I just did my work. I told a story; in the end that is what a writer does.

However, as I taught and discussed writing with students, it became clear to me that they needed guidance in understanding the art and craft of fiction. They had to get the craft down before the art showed. In order to do this, a writer must learn to bring characters to life, and to define those characters through dialogue and action. There are other aspects of fiction writing that had to be examined, such as point of view, and whether to write in the first person or third person. These are but some of the challenges facing a writer, and now I'm going to discuss the art and craft of fiction as thoroughly as I can.

The Art and Craft of Fiction

I
BEGINNING THE NOVEL OR SHORT STORY

All work must have a beginning, whether that work is a short story or a novel of over a thousand pages. Yet the same principles apply to both forms of prose.

There are three essential principles to consider when beginning a work: 1. Set the scene. 2. Introduce the character or characters. 3. Start the threads of the story.

All three must be present, and should be dealt with within a few pages.

Sometimes they can be presented in one page, or even one paragraph. Arthur Koestler, in his powerful novel, Darkness at Noon, was able to accomplish this in the opening sentence:

"The cell door slammed behind Rubashov."

Here, Koestler has set the scene, the prison cell, introduced the character, Rubashov, and started the threads of the story. Rubashov is imprisoned, but for what crime?

It doesn't really matter if the character is introduced before the scene is set, as long as the reader knows just what the scene is. A classic example is Herman Melville's classic, Moby Dick, where the narrator of the story starts the novel moving with the classic line:

"Call me Ishmael."

But immediately after, he tells us that several years before he was looking for a ship to sail on and is at a seaport town. The scene is set and the character is introduced.

1. Set the Scene

By this phrase we mean, show the reader just where the story or novel begins, so that the reader is comfortable and can follow the story. This is important in the craft of the story or novel.

Although a scene should be set, it is important that the character make his appearance in a short while, otherwise you have a travelogue. Many beginning and inexperienced writers fall in love with the description of the scene, and end up with just that, and no real beginning. An example might be:

"It was a beautiful summer day, and the sun was a yellow apparition hanging motionless over the beach. Fluffy clouds passed under an azure sky, and the breeze from the ocean blew softly."

And so forth, for five or six pages. Nothing is accomplished except boring the reader and showing an editor that the writer is an amateur.

Let's play with the above paragraph a bit. Suppose we began instead:

"It was a beautiful summer day, and the sun was a yellow apparition hanging motionless over the beach. John felt its heat as he paced aimlessly on the hot sand, knowing that today he faced a decision that would change his life."

Ok. Now we've introduced a character and the threads of the story are beginning to firm up. We no longer just have a description.

One mistake inexperienced writers make is not setting the scene in the immediate present. Several years ago, I was at an agent's office, where he had piles of manuscripts along one wall. I asked him about them, and he told me he had made the mistake of stating in some writer's magazine that he would accept unsolicited manuscripts. "Take a look at them," he said.

I did. I was immediately struck by a few which began almost in the same way. The characters' names were different, and the scenes were different, but all involved a character looking back in time to a previous event.

"Jane stared out the window, watching the rain hit the drab sidewalks in front of her house, thinking back to the events of the night before." Or

"Bill, sitting in his spacious living room before the fireplace, watched the flames lick at the logs he had just placed there, thinking back to the party at the Andersons."

Or

"The snow had been falling all morning. Jack Smith, his lean body taut with anxiety, clenched his teeth as he remembered the encounter in school with the principal the week before."

And on and on. All of these opening sentences relate to an event that occurred at an earlier time, and therefore lose the immediacy of the event. Why not begin with the event itself? For example, in the second example, suppose we began as follows:

"At the Andersons' party, Bill, nursing a drink in a quiet corner, was suddenly confronted by a very drunk Larry Anderson.

"I want to talk to you," Larry said, his voice slurring the words. "I want you to know what people have been saying about you."

All right. Now we have something, and we're right there watching the characters, not just in the mind of a character thinking back to a previous event, where everything must be filtered through the character's thoughts.

It is always best to show everything not from the mind of a character, but from the actions of the character and the accompanying dialogue.

That's why it's best to start with the immediate event. Inexperienced writers find it easier to go into the mind of the character rather than show the event from the outside, and so they often begin with characters thinking about previous events. This usually leads to a weak beginning of a story or a novel.

Of course, many great novels have begun with events that occurred days or even years before. Writers like Joseph Conrad loved to set a scene where men sit around and one of them, usually his great character, Marlow, begins a story that took place some years back. And most stories are told in the past, rather than the present tense, where events have already taken place. This is quite different than having a character think back to the night before or week before to tell a story.

Setting the scene and tying the character to the scene is something all great writers have done, no matter how big the book was. In Crime and Punishment, Dostoevski immediately lets us know that the novel begins in St. Petersburg and that Raskolnikov is a starving student in a desperate situation. He is on his way to a pawnbroker, evading a landlady he owes rent to. The scene is set, the character is introduced, and the threads of the story are woven. Raskolnikov will kill the pawnbroker, and that is the crime. His punishment will come later.

In another huge and famous novel, Great Expectations, Dickens introduces us to Pip, who is at a graveyard near the sea, where his family has been buried. A convict comes on the scene, having escaped from a convict ship, and demands that Pip bring him food. The scene is set, Pip, the main character of the novel, is introduced, and the convict's role is the thread running throughout the novel, even though Dickens tries to lead us astray purposely. Pip makes his way in the world with "great expectations" thanks to a mysterious benefactor. This benefactor turns out to be the convict he helped as a young boy. Finishing the novel, one realizes that the threads of the story were right there at the start. Dickens knew how to write a novel.

In both works, the writers start us off with immediate action, and so we are caught up at once in the drama of the novel. Another example is George Orwell's 1984, which begins with Winston Smith hurrying to work as the clock strikes thirteen. Clocks don't strike thirteen in our society. Obviously we're in a different kind of world, where strange things happen. What Orwell has done is set the scene, introduced the character, and started the threads of the story. Here is the beginning of 1984.

"It was a bright cold day in April, and the clocks were striking thirteen. Winston Smith, his chin nuzzled into his breast in an effort to escape the vile wind, slipped quickly through the glass doors of Victory Mansions..."

2. Introduce the Character

The character we introduce might not be the protagonist, that is, the leading character. It might be a secondary character who speaks of the protagonist, or is a character who narrates the story, where he is not the hero. But early on, we must introduce a character to the story.

And when we introduce that character, we must be sure that he or she is a human being, not a stick figure. The character must display something which holds our immediate interest. A good example is seen in the beginning of James Baldwin's fine novel, Giovanni's Room:

"I stand at the window of this great house in the south of France as night falls, the night which is leading me to the most terrible morning of my life."

Note how Baldwin immediately sets the scene, introduces the character and starts the threads of the story, right in the first line. The first paragraph continues:

"I have a drink in my hand, there is a bottle at my elbow. I watch my reflection in the darkening gleam of the window pane. My reflection is tall, perhaps rather like an arrow, my blond hair gleams. My face is like a face you have seen many times. My ancestors conquered a continent, pushing across death-laden plains, until they came to an ocean which faced away from Europe into a darker past."

Here Baldwin deepens the narrator, and makes us interested in him. This is not a stick figure, not merely a name, though we don't know his name. The description of the narrator is not quite precise, nor does it have to be. Many beginning writers feel that the protagonist must have a full description, but this is often a mistake.

Fine fiction is an involvement with the reader. The reader doesn't want to know everything about the character; what the reader wants to do is use his or her imagination. As Hemingway so aptly pointed out, "what you leave out is more important than what you put in." Leaving out the description is part of that truism.

The amateur writes like this when introducing a character:

"Bill Bryant was a tall man with the tight physical features of a former athlete. His hair was brown and full, and his eyes were hazel and piercing. He had a square jaw, and a hawk-like nose and when he disliked a person, his powerful facial muscles tightened."

So what? Are we looking at an ad for men's cologne in a slick magazine? I can't tell how many times I've read stories featuring men with square jaws, tight facial muscles and either classical or hawk-like noses. Or beautiful women with full busts and hair the color of golden wheat. For once I'd like the hair to resemble rotten wheat. All written by unpublished writers. Instead of these banal descriptions, the writers ought to deal with the inner soul and feelings of a character; those are the important things that hold a reader. Let the reader use his or her imagination to conjure up a description of the character.

Also, a description takes away from our enjoyment of a story. Sam Spade, the detective in Dashiel Hammet's The Maltese Falcon, is described in the pages of the book as a bear-like man with blond hair on his forearms. Hey, wait a minute! That's not Humphrey Bogart, whom most of us identify as the detective. The description, I feel, was unnecessary. Let the reader get involved; let the reader determine the description of the character in his or her's mind's eye.

3. Start the Threads of the Story

When I lived in San Francisco, I had a friend who had written a novel about the anti-war movement during the 1960s. He had sent it out to several agents and publishers, all of whom rejected it outright. He asked me to look it over, but he wanted to be with me while I read it. We went to a local coffeehouse, and he gave me the first few chapters of the novel, which ran, he told me, over 400 pages.

The novel began in New York City. The narrator is walking through the streets of Greenwich Village, an area I knew quite well at the time, having lived there during most of the '60s. The protagonist walks street by street, noting the White Horse Tavern, where Dylan Thomas hung out, the Lion's Head, where writers and actors such as Steve McQueen, spent time, and so forth.

For fifteen pages the character wanders through the streets. Then he gets to his apartment house, goes up a couple of flights of stairs and takes out his key, puts it into the lock, turning the lock and opening the door to his apartment. End of chapter.

"What did you think?" my friend asked me.

"Well...what you wrote about the Village is nothing new. All the character is doing is walking. I get no sense of where the story is going."

"So... what do you suggest?"

"Cut out the first scene altogether. Start the novel with the character turning the lock and entering his apartment. There's mystery to that...something is about to happen, I presume."

"Why don't you read the next chapter?"

After the protagonist enters his apartment, he looks around and describes all the rooms, and the view from each window. He notes the various objects he owns, such as paintings and his typewriter, and this goes on for twelve pages. Then the phone rings.

"Well..." my friend wanted to know.

"I'd cut out all the description of the apartment. Why not begin the novel as follows: the character opens the door and when he walks into his apartment, the phone rings."

I got a look bordering on hate. "You mean, take out twenty-seven pages and just have that?"

"That's what I think."

"You're decimating my novel."

He had asked my opinion. I will never be cruel, but on the other hand, I'm not going to waffle in my opinion. I'm not going to say that there's a good description of a table to lessen my criticism, especially if the description is superfluous in the first place. I said exactly what I felt; and would have done the same if this had been my own mother writing a novel.

That was it, however. He wouldn't let me read anymore of the novel. He told me adamantly that several other friends that he had shown the work to really loved it. None had criticized it the way I had.

I almost had to bite my tongue to not say, "well, if they liked it that much, let them publish it." That would be cruel and unnecessary. But what good was his friends' criticism? The work had been rejected and lay in his closet, he had told me, for three years. I guess he took it out now and then to impress someone with the fact that he was a writer and had finished a novel. I admired him for writing the novel; not many people can do that. But as I've written before, showing the work to friends is the kiss of death, especially if all you want is praise and get angry at criticism.

He stayed mad at me for a couple of weeks, then our friendship continued. But he never went back to rewrite his novel and never wrote another thing.

I don't write about this meeting to show my critical judgment but to make a point. What was lacking in his novel was simple; the threads of the story were missing. The reader had no idea where the novel was going. There was a character and the scene was set, but without that third necessary ingredient, the work went flat.

Let's look at the beginning of Bernard Malamud's "The Magic Barrel," to see how all three are integrated in the first paragraph.

"Not long ago there lived in uptown New York, in a small, almost meager room, though crowded with books, Leo Finkle, a rabbinical student in the Yeshivah University. Finkle, after six years of study, was to be ordained in June and had been advised by an acquaintance that he might find it easier to win himself a congregation if he were married. Since he had no present prospects of marriage, after two tormented days of turning it over in his mind, he called in Pinye Salzman, a marriage broker whose two-line advertisement he had read in the Forward."

Not only has Malamud set the scene and introduced the protagonist, but he has started weaving the threads of the story. Finkle needs a wife. What is going to happen? Malamud did what my friend failed to do; he got us interested in the plight of the character.

Often the threads of the story have to do with a character who is at the brink of a decision that will change his or her life. Or the character is about to do something, or take a journey. Or the character is a stranger in town. We become interested in someone who faces adversity or must make an important decision affecting his or her life. This is the meat of novels. In short stories, the character may act on a smaller scale, a mere illumination might be enough. By illumination, I mean a situation where the character discovers something about himself or herself, something that changes the character, makes the protagonist look inside himself or herself with a fresh perspective.

An important aspect of setting the scene is the tension created at the outset.

The best writers have the ability to draw us into the story at the beginning, by creating tension, tension that is like a taut wire running through the story or novel, never letting up.

Let's look at a few writers and how they do this. First, we'll examine the beginning of "The Killers," the famous Hemingway story, which, adapted to the screen, launched the career of Burt Lancaster as a major Hollywood star. A sidelight to this; Hemingway didn't use an agent and often didn't get the correct price for his work. He sold the screen rights to "The Killers" to Howard Hawks for $10,000. Hawks then resold the rights for $92,000. In any event, here's the start of the short story, just concentrating on the dialogue.

"The door of Henry's luncheon opened and two men came in. They sat down at the counter.

"What's yours?" George asked them.

"I don't know," one of the men said. "What do you want to eat, Al?"

"I don't know," said Al. "I don't know what I want to eat."...

"I'll have a roast pork tenderloin with apple sauce and mashed potatoes," the first man said.

"It isn't ready."

"What the hell did you put it on the card for?"

"That's the dinner," George explained. "You can get that at six o'clock."

As the conversation continues about the dinner menu and the time, which turns out to be five o'clock, the tension increases. The two men grow more impatient, and turn out to be hired killers, looking to kill someone named Ole Anderson. Hemingway, a master of dialogue, lets it be the catalyst for the tension of the story. Note how economical he is. Hemingway doesn't explain things; he leaves out more than he puts in, and this adds to the tension. He creates a closed world, and we, the readers, are caught up in it.

We always learn from the best writers. As I wrote before, you read junk, you write junk. If you read the best, it should inspire you to better work, and give you an insight into how the great writers begin their stories or novels.

II

CREATING AND DELINEATING CHARACTERS

1. Describing the Characters

I feel that it is unnecessary to describe characters, for I would rather have the reader imagine what they look like. This involves the reader and deepens his or her interest in your story. However, as we shall see from the next two examples, there are offbeat and unusual ways to describe a character.

I always think the best writing allows the character's actions and movements to carry the narrative and create the tension of the story. Note how carefully the point of view is dealt with by both writers. First, we have Carson McCuller's fine story, "The Jockey." Here are excerpts from the beginning paragraph:

"The jockey came to the doorway of the dining room, then after a moment stepped to one side . . . from the adjoining bar came a warm, drunken wash of voices. The jockey waited with his back to the wall and scrutinized the room with pinched, crepy eyes. He examined the room until at last his eyes reached a table in a corner diagonally across from him, at which three men were sitting. As he waited, the jockey raised his chin and tilted his head back to one side, his dwarfed body grew rigid and his hands stiffened so that his fingers curled inward like gray claws..."

There is a description of the jockey, but it is not a banal description. It concentrates on his eyes and on his clawlike hands, creating even more tension. As I reread this paragraph I was struck by the beautiful phrase, "a warm drunken wash of voices." Ladies and gentlemen, that alone is worth the price of admission.

The tension the jockey feels is clearly transmitted to the reader, and creates the tension of the story. He has seen three men, and something dramatic is going to happen, but what? Note how in this and the previous story, the writers immediately set the scene, introduced the character or characters that will carry the story, and wove the threads of the story.

In the last example, we examine the beginning of Sanctuary, a haunting novel by William Faulkner with the eerie character of Popeye dominating the book. This is not the friendly Popeye of the comics. This character is a dark creation. Here's the beginning:

"From beyond the screen of bushes which surrounded the spring, Popeye watched the man drinking. A faint path led from the road to the spring. Popeye watched the man-a tall thin man, hatless, in worn gray flannel trousers and carrying a tweed coat over his arm-emerge from the path and kneel to drink from the spring."

We see this from Popeye's point of view. He is watching a man who seems to be ordinary, wearing worn trousers and holding a tweed coat over his arm. After an intermediate paragraph, we now switch to the man's point of view. What we now get is quite a different and frightening description of Popeye:

"In the spring the drinking man leaned his face to the broken and myriad reflection of his own drinking. When he rose up he saw among them the shattered reflection of Popeye's straw hat, though he had heard no sound.

"He saw, facing him across the spring, a man of under size, his hands in his coat pocket, a cigarette slanted from his chin. His suit was black, with a tight high-waisted coat. His trousers were rolled once and caked with mud above mud-caked shoes. His face had a queer bloodless color, as though seen by electric light; against the sunny silence, in his slanted straw hat and his slightly akimbo arms, he had that vicious depthless quality of stamped tin."

Not a word is spoken, but the tension of the scene is palpable. Something terrible is about to happen, and although we don't go into the drinking man's mind, his point of view and way of looking at Popeye shows fear.

Faulkner was a Nobel laureate. Not for him the banal description of a man's face as taut, or strong-jawed or with a straight or hawk-like nose. Popeye's face "had that vicious depthless quality of stamped tin," one of the great and haunting descriptions in literature. It is an unexpected and brilliant image that astonishes the reader.

In all the above examples, the writers didn't really go into the thinking process of any of the observant characters, yet what they saw was sufficient to create enormous tension and move the story along. The cheapest and easiest way to create tension is to go inside the character's mind and reveal his or her thoughts, but it is the least satisfying. The best way is to show, not tell. If you learn nothing else, remember the admonition, show, don't tell. This is what the best writers do. The weak writers, unable to command the language and imagery necessary to show, simply go into the character's mind and tell. Or the narrator tells everything without showing us anything. This alone separates the strong from the weak writers.

As I wrote before, it is the protagonist and other characters which carry a story or novel. There may be some successful novels in which plot is predominant, but unless the protagonist is of interest, the plot alone can't carry a novel.

What kind of characters hold the interest of the reader? There is no formula to follow. In real life, each of us is attracted to certain persons. We may admire someone's looks or intelligence or guts or whatever. Few people are attracted to weakness, cowardice or stupidity. The same is true with the characters we read. We can easily lose interest in a protagonist who isn't as clever as we are, who is less brave, who is basically weak or who lacks humanity.

As writers, we generally create our protagonists giving them emotions and feelings we have been privy to, for we cannot realistically give a protagonist feelings we are incapable of having. That's why we must keep our feelings open, and constantly examine them. This is not to say that the character is the writer's alter ego, but bits and pieces of the author are usually in the protagonist, especially in the early work of the writer. The author must constantly go through the process of self-examination, which is one of the prices the serious writer pays for his craft.

When creating a character the writer should know everything about the individual. If the author has only a vague knowledge of the protagonist, the reader will be swimming on uncertain seas, and not be moved by an unformed character. But once you, as a writer, know your character thoroughly, you don't have to reveal all. Keep the mystery of the character by leaving out aspects of his or her persona. But don't do this because you don't know the character well enough; do it because you are enticing the reader to become interested in the protagonist.

It is akin to the situation in real life when you meet someone new and that person brags about all the things he or she has done. Within fifteen minutes you know all there is to know about that individual, and you quickly lose interest. How much more interesting a person becomes when he or she retains the mystery, and we learn about him or her piece by piece and bit by bit. Of course, in writing, as in real life, the first impression made by the character should pique our interest, so we want to know more about the protagonist or major character.

2. Feelings Appropriate to the Characters

Writing becomes weak when the writer doesn't really know what feelings are appropriate to a character and fakes the emotions. For example, we constantly are inundated with so-called tough characters who aren't afraid of dying, who, when faced with a gun, display bravado, baiting the gunman, daring him to pull the trigger. We can easily assume that the writers of this nonsense haven't really faced a gun, looking into the eyes of some cretin who can end their existence on earth by the pull of a trigger. I'd like to see how brave the author would be in that situation.

It's always correct to show true feelings, even if those feelings are not bravado in the face of danger. To be human is to be in touch with the entire world, and showing human feelings in a character allows the writer to get in touch with a wide range of readers who have experienced the same feelings. Feelings such as hate, anger, love, joy and so forth are universal. Touch this universal chord and you will touch readers.

3. What the Character's Reveal About Themselves

It is not necessary for the writer to mention that the protagonist is brave or interesting. That is "telling." The writer's task is to show, by deeds, action and dialogue, just what the character possesses in the way of interesting traits. Again, show, don't tell.

When I taught at UCLA, I usually told a new class a story. It went like this:

"When I lived in San Francisco in the late 70s, I had a small one bedroom apartment on Chestnut Street, in the Marina district. Each morning I'd go for a run down to the Marina Green and on a path leading to the Golden Gate Bridge. After an hour I'd return to my apartment, wash up and then grab a bite. Then I'd work on a novel. This particular morning I climbed the flight of stairs to my apartment on the second floor and took out my key, but noticed that the door was slightly ajar.

"What the hell is this, I thought to myself. I slowly pushed the door wide open and looked into my apartment. I could see the bedroom from the open door, as well as my living room. Both seemed to be empty. I stepped into the apartment, and then, to my left, I heard water running in the bathroom. And the door was slightly open. I closed the front door slowly and silently behind me, and pushed open the door to the bathroom.

"To my surprise, a young woman of about eighteen was sitting in my bathtub, with the water running. I stopped in my tracks and stared at her. Then she noticed my presence.

"Hi," she said brightly. She was tanned and had long auburn hair running almost to the center of her back.

Then she stood up in the tub and handed me a washcloth.

"Who are you, and what are you doing here?" I asked.

"Oh, don't look so worried," she said. "Why don't you wash off my back and I'll answer all your questions."

That was the story. There would always be a few moments of silence, and then someone invariably asked, "what happened next?"

"I don't know," I'd say, "I made it all up."

What was interesting was that no one ever was bored by the story in all the classes I taught. It certainly held their interest. It was really a simple story, and nothing dramatic happened, but a lot was said and unsaid. For example, the protagonist, the one who discovers the open door to his apartment, is a man who doesn't panic. He doesn't run down the stairs and get someone to call 911.

He's not afraid to go into his apartment, but he's not stupid. He looks around carefully. After all, his life might be at stake if a desperate burglar was in there. When he hears the water running in the bathroom he relaxes. Without me saying so, a dressed person always has an advantage over a naked one. So the protagonist has no qualms about opening the bathroom door wide, and what does he see? A young naked woman.

His reaction is also important in delineating the character. He doesn't get sexually excited; he doesn't grab for her. He has self-control, and his curiosity is aroused, rather than his libido. He wants to know who she is and what she's doing in his apartment. She probably recognizes that she's safe, for she offers to have her back washed by him while she's absolutely naked, without any qualms.

I told this story to show how subtly, just by actions and attitude one can delineate a character. I didn't say he was cool or self-controlled. I let his actions speak for him. I showed, and didn't tell. And I'm sure that my students, hearing the story, immediately thought of what they'd do in an identical situation. I had caught their interest and their feelings. I had done my job as a storyteller.

4. Revealing the Truth about the Characters

An important way to delineate character is to show the feelings and actions of characters so that the reader senses the truth about them. Characters in fiction shouldn't be different than people in real life. The emotions are the same, as I have pointed out, and it is the job of the writer to present them truthfully.

I used to give my classes another example:

"While Joan was pouring herself another cup of coffee at the sink, her husband, Frank, was sitting and reading the LA Times at the breakfast table. He was reading the sports section carefully, studying the story on the previous night's Dodger game.

"Joan sipped at the coffee, hesitated, then put the cup down.

"Frank," she said, "there's something I want to discuss with you."

She only heard a grunt in reply.

"Frank, I'm talking to you."

"Yeah," he said, not taking his eyes off the boxscores.

"Frank, would you please put the paper down. I'm talking to you."

He reluctantly did so. "Ok, I'm listening."

"Jane was on the phone with me last night."

"Who?"

"My friend, Jane. Jane, you know, she works in the bookstore."

"Oh, that Jane. The intellectual."

"Must you always say that? She merely works in a book-store."

"Ok, the bookstore worker Jane."

"She called me last night."

"So you said."

"She told me, that on the way to work, while she was driving on Sunset, she saw you."

"Saw me?"

"Yes, saw you. Saw you leaving a motel room with some blonde."

Frank picked up the paper and again began to read it.

"Frank, for God's sakes, didn't you hear what I said?"

"Yeah, I heard what you said."

"Was this true?"

"Was what true?"

"What I just told you. About Jane seeing you. It was about three in the afternoon."

"That's Jane the bookstore worker?"

"Frank, answer me."

"What's the question?"

"Were you at a motel with a woman yesterday afternoon?"

"You know," said Frank, putting down his paper and standing up, "I think I'm going over to McDonald's. At least I can read my paper in peace and drink some coffee, also in peace. I don't need this aggravation."

"Frank, I demand that you answer me."

"I forgot the question," he said. "Anyway I'm outta here."

This was also a made-up story. I wanted to show that in fiction, as in real life, people don't confess to anything that is against their best interests. You can see confessions on "The Perry Mason Show" even from spectators in the courtroom, but in real life, this doesn't happen. I should backtrack a bit. Of course, criminals confess to crimes for whatever reason, either guilt or being tricked or for some other reason. Generally, however, no one acts against his best interests.

In soap operas, confessions are the rule of the day, but it

has been my experience in life, both as a lawyer and as a layman, that even when faced with hard evidence, people will lie and deny their guilt. Sitting in courtrooms during criminal trials, I heard every excuse in the world from defendants charged with serious crimes. The bloody knife they held was picked up by accident, the gun found in their apartment was planted by some evil person, and so forth. When John Wayne Gacey's basement was examined and seventeen bodies turned up, he explained that some mass murderer must have been using the area as a burial ground. Certainly he had nothing to do with it.

In a divorce proceedings, my client caught her husband in bed with another woman, both naked and in the act of intercourse, yet he blandly turned and told her "this isn't really what it seems to be."

I guess he got lost while wandering around the city one afternoon and stumbled into this bedroom, looking for the local subway station. This was as likely a reason as telling his wife that "this isn't really what it seems to be." I guess he was practicing pushups.

What I also wanted to show in the previous example taking place in the kitchen, is not only that people don't answer questions when it isn't their best interests to answer, but that telling this story through dialogue reveals a great deal about the characters.

There is terrific tension between the husband and wife. The husband is scornful of his wife and her friends. At this point in their marriage, he couldn't care one way or another whether the marriage went down the drain. He was living life on his terms. The wife will have to make a decision, whether or not to put up with her husband's transgressions or drop out of his life. It all comes out of the dialogue.

What is unsaid can be as powerful as what is said. Scenes don't have to be played out to their inevitable end with both parties screaming at each other. In fiction, as in real life, people often don't say what they mean to say.

In real life, a person insulted or humiliated is often at a loss for words. Only later, in the privacy of a silent room, do the right words appear as the scene is played over and over in the person's mind.

I wanted the scene played as if a camera were stuck in the corner of the kitchen recording their movements and conversation. I didn't want to go into either mind to reveal their feelings.

This kind of scene is always a good exercise for a beginning writer. Play out a scene this way, as if a camera were recording everything. And realize that the camera cannot go inside the minds of the characters. Everything should be done from the outside.

5. The Character's Humanity

The most important thing in creating a character is to show his or her humanity.

By humanity, I mean the weaknesses and strengths inherent in all human beings. At one time, a tragic character needed a fatal flaw. Othello was jealous, Hamlet procrastinated, Lear was a foolish old man. The "tragic flaw" is sort of an old-fashioned concept in modern prose. Today the protagonist is often caught up in a situation where his struggle is not only against his flaws of character, but the dangerous outside world which is out to destroy him. A good example would be Winston Smith in 1984, caught in the world of Big Brother, a nighmarish society the opposite of the usual civilized world. Other examples are the protagonists of Kafka's works, especially in The Trial and The Castle.

The nightmares imagined by great writers have come true for modern man. Consider the Holocaust, or Stalin's reign of terror, or the frightening power of nuclear bombs. These threats from our own human species and from the science of modern man color our thinking in real life, and move in the same way through literature.

Despite the outside power of the world, the character we create still has to be of interest. He cannot merely be a pawn, for we don't identify with pawns. He or she must still hold on to human dignity in the face of terror. We must be able to identify with the character. But characters aren't created in vacuums. They come from the writers, and writers should be able to examine themselves closely, for this self-examination is the bread and butter of their craft, along with their talent.

Writers who are not blessed with great writing talent still can create memorable characters. Theodore Dreiser is a difficult writer to read these days, but his Clyde Griffith of An American Tragedy will remain one of the great characters of American literature. Dreiser, despite his limitations as a writer, was able to invest his protagonist with all the longing, fear and other emotions he himself felt. A writer like John Dos Passos, a much more innovative and polished writer, whose great accomplishment was USA, was more involved with plot and effects, and though I remember Clyde Griffiths vividly, I can't recall the name of a single character in Dos Passos' three volume USA.

Thus Dos Passos is largely a forgotten writer today, whereas both An American Tragedy and Sister Carrie are still widely read. Both of these novels by Dreiser have characters that still live and breathe.

It is natural for a beginning writer to use a great deal of himself or herself in the work. As a writer matures, the world he creates should expand, and his or her range of characters should also. This isn't always the case, even with great writers. Hemingway wrote about just a few characters. There was Nick Adams, who weaves through many of the short stories. There is Frederick Henry and Jake Barnes, who could be the same character at different times.

Hemingway was able to expand on these characters in his short stories. But basically, the protagonists lived by a certain code, no matter where they were placed in the novels or short stories. They took their punishment from the world and didn't complain about it. Those that did, those that wore their hearts on their sleeves, like Robert Cohn in The Sun Also Rises, were not only scorned by Hemingway but by the other characters in the novel. It is painful to see how Robert Cohn is set up in the novel; one winces as he makes a fool of himself by not living up to Hemingway's code of manhood.

This works both ways. Hemingway, as I wrote, was a firm believer in what was left out. In The Sun Also Rises, Jake Barnes, the protagonist, has been wounded in the First World War. His penis was shot off, and he is unable to consummate a love affair with Lady Brett Ashley, who is desperately in love with him. But he never really complains, and there are only a couple of allusions to his plight, but it is never expressed openly. When I first read the novel, at fifteen, as I mentioned before, I couldn't quite understand what was the matter with Jake. I had been reading inferior writers who spelled everything out, hitting the reader over the head several times to make sure he knew just what was going on in the novel.

Later on, I saw the power of Hemingway's story, and how he handled the protagonist. If you take your beating, and don't complain and don't brag, you are one of the select, in Hemingway's literary world. That Hemingway didn't personally live up to his own code is another matter. The work speaks for itself; one doesn't judge fine work by dissecting the character of the writer.

I firmly believe this. Of course, the bread and butter of all those in academia is to dissect the characters in the novels and the writer as well; otherwise how would all those PhDs be written? As for myself, the work is the important thing; the writer's character is irrelevant.

While Hemingway concentrated on a few characters, the greatest writer the English language has ever known, William Shakespeare, was able to create a world of characters, all different, all fascinating and all living and breathing not only on paper but in the theatre. Prince Hal, Othello, Falstaff, Richard II, Richard III, King Lear, Lady MacBeth, Viola, Coriolanus, Ophelia, Iago; the list could extend for several pages. It is well worth reading Shakespeare carefully to see how quickly he brings a character to life.

Many writers of prose, whose only reading of Shakespeare was required in school, have been turned off by this greatest of writers. Forget what you had to do in school; now read for your own benefit.

It is important in reading work, or even in seeing a film or going to the theatre, to think like a writer. When I go with non-artists to a movie, they talk about whether it was a good or bad film. What difference does that make? What is important is the characters presented, the vision of the writer and director. Did it work? What strengths and weaknesses were there? I want to always see a film or read a book that way, as a writer, not an amateur.

It is difficult, if not impossible to tell any would-be writer what characters to present in his or her work. The important thing is to make them human; to create a situation in which they must act, must move the story along. Characters are not in a vacuum; they are tied to the story itself. My best advice– read great works of art and see how the masters have created characters. Learn from them. Read Shakespeare and Dostoevski and Chekhov, Mann and Faulkner, Hemingway and Raymond Carver, Jane Austen and Katherine Ann Porter. Then there is James Joyce and George Orwell, Carson McCullers and Flannery O'Connor, Dickens and Stendhal. The list can go on and on. And above all, become a person who thinks like a writer. Read to learn. Observe how characters are created by these authors, see how they are introduced, what their actions and dialogue consists of.

And above all, when creating characters, always think of the human condition. Be someone who tries to understand and not judge. Characters are not there just to move the plot along. They are there to live and breathe and move the reader. If you create a memorable character your chances of being published increase. We always remember the great characters. Even a second-rate writer like Arthur Conan Doyle was able to create an immortal character, Sherlock Holmes. No one reads any of Doyle's romances or adventure stories these days, but Sherlock Holmes will live as long as English is read.

III

MORE THOUGHTS ON BEGINNING THE NOVEL

It always amuses me to hear someone say, "when I have nothing better to do, I'm going to write a novel." I rarely hear anyone say "when I have nothing better to do I'm going to write a symphony, or paint ten pictures to hang in a prestigous gallery."

Or else I hear a would-be writer telling me that all he or she needs is some free time to do some writing. Or that they're going to take a month off next summer and start a novel. As if beginning a novel is a matter of time off. Truman Capote had his own witty thoughts about this. He wrote "My point to young writers is to socialize. Don't go up to a pine cabin all alone and brood. You reach that stage soon enough."

As Floyd Salas told me, "you have to write the novel, because if you don't, you're going to die." The work you attempt should be something burning inside you. In my case, it smoked in my unconscious for years, and then burst out with some inspiration from a friend. It didn't matter to me that I was already working twelve hours a day; the novel, once started, had to be written.

Novels aren't something you do when you have nothing better to do. Nor should they be written to make a point, or get even with a job situation. I remember reading Gay Talese's book on the New York Times, and the one thing that stayed with me was his statement that several workers on the paper were all planning to write a novel about their experiences on the Times. I don't know if anyone of them did write a novel, but I doubt it.

A novel should be a work of imagination, an imagination that covers a wide spectrum of the human heart. It is not something to be done because you happen to hate your job or your circumstances and want to show the world just how unhappy you are. That is being pathetic. I knew several professors at various universities who were going to write their novels–basically stories of how they were trapped in the academic world. Who really cares? Just as we don't want to listen to whiners, we don't want to read their work.

As I mentioned, the novel is not that far different from life. In life, we avoid people who moan and complain about their lot in life; we avoid them like the proverbial plague. Why should we bother to read about their plight in a book?

The great joy in writing is to create a world of your own, people it with your characters, and feel, as you are writing the novel, that your very soul is involved in its creation, because this is vastly more important than the mundane actual life you live. The world of the novel then takes on a life of its own, and who is to say that this life is less important than so-called "real life?"

Now and then I come across an article which asks, "is the novel dead?" In my opinion, it is far from dead. What is endangered is the serious novel, because many major publishers are now dominated by international corporations which think only of the bottom line, not the quality of the work. They would prefer bestsellers and blockbusters to serious work.

So a lot of trash is published and promoted these days. In the local library I see this garbage prettified in gaudy covers. Romances, cheap violence, Hollywood pseudo-exposes, the whole gamut of junk. However, the human heart and human intellect has not changed. There will always be a pool of readers, in the millions, who want to be touched and moved by fine work. A novel isn't just a weaker kind of book. As a character in Jane Austen's Northanger Abbey states:

"Oh! it is only a novel!...Or, in short, only some work in which...the most thorough knowledge of human nature, the happiest delineation of its varieties, the liveliest effusions of wit and humour are conveyed to the world in the best chosen language."

That statement says it all. The character is talking about a serious novel, not a trashy bestseller. To paraphrase Hemingway, "if I could bring back Joseph Conrad to continue writing his novels, by grinding up the bestselling authors of this day, I'd immediately buy the biggest meatgrinder I could."

Although I have disparaged whiners who write novels, or threaten to write them about their unhappy lot at the university or at work, it is often this unhappiness that propels the serious author into writing a novel. The novel should relate to the human condition, and not moralize, but attempt to relate that condition in all its variety, both the horror and the joy. Putting down the truth in that way, touching the reader's feelings, is the work cut out for serious writers.

1. Write Truthfully

When students would ask me what they should write, I'd simply say, "the truth." What is the truth? I believe I said before that we don't know what the truth is, but we do know what it is not. We know when we're faking.

The journey of the writer must be, as Thoreau stated, "though his own mind." That, Thoreau wrote, was the longest journey he ever took. In the mind of the writer is all experience, and all human feelings. This is the meat which he digests in his art.

A good exercise, which I had my students undertake, when they didn't know what to write about, was to have them recall an event that changed their life. Then I asked them to put it down as truthfully as possible, whether or not it reflected well upon themselves or not. This is difficult to do, but well worth the trouble.

Or else, I'd advise, "try and write your most humiliating experience ever." I gave this advice to some students who wanted a writing assignment, and as they wrote down my suggestion, I said, "what is going to happen is this. You'll get home and start thinking about it. Perhaps you'll come up with your third or fourth most humiliating experience, because the worst is probably buried somewhere in your psyche and you don't even want to bring it up again."

I felt this was true. Then I told them, "even if you finally get down to that worst experience, you're going to start thinking– 'hey, why write this down so the other students and the teacher know about this. It's best left buried. The hell with them.' "

But the great writer tries to reveal all. A poet once wrote, "the ugly clerk I see in the mirror is myself." Search your soul, and put down whatever it reveals. In that way you'll deepen your work and free yourself up as an artist. When I was in London, I always went to the National Gallery and looked at several Rembrandt self-portraits displayed there. The later portraits showed a beaten, bankrupt old man. A defeated man. Only a great artist like Rembrandt could look at himself this way and reveal the essential truth about himself.

Those self-portraits inspired me. That's why, when people say, "I don't want to know about this or that," I know they'll never be writers. People who close off their minds will not open their hearts to themselves. They'll bury what they don't want to know, and never reveal it. All they'll show is a wash of grayness, of no interest to anyone.

You must, to be a writer, look deep into yourself. And don't be afraid of what you see there. Feelings are our common lot as human beings, and we are moved when they are displayed truthfully and appropriately. I think now not of a book but a film, "On the Waterfront." Marlon Brando says to Rod Steiger, who plays his older brother– "you let me down. You were my brother, you should have taken care of me, watched out for me. I could have been something, a contender, instead of the bum

I am."

I'm paraphrasing the dialogue, but who cannot be moved by it? How many times have we wanted to cry out to our parents in moments of despair, "why didn't you teach me to be able to love, why didn't you allow me to fulfill myself?"

How many thoughts have strangled in our throats instead of being said, to a lover, a friend, a sister or brother, a child or grandchild? When these are put into a book, they touch a universal chord. But we must, as writers, have the courage to do this.

2. Interrelationship of Characters and Plot

To repeat what I wrote before, it is the characters and protagonist, rather than the plot, which eventually carry the novel, though both become interrelated. When I begin a novel, I think of the protagonist or of several main characters and their interrelationship as well. I also try and put a protagonist in a situation where he must act, where his actions push the story forward. He or she is either outside of society or up against the wall, and is faced with decisions he or she can only decide to make.

In my last novel, Abandoned, the protagonist was a failed Hollywood writer who was out of money, was bitter and blamed everyone but himself for his failures. Then a mysterious stranger approached his agent offering to finance a trip to a deserted desert island so that he would write a modern Robinson Crusoe story. My character had a number of faults, but he was human, and it is important in a novel that the character learns and changes from his experiences. At the outset, Tom DeWinter (his name) was incapable of love, and thus, was consigned to Dante's 9th Circle of Hell, for those unable to love. All this was unsaid, and only after I finished the novel did I realize this. But DeWinter went to that island; and on that island, alone and abandoned, he had not only to survive but to resurrect himself as a human being.

In another novel, Nightmare of the Dark, the main character, Robert Lindner, only a boy at the outset of the story, is taken with his mother to a concentration camp. Unlike DeWinter, this was not his choice. But once there, he must learn to survive as he grows into his adolescence, and his story is tied up to the most rudimentary facts of existence, the struggle for life in the face of death. Here outside forces control much of his destiny, but not all of it. His decision to resist and live as a free person color much of the story.

3. Where to Open the Novel

When beginning a novel, it is important to know just when it should open. My advice is this–delay the opening to the last possible instant, when something is about to happen. I think of the opening lines of a novel the way I think of theatre. The curtain rises as events are about to unfold. We don't see a character shaving on stage, wiping off his face, watching TV for ten minutes, and then the doorbell rings and another character comes on stage with a dramatic announcement. What happens when the curtain opens is that a character comes on stage to make that announcement at once. The same is true in a novel.

Something is about to happen. The writer may delay it a bit by having a narrator talk about another character, as in Hemingway's The Sun Also Rises, where Jake Barnes starts off with a description of Robert Cohn. Or the writer gets right to the point, as Carson McCullers did in The Heart is a Lonely Hunter, with the line:

"In the town there were two mutes and they were always together."

In Franz Kafka's famous short story "The Metamorphosis" written in 1915, the opening line gets the story off immediately:

"As Gregor Samsa awoke one morning from uneasy dreams he found himself transformed in his bed into a gigantic insect."

IV

THE NARRATIVE DRIVE

Narration, in its simplest terms, is the telling of a story. The narrative drive is the movement of that story forward. This drive is often intertwined with a character's plight, and we read on to find out if that character will survive or will endure, in extreme cases. In others, we read on to see if the character will reach his or her aspirations, whatever they are.

This drive is tied up to imagination. Many writers must have thought of the phrase "what if" in writing their novels. What if a man, dreaming of a rival's death, actually decides to commit a murder? What if a woman woke up one day and found that she didn't recognize the person she saw in the mirror? What if...? The list of possibilities is endless, and if we portray a character that we can be interested in, then the story often moves of its own accord.

From the moment the novel begins it must move forward. There must always be tension, and unresolved conflicts and issues which engage the reader's interest and propel the story. Once the tension is relieved, the novel sags. Events may occur tangental to the main story; there may be subplots of course, but the threads of the story, which I mentioned at the beginning, must be tight and taut throughout.

In order to do this, a writer must separate the "dramatic truth" from "real life truth." Let's assume you're writing a novel about an important time in your life; let's say it's about your adolescence and your relationship with your family as you attempt to move by yourself into the great world. You use your experiences and your feelings as a basis for the novel, but you cannot let go of the tension or the unresolved issues even though these same issues were resolved in real life. There must be a dramatic truth, in which those issues stay alive and unresolved. Otherwise the novel starts to fall apart and you lose the interest of the reader.

If you want to write an autobiography, that is one thing, but if you're working on a novel, the tension must be there, and the reader must turn the pages to find out what is going to happen. By reader, I mean the editor or agent you send the novel to. He or she is your first, and most important reader. If he or she loses interest, because the story lacks tension, then you've failed. I think back to my first novel. In Rapt In Glory, I was unaware of the principle of tension and unresolved issues, but instinctively I was working on a novel where I didn't know what was going to happen next. I had to keep writing to find out how events would be resolved. As a result the tension stayed in the work. The editor I originally gave it to told me he couldn't put it down, he had to find out what would happen next. There was no mystery to what I did; I simply told a story.

A good example of this effect is telling stories to children that you make up on the spot. I have two grandchildren named Melissa and Stephanie. When they were younger, I could entertain them for hours with stories I made up. It was simple. I'd tell them about two girls with their names who go to stay in a house with a kind old woman, roughly based on their great-grandmother, my mother. The woman tells them they can play in the fenced yard, but warns them not to go into the woods beyond the fence.

Of course, at this point, the kids would ask me why they couldn't go into the woods, and I would say, "wait to see what happens." I had already hooked them in a simple manner. To tell them the danger lurking in the woods would break the tension. So, in my story, the grandmother falls asleep and the kids go into the woods. The tension builds; what will happen remains unresolved. Telling a story to kids and writing a novel involve the same rules. You don't let up on that tension at any time, and the kids have to listen closely to find out what is going to happen.

I listen to people closely when they tell stories, no matter what the story is. It is my feeling that those who can't really tell an interesting story can't write well. This is not an ironbound rule, but writers I have known who have been successful always were great storytellers. I love to tell stories. My second wife complained after I told a story that I made the experiences we shared, if that was the basis of the story, more interesting than what really happened. All I was doing was telling the dramatic truth of the story, which was much more interesting than the real-life events.

The easiest way to get anyone to read what you write is to use the title, "What I think about ..." and fill in the blank with the name of someone close to you. Write about them and give it to them. They'll grab it out of your hand to read it in full. In writing a novel, we cannot do this, but we can, through putting down the truth and relating appropriate feelings, accomplish the same thing. If we touch another person's feelings through our writing, we have hooked them as readers. As long as their feelings are engaged, they will continue to read the work.

I cannot emphasize this last statement strongly enough. Deal with feelings, write with understanding, create characters touched by humanity, and keep the tension of the story throughout the narrative. These are essential elements of the novel.

V

FIRST OR THIRD PERSON NARRATIVES

One of the first decisions a novelist is faced with is the voice he or she will write in. Will it be the omniscient third person, having total knowledge and seeing all, covering a host of characters and situations, changing from scene to scene, or will it be the first person, more limited, but more intimate.

When I wrote Nightmare of the Dark in the first person, the editor at Knopf thought it was a true story of a boy that was imprisoned and subsequently escaped from a Nazi concentration camp. And he thought that since I wrote the book, I was the boy. That is the power of the first person, the powerful "I."

Many great novels have been written in the first person. For example, two of Dickens' greatest works, David Copperfield and Great Expectations, come readily to mind. Hemingway's two most successful novels, The Sun Also Rises and A Farewell to Arms, were also written in the first person. For Whom the Bell Tolls, in the third person, was a much weaker work. Other novels, such as Heart of Darkness by Joseph Conrad, Moby Dick by Herman Melville, The Adventures of Augie March, by Saul Bellow, The Adventures of Huckelberry Finn, by Mark Twain, and of course, Marcel Proust's monumental work, Remembrance of Things Past, were in the first person. The list could go on and on.

Writing in the first person has that great power of intimacy with the reader, but it has its drawbacks as well. The events portrayed are usually limited to what the narrator is perceiving, though great writers expand upon this. By limited perception, I mean that the narrator can only relate what he or she knows, hears about or sees. In the hands of a poor writer, the first person becomes a tedious event, with the "I" of the narrator intruding constantly.

Conrad, a master of the first person, would expand the narrative by having someone, usually his main character, Marlow, start a story at the outset of the novel, as in Heart of Darkness. As the novel progresses, Marlow relates his story of meeting other men who talk of the mysterious Kurtz, and gradually the narrative, still in the first person, changes to other men relating a story in the first person. The story skips from one narrator to another; in one novel, Conrad's final narrator was the sixth person to tell the story. This is involved, and perhaps only a master such as Conrad could pull it off.

Even if the novel starts in the first person, there are devices open to the writer to change it to the third person. Another character can tell a story in the third person; a manuscript can be found in the course of the novel, telling a tale in the third person. Or today, with the boundaries of the novel as flexible as they are, a story beginning in the first person can change, at the author's whim, to the third person in a subsequent chapter.

However, I suggest, that, if you start in the first person, that should be your voice throughout the novel. First learn the craft, then once that is down, you can move to experimentation.

1. Expanding the First Person Narrative

I mentioned that one of the limitations is the constant use of the word "I" in the narrative. This can easily be dealt with. The narrator can relate conversations between other characters, can listen to stories told by other characters, can perceive events carried out by other characters. Let's just make up easy examples of each of these situations:

a. Conversations Between Other Characters:

"I was sitting in the restaurant finishing my second cup of coffee, just killing time. In an hour I had to go out for a job interview, a job I desperately needed. I told myself, "relax, don't get anxious, be self-assured or that job will disappear" but this pep talk wasn't working. I sipped the coffee, thinking that all this caffeine wasn't a good idea. I felt like smoking a cigarette–I had given up on them six months before, but now, with the anxiety and the warm wash of coffee on my tongue, I craved a smoke.

"As I sat there, I became aware of two people talking behind me. The restaurant was pretty empty, it being after lunch hours, and I could hear them distinctly. They were a couple, and sounded as if they were in their early thirties, just a guess. I didn't want to turn around and be obvious, so I just sat there, drinking the coffee, thinking of having another cup.

"You know what I thinks the matter with you," the woman behind me was saying, "you're very depressed."

"Depressed?" The man's voice was a little high-pitched, then after the question, it settled down. "Why am I depressed? How can you say I'm depressed?"

"Well, you keep complaining about this city? All I hear you do is complain, complain, complain. That's all you do."

"Oh, is that right, that's all I do? You think I have no life but that, is that what you're saying?"

"It"s just that you complain all the time."

"Till you brought it up, I wasn't complaining. I was just telling you about the birthday card my kid sent me. I wasn't complaining then, was I?"

"You're just disguising it; disguising the fact that you're depressed."

"What is this depression bit? Jesus, Kathy, you know what you remind me of? A dog with a bone. You get on a topic and you won't let go. Depressed? I'm not depressed. I was happy today, getting that card."

"You're just talking about the card, because I forgot your birthday. You're just bitching again."

"Am I?"

There was a silence, and I was tempted to turn around. As I thought about it, the waitress came over with the check. "Anything else?" she asked.

That's it. Just a little scene in which the writer is able to expand the narrative out of the first person into a conversation between two other characters.

b. Stories Told by Other Characters:

"We were sitting around, the three of us, all wearing tuxedos, a bottle of rather sweet American champagne on a table in front of us. Around us was a clamour of voices and people in motion. From another room the sounds of the band playing "Mona Lisa," was muted.

"I can remember the first time I heard that song," Billy said. "Definitely remember it."

"You're drunk."

"No I'm not, Al, just tipsy. Just a little tipsy is all. Hey I have a right to be tipsy. I have every right."

"Tipsy," said Al, "where the hell did you come up with a word like that. A man says 'sloshed' or 'tanked,' not tipsy."

"Well, I'm a poet," said Billy, "I have a right to say tipsy if I want." He picked up the champagne glass, drained it and then poured some more of the champagne. "This stuff is terrible," he said, "you would think Larry would buy better stuff for his wedding." He drained that glass as well and turned towards me.

"Frank, do you remember my wedding?"

"Sure."

"That was a long time ago. Shit, it was twenty five years ago. You know where the bitch is today?"

"Millie? No."

"Florida. She lives in Boca Raton. You know what that

means?"

"Rat's mouth," I said.

"Very good, very good. And you know something, Frank. Sometimes when I think of her, I think, boy, every day that she's alive she ought to thank God on her bended knees. Did you know that?"

"What are you talking about," asked Al.

"I'll tell you what I'm talking about. And I'm only talking now because my two buddies...we know each other, what, thirty years now. Thirty years at least. Well, after I got married...I never told anyone this story before, but screw it, the statute of limitations probably ran out. Anyway, you know Millie started to cheat on me. Not that it was her fault entirely, you know, I was a stupid shit in those days. I was young and able, young and hung."

I leaned back. Al, who was sweating freely in his tux, took out a handkerchief and carefully wiped off his face.

"So anyway, Millie...yeah. So I know who's she's cheating with, it's some sonofabitch who comes to our house about twice a week, a so-called friend of mine. So I'm at work; in those days I worked for that agency on East 48th Street. And I get this incredible idea, just out of the blue. You want to know what it was?"

We didn't answer. I leaned back and closed my eyes. It was awfully hot in the room. I opened them again. A couple walked by, people I recognized vaguely. They waved to Al and went on.

"Anyway," continued Billy, "I'm sitting at my desk on the fortieth floor, and looking out at a sunshiny day, and thinking, that bitch got to pay, and that guy also...you know, it's funny, I don't even remember his name today. So I get up and leave the office and go to a nearby bar and drink about five scotches, one after the other."

"Why?" asked Al.

"To get up nerve."

"Nerve? For what?"

"Come on, Al, let me tell my story. So I'm looped and I leave this dismal bar and walk down to Times Square and go into one of those stores...you know, they sell knives, and in those days you could buy a switchblade knife, and I buy this big mother, and put in in my jacket pocket."

"Are you serious?" I asked.

"This is the God's honest truth."

"So..." said Al. He was now leaning forward. The band was now playing "Love is a Many Splendored Thing."

"Yeah, so where was I? At Times Square. I get into the subway there, take the BMT and go all the way down to where I lived, you know, in those days, on Ocean Avenue and Avenue M. I get off, and walk to my house. I'm thinking, two people are going to die...and I'm feeling good about the thought. Two people are going to die. I get to my house, and let myself in. I open the front door real quiet-like and close it behind me, no noise. I'm a killer and I got to surprise the bitch and her ...whatever."

He paused and poured himself another drink. Billy put down the glass and rubbed one hand across his brow, then continued. "I go looking for them. My plan is this; if they're both together, I kill them both."

"So," said Al, "what happened?"

"Millie is in the kitchen, cooking some shit or other. It's about two in the afternoon; the kids are in school. She looks at me, and takes a double look. 'You're drunk,' she says.

"I don't answer. I walk through the rest of the house, looking for that bastard destroyed my happy home. But he's not there. I think, maybe just kill her, but that was stupid. Now I'm coming to my senses. She's the mother of my kids for God's sakes. So, without another word, I just walk out."

"Well, that was wise," Al said.

"I don't know."

"What if the guy was home?" I asked.

"Oh, I kill them both. No doubt about it."

"I don't think so," said Al. "I know you too well, you're not a killer. As you said, you're a poet."

Billy closed his eyes and kept them shut for a couple of minutes, then opened them again. "I would have killed them," he said, his voice dropping. "Yes sir, I would have greased the both of them."

Al and I said nothing. We sat there, listening to the music from the other room. I didn't recognize the tune.

Note how the narrator, who is Frank, the "I" of the story, fades into the background, and Billy takes over, telling his story. This is another way of expanding the narration without the "I" predominating.

c. Events Carried Out by Other Characters:

Pete, Dominick and I went down to Coney Island. "We've got to see a man there," said Pete, driving the Ford. "We gotta take care of some business."

Dominick always hung around with Pete and now sat in the back seat, smoking a Lucky Strike. Dominick had a thin face and a bad cough, which he blamed on everything but the three packs he smoked daily. Pete, in great shape, a natural middleweight, didn't smoke or drink. He took care of himself. Pete had fought in the Golden Gloves at 160 pounds, and knocked out three guys before losing in the finals.

"I had the bastard where I wanted him," Pete had told me. "When I dragged myself off the canvas, that's what I told Big Lou, my trainer. I had him where I wanted him. Lou thought I was nuts. Maybe I was. That bastard could hit. And could take a punch. I gave him my best shot, and it was like...ah, the hell with it. The point is, he's the champ and I'm a runner-up, an also ran. That's my fate."

We were in Coney Island now, on Neptune Avenue. Pete drove slowly, one hand on the wheel, the other hanging out the window. He made a few turns and pointed out a couple of tough looking dudes in leather jackets standing near an empty lot.

"See those guys," he said.

"Yeah."

"One of them whacked out a guy I know."

"No kidding, which one?"

"The one in the leather jacket," said Dominick. "He's gonna get his one day. And I know who's gonna give it to him."

We passed them and kept driving. On West 12th, Pete made a left and drove toward the boardwalk and parked the car on a dead end street. No one was around. Dominick and Pete got out of the car. "You stay here, Bobby," he told me.

"Ok."

They walked toward the boardwalk. A man came out of the shadows, a bald guy, maybe in his forties. He waved toward Pete and Dominick, and they all went under the boardwalk. I strained to see what was happening. I could see them standing and talking, then suddenly, Pete hit the guy. The guy fell back a little and Pete hit him again. The guy went down. I could see Dominick kicking the guy who was down. Then both of them bent down over the fallen guy. A few minutes later they were coming back to the car.

"Jesus," I said, "what happened?"

"You don't want to know," said Pete. He started the car. I looked toward the underside of the boardwalk but the guy hadn't gotten up yet. Had they killed him? I got a little panicky then. Accessory to murder. I had bad thoughts then. But Pete turned the car around, and we drove out of Coney Island. Later, we went to Stanley's Diner on Avenue X and had burgers and coffee. They never talked about what happened and I never brought it up again.

This is but another example of the expansion of the first person narrative. Like the third person, it's really not necessary to get too much into the mind of the narrator. What he sees and how he reacts to a situation speaks volumes about his feelings. His character is also delineated by the men he hangs around with. This is another good way to delineate a character. As in real life, we judge someone by their friends and how the friends treat the person we observe.

2. Third Person Narrative

In the third person, the "he" and "she" predominate. For example, the story is told by the author, not the "I" narrator. For example, my novel Sweet Land of Liberty, begins:

"He used to sit in his room on the farm near Lamoni, Iowa, staring up at the wall map of the United States of America..."

By writing in the third person, the author can expand his narrative since he's not restricted to the perceptions of the "I" character. The writer can follow the lives of a few characters in one scene, and a few more in the next scene. Then he can observe other characters in yet another setting. This allows a writer to be omniscient, seeing all and revealing what he wishes to reveal.

Tolstoy, in his masterpiece, War and Peace, perhaps the greatest novel ever written, followed various members of Russian society, from vassals to aristocracy, from soldiers to generals. He was able to present scenes ranging from drawing rooms to battlefields by writing in the third person, and presenting an array of unforgettable characters in the process. It would have been impossible to carry out the scope of this novel in the first person.

Nearly all writers have written separate books in the first and third persons. Even if the writer means to show a limited view of society, he may be more comfortable in the third person, as Orwell was in 1984. In many of these novels, the writer prefers telling the story this way, rather than having a narrator.

When you begin a novel, this is a basic choice you will face. I faced it and chose the third person with my first novel, because I was interested in following a number of diverse characters in various locations, and couldn't accomplish the same result in the first person. With my second novel, I chose the first person, because basically I was following a boy's life, and it was unnecessary to show anything other than what the boy, the narrator, perceived.

Though a novel may begin in the third person, there are a number of ways to switch to the first person. The easiest is to have a character tell an extended story with himself or herself as the narrator. Another method would be to have a character keep a journal or diary, in which the narration takes place in the first person.

As you become more confident of your craft, you can even alternate chapters, one in the third person, another in the first person. This is tricky to do, and my first suggestion would be to avoid this device. Learn the craft first, and learn to write separate works in the first and in the third person. After you've written a novel or two and gotten published, then you can experiment. But learn the craft first. Without the craft down pat, there can really be no art.

It is best, before thinking of writing in either the first or third person, to read the best work by the greatest writers, to see how they accomplish their goals in either voice. I have named writers continually in this book, whose work I respect.

I'll name some writers to study:

Dickens, Orwell, Austen, Mann, Stendhal, Camus, Conrad, Hemingway, Faulkner, Steinbeck, Malamud, Tolstoy, and the list goes on and on. Study the best work as a guide to what can be accomplished, then strike out on your own, with your own voice and vision. Don't imitate. I mention these great writers only as a roadmap.

3. Past and Present Tenses

Most novels are written in the past tense, though there are exceptions to this, and one we have shown previously was James Baldwin's Giovanni's Room, which is in the present tense.

The difference between the two tenses is obvious, but we'll write a couple of sentences; the first in the present, and the second in the past tense, to make them absolutely clear.

"He stands by the window looking out at the falling rain."

"He stood by the window, looking out at the falling rain."

It is difficult to write a complete novel in the present tense, but writers like Baldwin have done so. More often, a short story can more easily accomodate itself to that tense. What the present tense gives us is an immediacy of action, and combined with a first person narrative, we get both the immediacy and the intimacy of both forms. Here's a quick example:

"He sits on the bed, staring at a wall. The wall is blank, though behind him is a print of Rousseau's "After the Ball." He does not want to look at the print. He really doesn't want to look at anything. All he wants to do is close off his mind, but that, he knows, is impossible.

"There are other things he knows. He knows that in the top drawer of his dresser is a Ruger .38, of stainless steel, with a four inch barrel. He knows it is loaded. He knows he can get off the bed and walk over to the dresser and take out the gun. He knows he can put it in his mouth and pull the trigger. He knows this is a sure way to die.

"He knows all these things. He is amazed at all he knows right now. He gets up, feeling weary. He is tired, but that is nothing new. He is always tired. He walks toward the dresser. It would be simple to just open that top drawer. Just open it. But just then the phone rings."

I would suggest to the beginning writer that he attempts a short story using the present tense, either in the first or third person. This should be another weapon in the arsenal of a writer.

VI

FLASHBACKS

A flashback is a device in which an earlier event is inserted into the normal chronological order of a narrative. A flashback, in my view, should be used sparingly, and only in a situation where there is no other way to reveal the earlier episode.

For one thing, a flashback stops the action cold, halts the narrative drive and brings the reader back in time. It can be effective in the hands of a skillful writer, but as I wrote, the flashback should be used when there is no other alternative.

I used to illustrate the pitfalls of the flashback to my classes with this story:

"On a hot summer day, I was in my study, working on a new book, when the front doorbell rang. At that time I lived in Studio City, in a house I had bought several years before, and since there was airconditioning only in my bedroom I worked in shorts with the doors and windows open, trying to get some relief from the heat by cross ventilation.

I left the desk and typewriter and went to the front door, which was open, though the screen door was clasped. Standing there was a young woman with long blonde hair, wearing shorts and a halter. She looked like an actress or model.

"Yes?"

"Are you Ed Silberstang?"

I nodded.

"I'm Julie. I read one of your books and decided to look

you up."

"Really? Which one?"

"Losers Weepers."

I stood there awkwardly and then opened the door. "Come on in," I said.

She stepped into my living room. "Do you rent this place?" she asked.

"No, I own it."

"I love fireplaces," she said, pointing to the one in the living room. "I used to live in Minnesota. In fact I was Miss Minnesota some years back."

I could believe that.

"What can I do for you?" I asked.

"I want to talk about the book you wrote. I have an agent and he wants to get me in pictures and is always looking for material for me. The role of Laura would be perfect for me, don't you think?"

"It might be."

She stood in the living room, fanning herself with her hands. "Ed, it's so hot in here. Don't you have airconditioning or something?"

"Only in my bedroom."

"Can we talk in there?"

"OK." I led her to the bedroom and turned on the air conditioning unit there.

"I swear," Julie said. "I'm soaked to the skin. If you wouldn't mind, I'd love to get out of these clothes."

"What?"

"If you wouldn't mind. I'm just all soaked. I'm just not used to this hot weather." And with these words, she took off her shorts and halter, and crawled into my bed.

I looked at her on the bed. I thought about that bed. Where had I bought it? At the Broadway or at May's? It was hard to remember, but I knew that it was on sale, along with the other bedroom furniture. The salesman was a tall man, I remember now, with a walrus mustache and warm brown eyes.

He was wearing a checkered jacket..."

What about the girl on the bed? Well, time out for the flashback. That's what I mean about the danger of a flashback. First you set the reader up, and then leave him high and dry as you devote yourself to the flashback. This is not to say that a flashback isn't useful at times. I've used it in novels. But it must not interfere with the narrative, and must bring information and deepen the story and character.

VII

THE LANDSCAPE OF THE NOVEL

A novel is a large undertaking, unlike a short story. Many beginning writers make a crucial mistake at the outset of the novel. They write one or two chapters, which are interesting, and then they have nowhere to go. I've seen that time and time again. Students would read a chapter or two in a workshop, holding the attention of the group, then plaintively ask "what do I do now?"

What they have done, in essence, is round out the story without leaving unresolved issues or tension in the work. They've closed up the novel and a novel must have a broad landscape. By broad, I mean an expanding landscape. There is the basic story, there may be subplots, other characters introduced, stories examined and told within the framework of the novel.

To prepare this broadening, the writer, at the outset must create a world that will accomodate all of this. The world can be narrow in the sense of space or time; two examples that come to mind are Darkness At Noon, by Arthur Koestler, where much of the action takes place in a prison, and James Joyce's great masterpiece, Ulysses, where all the action takes place on a single day. No one could say that Joyce's work was limited in scope because of the narrow time element; in many ways it is as far ranging as "The Odyssey," Homer's epic poem, on which it is based.

At the outset of the novel, there must be an unresolved issue. A woman wants to find romance, a man returns to the scenes of his youth in search of his past. Or a stranger comes to town on a mysterious mission, or a person goes on a voyage of discovery. The choices are endless; but the protagonist whom we are to follow must hold our interest, and engage our emotions and feelings.

I wrote before that we might not be interested in a character who is not as clever as we are. There can be exceptions to this when we follow someone who is buffeted in the world because of his or her weakness of intellect. This same protagonist may have a good heart, and we will be engaged, as in real life, by a kind and good person. Cleverness and intelligence are not always the hallmark of an interesting protagonist.

In the course of the novel, it is better that the protagonist moves the story, rather than he or she being buffeted by fate. The line here is thinly drawn, for in modern society, the great forces around us move us and push us into situations we might not take on our own. The whole idea of a good simple person trapped by society is evident in the great films of Charlie Chaplin. The tramp is a sorry figure, who is not particularly bright. But what he possesses is kindness and a great humanity. These same qualities will be those we will follow in a novel.

As we wrote before, we begin the novel at the last possible moment, that is, we open the curtain on the world we're writing about when something is about to happen. In "Hamlet" the late king's ghost has been spotted, and Hamlet is called to the scene. The ghost cries out for revenge for his murder, and the story is underway. Hamlet, the slain king's son, must revenge his father's death.

In a novel, a character may find himself forced by circumstance or by pressure to right a wrong done to his family, or to himself. This propels a story forward. Once the story moves forward, the tension should not let up. Nothing should be resolved, and subplots should spring up. There may only be one subplot; for example, a man might have a certain mission he must accomplish; during that time he meets a woman, and their love interest becomes a viable subplot.

A writer is not forced to have only one protagonist. There may be two, who together face a common fate or enemy, or who are aligned against each other. In the latter case, the reader will read on to see who is triumphant in the end. When dealing with subsidiary characters in a novel, be careful to flesh them out. Don't just have them as names or stick figures who make plotpoints and move a plot along. Each character must have a soul and be interesting. I first became aware of this principle when reading the novels of Dostoievski. Each character he introduces is fully realized and stands on his or her own.

When a protagonist has a mission, this moves the story along and contributes mightily to the narrative drive. The mission may be to land a husband, to avenge a wrong, to break out of poverty, to make something of oneself. Again, the possibilities are endless.

In real life, we may have the same missions, and within a short period they may be resolved. But this can't happen in a novel; the work must be strung along, not artificially, but within the framework of the story. The line of the main story must always stay taut, even though there are valleys and hills within the story itself.

Sometimes the main story is rather subtle. In Hemingway's finest novel, The Sun Also Rises, Jake Barnes, the narrator of the story seems to just be floating around Paris. He has a woman interested in him, Lady Brett Ashley, and a group of friends are going to visit him and all of them will eventually go to Pamplona to the racing of the bulls and the subsequent bullfights. Jake and friends go on bus trips in Spain, go fishing, go drinking in cafes. Nothing much seems to happen.

However, a great deal is happening, and the narrative drive never lets up. Jake Barnes, emasculated during the First World War, cannot consummate his love for Lady Brett, and as the novel progresses and she lurches in and out of sordid affairs, we feel the anguish and frustration of both of these characters. Hemingway uses Gertrude Stein's statement that "you are all a lost generation," as one of the epigraphs of the novel. These people are a lost generation, damaged goods as a result of the World War I.

In some ways, Jake's wound is a symbol of the aimlessness and loss of that generation. He has been made barren, and the generation around him is barren in a different way; they are world-weary and aimless. In this novel, Hemingway subtly deals with the narrative drive in a fresh manner, and our interest is never lost.

In The Great Gatsby, F. Scott Fitzgerald's fine work, which many consider the greatest of all American novels, Nick Carraway is the narrator, but really a minor character. The story is about Gatsby and his love for Daisy Buchanan. Gatsby is rich, and made his way above his ordinary station in life, unlike Jake Barnes, as a result of the First World War and various shady ventures.

There is the same aimlessness as we see in The Sun Also Rises, but whereas Hemingway's characters are expatriates in Europe, the action is limited to New York City and Long Island, where Gatsby has built a sumptuous home that overlooks Daisy's across the Long Island Sound. The drive of the novel deals with Gatsby's infatuation for Daisy, and the futility of his desperate search to win her over. He fails, because he is of a different class, and all his money is new money. He is gauche and doesn't have the veneered manners of Daisy and Tom Buchanan, with their old money and old connections.

Fitzgerald has several subplots in the story, and the narrative drive never lets up. This novel is highly recommended, and should be read, as all work recommended in this book, as a professional writer reads a book. Don't read it to see if you like it; read it to see how Fitzgerald weaves together the story, and presents characters that have worked their way into the American consciousness. There is hardly a big city without a place called "Gatsby's." And Daisy Buchanan is an unforgettable character.

In earlier centuries, and even in the early part of the twentieth century, before the advent of radio, motion pictures and television, the novelist wrote on a larger scale than he does now. Today's writers tend to write tauter, more focussed books. There is a reason for this.

Prior to the media age, the writer was a teacher as well as author. Dickens introduced us to a world that few people, even those who lived in London, knew about, the world of the debtor prisons and blackening factories, the world of Fagin and his band of juvenile thieves. Dostoevski and Tolstoy wrote enormous novels that covered great swaths of Russian society. Readers knew nothing of these people before reading these great masters' works. Laymen often got their information about the world from novels. Of course, this is not the case today.

In this information age, we get our news from visual images for the most part, not from the printed word. Therefore, the role of the novelist has changed. He is no longer a teacher or a moralist, as in the case of Upton Sinclair or John Steinbeck. The novelist's scope has narrowed. He or she now deals with smaller segments, but still deals with the human condition. That will never change.

VIII

GET YOUR FACTS STRAIGHT

A mistake many beginning writers make in their work is presenting facts that are already well known by the readership. For example, there is no point in describing the Notre Dame football stadium in detail because millions of people know what a football stadium looks like. Nor does a prison cell have to be detailed in full. However, not many people know what the Notre Dame football team does in the locker room before a game, and the daily routine of prison life is likewise not generally known.

In other words, what facts you present as a novelist must be carefully chosen so that the reader doesn't feel you're wasting his time writing five pages on something he has seen dozens of time on television. Another thing to watch out for is putting down as fact something you don't really know. It can be the most trivial thing, but to a discerning reader, it may be the excuse to summarily close the novel and not read anymore.

I think of a few examples. I was once given a novel to critique and possibly pass along to an agent. In this novel, the main character was a stock broker, and in the opening chapter he buys 5,000 shares of American Telephone stock for a client. He describes watching the ticker go by with the trade, 5,000 ATT. I and millions of other investors know that the symbol for telephone stock is T. He lost me right then and there.

Once, watching a play in Los Angeles I was equally annoyed. The woman who took me knew I was from Brooklyn originally, and the play dealt with the building of the Verrazano-Narrows Bridge. In the opening scene, the hero is asked by a woman what he does for a living. "I'm a steel-worker," he tells her.

Now, when I lived and worked in Brooklyn, I represented a couple of men who worked the high steel on bridges. They called themselves "ironworkers," never "steelworkers." I couldn't understand, sitting in that theatre, how the author didn't even know this and yet the whole play revolved around the hero's work. Immediately I felt the play was phony. Maybe I judged too quickly, but if he didn't know this, what did he know?

It would be the same as if a person who drove a truck said he belonged to the trucker's union, not the teamster's union. Another example was a manuscript I was given because I had written about the Mafia in a couple of my novels. It was set in New York, and written by someone in Los Angeles. The main character is supposedly a mob guy. At a party, to impress someone, he tells this person he's in the Mafia. Reading this, I thought, "come on now, this is nonsense." First of all, anyone in the organization denies there's a Mafia. And if they rant against the Feds, it's because the FBI cracks down on "O.C." and not the Mafia. O.C. stands for organized crime.

In my office one time, a client who wanted to put a scare into me told me he was in the Mafia. I suppose he thought I'd shake in my boots. At that time, after my father's death, I was representing several mob guys, and one was in the vestibule waiting to see me. I called him in.

"Augie," I said, "you told me you always wanted to meet someone in the Mafia. This guy says he's in the Mafia."

"Oh," said Augie, "so you're in the Mafia."

Augie, who looked like a miniature John Gotti, was a pretty scary guy. The other guy mumbled something and was quickly out the door.

So, my point is this; if you're writing about a segment of society, be sure to know what you're writing about. The quickest turnoff to an editor is someone who doesn't even know the facts about the small world he's putting on paper.

Sometimes editors, who don't have a particular knowledge of a subject, let false information slide through.

Years ago, I read a memoir of a gambler, published by a major house. Now, if there's something I do know, it's gambling and games. I've written over forty books on the subject. In this book (not a novel but supposedly a true story) the author tells of looking at the Golden Nugget hotel from his window at a hotel in the middle of the Strip. Of course, to see the Golden Nugget from there, he would have to beam his eyes to the nearest satellite. And when he gambles on the Strip, he bets with $20 chips. Unless he manufactured them himself, he can't find them in Las Vegas. He had probably visited the card clubs of Los Angeles, where one can play with $2, $3 and $20 chips, all denominations not found in Vegas, and thought he could fake it. Once I read these sections, I figured that much of the book was fake. The editor didn't catch these mistakes, which I felt was the editor's fault. If you're an editor and faced with a topic or subject you don't know about, at least call in an expert to verify the facts. And if you're a writer, verify your facts and do a little research. There's nothing so embarassing as presenting as facts something that doesn't exist or is untrue.

IX

REFLECTIONS ON THE NOVEL

1. The Protagonist's Internal and External Struggles

A solid way to contribute to the narrative drive is to force your main character to encounter various difficulties. In this psychological age, often the struggle is internal, as the protagonist becomes aware of his or her own weakness. If you combine this with the struggle against external forces, then the movement of the story can be relentless. The ideal example is not from a novel, but from "Hamlet." Not only must Hamlet try to avenge his father's death at the hands of the murderous Claudius, but he must, within himself, overcome the paralysis of will that prevents him from carrying out his mission. When these two struggles dovetail, not only do they deepen the character of the protagonist, but they impel the story forward.

For those readers who like to be entertained, the hero's struggle against outside forces often holds their attention. For those readers who are more involved in the internal psychological emphasis on character, the internal struggle is the mainspring of their attention. Some novels simply pander to the former, with a big adventure story, the hero against evil forces. To me, this kind of book is uninteresting. What holds me is the internal struggle of man in all its colors, for humanity with all its failings is the stuff of great work. Both the internal and external struggles can be meshed, and then the work becomes fuller and satisfies a wider readership.

2. Dialogue vs Narration

When I taught, a question that often was asked was this: "how much of the work should be dialogue and how much narration?"

There is no simple answer to that question. Just as I cannot answer a question, such as: "how big should a novel be?" in quantitative terms, so I cannot give a cut and dried response to the first query. To me, a novel should be as long as it has to be, no longer and no shorter. As Albert Einstein so succinctly said, "everything should made as simple as possible, but no simpler." This is a Zen answer to many aspects of life. Let's get back to dialogue vs. narration.

The one thing a writer must avoid is this—setting up or dividing his work according to a formula. When dialogue is called for, then there should be dialogue. When narration is necessary, then there should be narration. It's as simple as that. If dialogue runs for ten pages, then that's what's happening. If narration runs for the same length of time, and there is no necessity for dialogue, then stick with that length. Don't ever bind yourself as a writer. Don't feel that the dialogue has gone on long enough and now it's time to change to narration. Or vice versa. Do what is most effective in presenting the work, without worrying about proportions.

It may be that almost the entire work will be in narration, or most of it in dialogue. If that is the case, and you've effectively told the truth, then trust in what you have written. Any critic or editor who will say "there's too much dialogue," or "too much narrative" isn't worth listening to. The only important response to work is this— "it moved me," or "it held my attention," or "it caught hold of my feelings" or "it didn't." Telling you that you've put in too much dialogue is like criticizing the number of commas you've used. It's worthless criticism.

3. Effective Dialogue

Dialogue which is stilted or doesn't sound realistic is the kiss of death for the serious writer. How does one then write effective dialogue? For one thing, study the masters, but don't imitate them. See how effective dialogue is written. To get a fresh perspective on this subject, the writer should be out in the world, listening. I carefully listen to what people say, not in movies or on television, but in real life. I listen for inflections, for subject matter, for common and contemporary speech patterns. I listen to lyrics of the latest songs. I listen to whatever I can, but not the artificial dialogue of weak television or movie writers.

Sometimes a vulgar expression can spoil the whole effect. In the movie "Crossing Delancey," the main character is played by Amy Irving, a fine actress. She works in a bookstore and is infatuated with a writer, who really is unworthy of her. When she realizes this, she mutters the word "asshole." This vulgarity is a favorite one of scriptwriters. And each time I hear it, it rubs me the wrong way. When Amy Irving's character said it, I felt let down at once. All that had been built up in sensibility was torn down with one word.

Weak writers and Hollywood hacks take the same tack. When they have to express a deep feeling they use a curseword, not being able to express feelings any other way. Even silence would have been better, for example, to express Amy Irving's character's anger. She's an actor, and should have used or been permitted to use her talents to convey her anger and unhappiness. Instead the cheap word "asshole" is meant to explain everything. It explains only one thing—the inadequacy of the screenwriter.

Now that books and films have been released from the artificial morality that prevailed for too long, many writers have gone to the other extreme, with a wild range of profanity running like spittle out of their characters' mouths. This garbage isn't dialogue; it's nothing but filth. I'm not a moralist by any means, and my characters aren't goody two-shoes, but if they curse, it's indigenous to the situation, not something imposed on the scene.

Cursing in real life, when other forms of expression could

be used, is generally a sign of a vulgar, uneducated person. It often takes the place of wit, and reflects badly on the curser. Wit is so much more interesting and evokes a stronger reaction.

When Oscar Wilde was asked by a minor poet what he should do concerning a conspiracy of silence against him becoming poet laureate of England, Wilde told the poet, "join it."

That is true wit. In this day and age, the hack writer would have him answer, "go screw yourself with your shitty request." This isn't wit and isn't a worthwhile answer.

As I wrote before, I listen carefully to people when they hold conversations, in all types of situations and in all walks of life. I eavesdrop a great deal, not to hear personal matters, but to listen to patterns of speech. I'm not going to imitate them in my work, but they keep me alert to the uses and power of dialogue.

What I've noticed is this–people don't always talk in set patterns, nor do they stick to the point. In badly written dialogue, everything is to the plotpoint. The purpose of this second and third-rate dialogue is to move the story along, and it exists for no other reason. But the trouble is, no one speaks like these characters in real life.

Even in the most dramatic situation, people don't speak to the point. I tried to show this in my novel, Losers Weepers in a scene where two men are waiting to kill some bikers in New Jersey. Carmine Abatto, one of the two main characters in the book, is sitting with his pal Vitale in a car, waiting for the bikers to come out of a bar. Do they talk about the imminent killing? Let's listen in as Vitale speaks first:

"When I was a kid, hell, you remember, when we stole that bike from that spick."

"That ten-speed one."

"Yeah. Aah, the fuckin' spick stole it himself. What a bike, remember that one?"

"Yeah,. Rode it all day around the schoolyard. What we do

with it?"

"Tony Balls busted it up."

"Yeah, that jerk. Where is he?"

"Got life in Oregon."

"Oregon?"

"No shit. Killed a cop out there. Pulled a bank job, killed a cop."

"What the fuck was he doing in Oregon?"

"Some broad, what else? Ran after some tail to Portland."

"He was always a jerk."

"Yeah, old Tony Balls. He used to be called 'One Ball,' you know. He lost one to mumps."

"No shit, didn't know that," said Carmine.

"Yeah. Hey, I used to bust my old man's chops to get me a bike. He'd say,"Whatta bike, it costa money."

"You should have told him everything costa da money."

"Huh. How you gonna speak to the old man when you're a kid. That's the trouble with being Italian..."

Then, a few minutes later, the bikers come out and they assassinate them.

What I didn't want to do was have these men talk about the future killing while waiting. That would be the cheap and incorrect way to have them speak. Again, as I have pointed out, dialogue isn't always to the point. It serves two purposes; one, it moves the story forward and two, it deepens the characters. We can even add a third purpose; it adds texture to the novel. By texture I mean deepening the story, going beyond the surface of the story to reveal something else, something fresh and unusual. A good example is our old friend "Hamlet," where Hamlet, feigning insanity, watches helplessly as his love, Ophelia, actually goes insane.

A good example of all three elements is in the beginning of The Friends of Eddie Coyle, by George V. Higgins, which I recommend to the beginning writer. In the beginning of the novel, Jackie Brown is trying to sell guns to the protagonist, Eddie Coyle. The scene, complete with dialogue, fulfills all three criteria of effective dialogue. The plot is moved along, the characters are deepened and there is added texture to the novel, all in the dialogue.

There are some writers, such as Hemingway, who have fine tuned the art of dialogue. In a number of short stories, such as "Fifty Grand" or "The Snows of Kilimanjaro," Hemingway begins with dialogue and lets it run for awhile. The reader is forced to carefully follow what is said; nothing is made easy for him or her. The beginning of "The Snows of Kilimanjaro," one of Hemingway's greatest short stories, illustrates this:

"The marvellous thing is that it's painless," he said. "That's how you know when it starts."

"Is it really?"

"Absolutely. I'm awfully sorry about the odor though. That must bother you."

"Don't. Please don't."

"Look at them," he said. "Now is it sight or is it scent that brings them like that."

As we read on, we realize that the man speaking is dying and is infected with gangrene. The "them" he refers to are carrion, which sense the dying of a human or an animal. The man is talking to a woman. We have to read carefully to see just what is going on in this story. Hemingway writes sparingly, and explains nothing in his marvellous short stories. As he once said "it's what you leave out that is more important than what you put in."

An exercise I would suggest is to write an entire scene strictly with dialogue, without any narrative or inner thoughts of the characters. Try more than one scene; this is a solid way to deal with dialogue and master it.

When writing dialogue, don't have all of the conversation go to the plotpoint or to the situation on hand in the novel. Real people, when speaking, will vary the range of their conversation to all sorts of subjects, some of which may have nothing to do with what was originally the point of the original dialogue. Let's give an example of how this might be done:

"So you're really leaving town," I said.

"Yes," Marie said, "I'll be out of here by the end of the month."

"Going to Phoenix."

"That's right. Phoenix, here I come."

"It's awfully hot in Phoenix."

"I'll get used to it," Marie said. "It gets hot here in LA in the summer."

"But not like Phoenix."

"That's true. But it'll be ok. The job offer is good, and I can use the money. I'm not going to live from paycheck to paycheck the way I've been doing for the last four years."

"That's a consideration," I said.

"A big consideration. Listen, I'll be ok. Don't worry. I've thought it all out."

In the above conversation, everything is to the point. The weather, the job in Phoenix are discussed. But the dialogue is essentially uninteresting, in the sense that the characters aren't deepened. Let's play with this dialogue to add more interest.

"So you're going to Phoenix," I said.

"That's right. Phoenix, here I come."

"It can get awfully hot in Phoenix."

"Sure it can. Why are you bringing up the heat?"

"I just want to warn you," I said.

"Do you think I was born an hour ago? I know what it's like there. For God's sake, I made two trips there for job interviews last month. That was July. I know what it's like there."

"I just thought..."

"Look, what are you telling me? I'm making a big mistake? Is that what you're telling me," said Marie. She leaned back in the booth and pushed her iced tea to one side. "You know what this conversation reminds me of? Ah, forget it."

"What were you going to say?"

"It's unimportant."

"No, really..."

"Never mind. You know, Charley, when I was a little girl, I

was about five or six, my father used to come into my room before I went to sleep and read to me. He'd read from Mother Goose. He had bought this big book of Mother Goose in a second-hand bookstore, and every night he read to me, and when he left the room, first I felt good, then very sad." She glanced around the restaurant. "Very sad...you see that woman over there, don't turn your head and be obvious..."

"Where?"

"To your left, near the window. The woman in the pink outfit."

I turned my head slightly. "Yeah? What about her?"

"She's been staring at us."

"Really?"

"I don't like the way she's staring at us. I don't know. Maybe I'm getting paranoid. I miss my father. I wish he hadn't gone and died on me. I miss him a lot."

"Sure, I can understand."

"No you can't." The woman she had pointed out was getting up and leaving the restaurant. Marie watched her out of the corner of her eyes. "She's still watching us," she said. "I have bad feelings about her."

"What's going on?" I asked.

"Never mind," said Marie, "just do me a favor. Ok?"

"Sure."

"Stop asking me questions and stop giving me advice. Ok?" Marie scratched one wrist with the fingernails of the other hand. "I've got to get out of here."

I didn't say anything. The waitress came by and I asked for the check. Outside, through the big front glass window, I could see the woman standing in the sun, motionless, adjusting her sunglasses. Then she turned and walked out of view.

The dialogue is full of fits and starts. Topics are brought up, dealt with partially and discarded, then brought up again. The woman pointed out by Marie has no relevancy to the story, or does she? An aura of uncertainty and irresolution hangs over the scene.

Dialogue, like the other literary devices used in the novel, should expand, not contract the action or the story.

Be aware of this writing your novel or doing an exercise in dialogue. Conversely, try a scene with only narrative, without any dialogue and without going into the mind of any of the characters. This, plus the previous exercise, will expand your range as a writer.

4. Point of View

A point of view can be defined as a position from which something is observed or considered; a standpoint. It is also defined as an attitude or outlook of a narrator or character.

When writing in the first person, the point of view will be that of the narrator, but as we have seen in my examples of expanding the first person narrative, it can easily be switched to another character. An example of this would be a woman sitting at a table with an older woman, and though the first woman is the narrator, she listens to the older woman speak about an earlier marriage and divorce. By having the second woman speak, the point of view has changed, and we see all from the second woman's viewpoint.

When writing in the third person, the "he" or "she" of the story may be given a point of view. Or the omnipotent and all seeing writer may take over. Here's an example of this:

"On the bus, staring out of the window, a young man sat, his face serious, his eyes on the banks of dirty snow at the side of the road. Now and then he'd wipe the window with the tips of his fingers to clear a space, for his breath was constantly fogging it up. It was warm in the bus, and the young man wore a thin sweater over a shirt. Folded on his lap was a heavy plaid jacket, a popular item in the small town in Ohio he had come from."

The writer is narrating the story, and it is this all–seeing viewpoint that we follow here. He, the writer, knows everything about the character. He knows where he's from, what he's wearing, and could even, if he wished, reveal his thoughts. The viewpoint can remain with the writer, or it can be switched to the character. Let's now switch it.

"At the next reststop, the young man, whose name was Henry Oulette, got off after carefully putting on the heavy jacket and zipping it up. Outside the weather was clear, but the cold wind blew into his face and mussed his hair. Henry walked into the building housing the restaurant and went to the counter and asked for a coffee and doughnut.

Standing there, he noticed a pale young woman sitting by herself at a nearby table. He thought, should I go and sit at that table? Maybe she was a passenger on the bus, but he hadn't seen her before. She had freckled skin and her hair was a pale red, almost pink. He wondered if it was her real color.

Holding the coffee and doughnut awkwardly, Henry made his way to her table. She was staring at the tabletop and didn't look up when he approached.

"Do you mind if I sit here?" Henry asked.

The young woman, without looking up, shrugged."

We are now in Henry's viewpoint, sliding from the author's easily. We could go on, and move into the young woman's viewpoint as well, through the omnipotent author, but that would be a mistake. When writing a scene involving two or more characters, the author should choose from whose viewpoint the story will be told. It is of course possible to tell a story from everybody's viewpoint in a scene, leapfrogging from one to another, but it is bad form, and confuses the reader.

Generally speaking, the more important the character, the more that character's viewpoint should be honored. When a reader looks at a work, he or she naturally assumes that the character whose viewpoint he or she is following, is important to the story or novel. This is true, especially in third person narratives. In the first person, the "I" narrator may not be the important character, merely someone relating a story involving more powerful characters. We see this in The Great Gatsby, where Nick does the narration, though it is really the story of Gatsby and Daisy.

5. Stream of Consciousness

This is a literary device that presents the thoughts and feelings of a character as they develop. With its use, we are in the character's mind, as he observes and perceives the world around him, commenting on what he senses, and also at the same time, examining his feelings. It is the inner voice of the character that is revealed in a stream of consciousness. One of the first successful uses of this device was made by James Joyce in Ulysses, while he followed two main characters, Stephan Dedalus and Leopold Bloom, as they wandered around Dublin on one day, and wandered at the same time through this powerful work for close to a thousand pages.

The success of this book spawned a host of imitators, none of whom could match the power of Joyce's words or characters. For many imitators, it was an easy way out–they didn't have to deal with dialogue or narrative; they thought their work was accomplished by gushing out what often has been described as a "diarrhea of words." Writers with little or no talent figured that putting down what they thought was in a character's head for two hundred pages, was a work of art instead of the intense bore it really was. For a while, after Ulysses was published, the stream of consciousness method of writing was all the rage. Today, outside of Virginia Woolf's work, and of course, Ulysses, most of these works have faded into their proper insignificance.

The cheapest method of writing is to go inside a character's mind and reveal his or her thoughts. This would be akin to watching a film in which the actor, instead calling on his craft to present an emotion, merely had a "voice over" tell what he was feeling. The art and craft of a writer is in revealing inner emotions and feelings without going directly into the mind to make them perfectly clear. I would avoid stream of consciousness writing, as I would avoid "automatic writing" which is taught sometimes in writing workshops. With automatic writing, whatever comes into the writer's head is put down on paper and called "art." To me, it's nonsense, and another way of avoiding the fine art of creative writing.

6. Death and Violence

Violence is the mantra of modern life, and has worked its way into the arts. Just turn on any television program, or go to the movies and you're inundated with violence and its partner, death. Like any other assault on the senses, the volume has to be constantly turned up for the audiences, because they quickly become old-hat. After a while, the viewers become jaded, and whereas a single death used to suffice to engender some kind of emotion, now mass deaths leave them bored. More deaths, more violence, more more and yet more, cries the audience, and the more that's thrown to them, the less influence it has. So, who cares if a character in a television show or film dies? No problem. On to the next scene.

I'm always amazed at the number of deaths that become meaningless in films. A person is killed in someone's residence and is just left there. The hero of the film steps over the body, as if he is stepping over a dead cockroach. The story goes on, and the body is forgotten. The police never question the hero. What happened to the body? The man who made the film knows. He got up and went home; his work on the film over.

Who really cares if a human being has been wiped out? The hero goes on his way, for there are more important things to think about, mainly the plotline. When I was in London some years back, a producer I had been introduced to was going to do a series on Sherlock Holmes. He had made a couple of pilot episodes, and invited me to a screening.

In one of them, Sherlock Holmes, played by Ian Richardson, was with his sidekick, Dr. Watson. Someone has been bludgeoned and the two men jauntily step over the victim. Dr. Watson is involved at that moment in light conversation with Holmes. The person on the floor may or may not be dead, but looks dead.

I sat there in stunned silence. Dr. Watson, after all, is a physician. He couldn't even bother to see if the person on the ground is alive or dead. He, as a doctor, has an obligation to help those in distress, but he's too busy talking about some trivia. The producer asked me what I thought of the episode, and I expressed my outrage at the behavior of Dr. Watson. How could I be interested in a character who is allegedly a physician, yet shows no interest in a person who could be mortally hurt? The producer looked at me as if I were crazy. What was I talking about? Why was I making such a fuss over Dr. Watson being a physician?

I don't know what movies or television programs he had made previously, but he couldn't even see my point. After all, what was another dead body on the screen? To these people death is some sort of temporary condition, because after the take the actors get up and leave the set and go home, dead or not dead in the script. However, if you are going to touch the audience, the death must have some significance. Movies aren't made about statistics, and neither are novels.

Yet over and over again, I am assaulted by this indifference to mortality in films, television and books. If a man dies, so be it. On to the next scene. To anyone in real life who has seen a dead person, it is a sobering experience. The hardest lesson to learn in life is one's mortality. It is difficult to realize that once a person dies, that is the end. There's no way to bring him or her back. No way. That finality will affect us all, and no matter who we are, if we are thinking, feeling persons, we ponder our own death and that inexorable moment when life ends.

Our own death is difficult to contemplate. One instant, we are living and breathing, in full control of our emotions and feelings, and the next we are dead meat, cold and lifeless, impervious to the world. At that moment, the world truly ends for us. And unlike a mechanical device, which, after failing, can be brought back to life with new parts or the experienced hands of a mechanic, it is all over. Our short time on life's stage has been played out; we are gone to dust for eternity.

Hemingway once wrote, "if you tell any story long enough, it always ends in death, and no real writer would keep that from you."

Every story we write doesn't have to end in death, yet in literature, as in life, mortality hangs over us. Time is our great enemy and cannot be stopped. As the English poet, W.H. Auden wrote, "time coughs when you would kiss." Time and mortality are always in our lives, unwelcome visitors to our joy and happiness. As a writer, you must be aware of mortality and touch the reader in this regard.

Don't be like the cheap moviemakers, to whom death is just a moment in a plot, where dead bodies are just another establishing shot for the cameraman. In all the old John Wayne movies, he was the big hero, impervious to death. The men who served with him in the movies didn't worry about their own mortality. They were too busy being heroes. Of course, John Wayne never served in the military and took steps to avoid serving, and the actors he played with in the movies were also non-combatants.

How easy for these guys to not worry about death. Death is part of a script to them; and bodies lying on the ground, well, that's just part of the scenery. Anyway, they're probably Japs or gooks or whatever. Their deaths don't count. Body counts are important, the objective is important. What is death after all, but something scripted? After a while, a young viewer must think that people who die are like the roadrunner in cartoons, who is flattened, burned and demolished, but still jumps up in the next scene and shakes it all off.

Only in life, this doesn't happen, and a dead body reminds us all of our mortality. I have often felt that the transition from childhood to adulthood is that moment we realize our mortality. Yet, on television and in the films and in cheap novels, we are always in that state of suspended childhood, where mortality makes no difference.

As we have stressed over and over again, the characters we

create must have humanity, and must be connected to the readers' emotions. When such a character dies, it must have an effect upon the reader. The death isn't just another statistic, anymore than the death of a loved one is, but a heartfelt tragedy. When this occurs in fiction, the writer has succeeded. I think of the ending of Erich Maria Remarque's All Quiet on the Western Front, where Remarque moves from the first person to the third person narrative to describe the death of his protagonist, on a day that all the papers proclaimed was "all quiet on the western front." Who could not be moved by that final scene where Remarque writes:

"Turning him over one saw that he could not have suffered long; his face had an expression of calm, as though almost glad the end had come."

Many writers have dealt with death, and though writers have written in myriad ways about that moment, the serious writers have all moved us. I think of Rubashov in Darkness At Noon, Arthur Koestler's fine novel, or Thomas Mann and von Aschenbach's death in Death in Venice or Prewitt's death in James Jones' From Here to Eternity. A revolutionary who died at Stalin's orders, an obsessed homosexual who died peacefully on the beach watching the beloved object of his affections, and a soldier who was shot mistakenly by his own men, all of these deaths have moved us. The writers who created these memorable characters were serious when it came to dealing with mortality; death was not a joke to them.

Koestler's final lines in Darkness At Noon show his profound respect for life's demise.

"A second, smashing blow hit him in the ear. Then all became quiet. There was the sea again with its sounds. A wave slowly lifted him up. It came from afar and travelled sedately on, a shrug of eternity."

To me, these are beautiful lines, especially the description of a wave travelling sedately, and the final "shrug of eternity." Of course, unlike John Wayne and the men who wrote his war movies, Koestler had seen war firsthand. He had even faced a firing squad and been given a last minute reprieve. Not for him the aimless senseless reporting of the dead, but instead the careful delineation of the end of a man's life.

Violence, like death, is overdone in today's media. On every screen, large and small, is a constant barrage of bodies being battered, burned and smashed to pieces. Faces are shattered, midsections ripped apart, knives stuck into flesh, bullets plunging into bone and so forth. After a while, it seems meaningless. Pain becomes an abstraction, which is quickly forgotten and overcome. Recently I watched a film, "Batman Forever," an insipid Hollywood product. In it, Batman's butler is smashed in the head by a couple of villians. The next day he is back serving his master, as if nothing had happened.

When I was smashed in the head a couple of years ago, it took me three months to recover. I couldn't even touch the left side of my skull because of the intense pain. I had searing headaches. But in the movies, what's a blow to the head with an iron rod? Nothing. What's several punches to the face? Nothing at all, just an excuse for the character to fake injury and come fighting back. In the movie "Taxi Driver," the character played by DeNiro, blows one man's fingers off with a gun, and another man is shot in the stomach with the same gun. Yet these men come back fighting. Absurdity after absurdity.

Violence has become so abstract a concept that it no longer brings pain, just a momentary pause in the action. I wondered how the writer would have scripted this scene if he had ever suffered a gunshot wound to his stomach. With a great deal more respect, I would assure you. And to have one's fingers blown off–a frightening prospect. When that happens, the victim is lucky not to go into immediate shock, let alone chase the guy with the gun.

It is this disrespect for the truth of violence that has produced a fairy tale view of what life is all about by filmmakers, television writers and hack writers in general. Pain is one of the necessary facts of life, an early warning system of danger and illness, as well as a cross for mankind to bear during violent times, and at the hands of sadists and torturers. It should be treated with great respect, whether it a dull pain in an extremity or a frightening searing pain in the middle of the chest. But filmmakers and hack writers treat pain with the same offhand attitude in which they treat death.

It's important for the writer to always be in the scene when writing about pain or death. By this, I mean that the writer must sense and feel all that is happening to the characters he is portraying. If a man is hurt, the writer must feel that pain. If a character is dead, then the writer must stand in awe of death itself, which, a poet has written "subdues the entire world."

When looking at students' work, one of my main criticisms has been "you weren't in the scene." The writer didn't feel what the characters were feeling. The writer stood above the emotions of the people he created, and therefore the writing was pallid and without strength. Of course, as writers we can't experience everything. We might not have been shot in the stomach, or have our nose broken in a fight, or been stabbed in the throat. But we have to, at the moment of writing about this, pause, and reflect on the enormous pain these acts engender.

We have to recall, as I'm sure we all can, the feeling of going under, of panic, of a coldness running through our body when we are very ill or hurt. We can't disregard this to make a character more heroic. No one can be heroic with his throat cut, or a bullet in his large intestine. We revert to an animal-like status then, and survival is our only goal. We fight to stay awake, as the body goes into shock. We struggle for breath, as blood runs out our mouth. We try and hold on. That is heroic enough, to fight for life, the most precious of all our commodities. As a writer, don't cheapen the struggle or life itself. Put down the truth; portray the reality of the human spirit in the face of its' mortal enemy, death.

7. Sex

Like violence, sex has been liberated during the media age, and is one of the "come ons" in a multitude of television shows and motion pictures. It is also a mainstay of cheap novels, where the so-called "real goings on" of Hollywood or New York, or some industry is "exposed." In the hands of third-rate writers, their portrayal of sex is written primarily to titillate the readers of the trash they turn out.

Sex, of course is one of the pleasures as well as curses of mankind. Serious writers like Sigmund Freud have examined it in light of the human experience at its highest and lowest levels. Sex brings a lot of baggage with it; guilt, regret, fear and many other emotions. It is also one of the great joys of life. Just how should a writer treat sex?

There is no single answer, but like all other acts of humanity, it should be dealt with seriously and with respect for the feelings it engenders. And in good work, it should always be indigenous to the story, and never imposed on a novel because sex will sell more books. When a writer does that he sells out, and cheapens himself and his art.

Bad writers of sex scenes imagine they have to describe each movement, each act, as though they were describing something the reader has never experienced before, as though this is new territory. But basically it is old hat. The reader has had sex, and perhaps several variations of the sex act. He or she isn't going to learn anything new from what is written; at best, the reader will be "turned on" if that is the goal of the reader in reading about sex.

However, if a reader wants to be sexually aroused, there are many ways to accomplish this through the reading of outright pornographic work. There are thousands of porno videos available as well, as cheap works by writers whose only purpose is to supply material for masturbation. The serious writer should be above all this; he or she is not writing to give the reader cheap thrills. He or she is writing to move the reader by an examination of the human heart and experience.

I liken the writing of the sexual act with all its complexity to writing about a good meal. Suppose a writer were to describe a fine meal in an elegant restaurant. He might write that the shrimps came drenched in a butter sauce saturated with garlic and wine. A hungry reader might start salivating if he liked shrimps made this way. But could this same reader endure a scene where the writer describes eating the shrimp, biting down with teeth on each morsel, chewing slowly, the saliva engulfing the food, the shrimp being ground out in the mouth and finally swallowed.

That's the way food is masticated and eaten, but who wants to read about it? It is a common experience, known to practically all living creatures. Food has to be broken up in the mouth, using the teeth, and when it is fine enough, it is swallowed. Sex isn't much different. There may be several variations, but intercourse is intercourse. Human desire is basically there to propagate the species. With most creatures, sex is just that and not a constant raging desire that must be quenched.

Mankind, fortunately or unfortunately, has the ability to perform sex for pleasure, rather than for procreation. Thus sex is a constant in our society, and one of the great motivators of practically everything we purchase. We buy things to look good or to attract the opposite sex. Sex sells, and it sells particularly well in books, television, movies and other media.

The serious writer, who must be aware of all that is involved with humanity, should not exclude sex from his or her work, but it must be there for a purpose, and not added on. And what should one write about the sexual act? As with all good writing, what is left out is more important than what is put down on the page. If a man and woman are to have sex, the act doesn't have to be described in detail, with the foreplay leading to the caressing to the ultimate act of intercourse and orgasm. The world has experienced all this, and unless the writer can show something about sex in a fresh way, he or she should not go into every detail of the sex act.

In life, the anticipation is often greater than the event itself. We may hunger for intimacy with a particular person, only to find, once we've accomplished the sex act, how disappointed we are. Anticipation moves a story along and is useful for the narrative drive of a novel. The final act need not be shown in full; a whisper of delight, a momentary glimpse, a breathed word, may be more erotic than a full description of the penis entering the vagina.

For centuries, the great writers were foreclosed from showing actual sex scenes. And yet, in the work of many writers, there is an erotic element that has moved the reader. "Romeo and Juliet" is considered the consummate love story, yet there is no sex in it. Love can be expressed in many ways other than the sexual. The actual act doesn't have to be depicted in order to involve the reader. Think of all this when you put sex into your novel. Instead of the sexual act, a writer can show the man staying over at the woman's apartment, and awakening in the morning in her bed or in her arms. A languid pose, a movement, a word or two can be more erotic, as we have pointed out, than that erect penis doing its usual chores.

8. Language and Imagery

Often, the one difference between the great writer and the average one is the use of language. Language's glory is imagery, which has been defined as the use of vivid or figurative language to represent objects, actions or ideas. The use of expressive or evocative images is one of the hallmarks of great literature.

Generally speaking, two types of images are used quite often. The first is the simile, which can be defined as a figure of speech in which two essentially unlike things are compared, often in a phrase introduced by "like" or "as."

An example: "How like a winter has my absence been," from Shakespeare.

The other image is a metaphor, defined as a figure of speech in which a word or phrase that ordinarily designates one thing is used to designate another, thus making an implicit comparison. Two examples from Shakespeare come to mind here– "a sea of troubles," and "all the world's a stage."

Language by itself, in the hands of a master, has a richness and beauty that pleases the reader and makes the work immortal. I think of the ending of the short story "Araby" by James Joyce.

"Gazing up into the darkness I saw myself as a creature driven and derided by vanity, and my eyes burned with anguish and anger."

Joyce was a master of language. Here is the ending of "The Dead," one of the masterpieces of short story writing.

"His soul swooned slowly as he heard the snow falling faintly through the universe and faintly falling, like the descent of their last end, upon all the living and the dead."

How evocative and powerful are those lines. We are not all blessed with that kind of writing talent, but we can improve our work with imaginative language. As I wrote earier, if you read junk, you write junk. Therefore, it is to the writer's benefit to read the very best, and not only the best in prose, but poetry as well, for in poetry, the image is the substance and meat of the art. I have quoted Shakespeare often–Shakespeare is mandatory. Shakespeare's power is in the unexpected image. When Hotspur is slain by Prince Hal in "Henry IV, Part 1" his final words aren't "thou has slain me," but include the wonderful, "Oh Harry, thou hast robbed me of my youth."

Try and think of the unexpected image, rather than the banal and expected one. When I held my workshops, I asked my students to complete a line of one of W.H. Auden's poems, which began, "Lay your sleeping head, my love..."

I received all sorts of answers. Generally, the students thought of romantic love, and would state something like "because your beauty inspires me," or "lie next to me on this pillow," and so on. But Auden, one of the great modern English poets, would never have been satisfied with these kind of expected images. The whole line he wrote is:

"Lay your sleeping head, my love, human on my faithless

arm."

"Human on my faithless arm..." This language separates the great from the average writers.

Adjectives, which are defined as a class of words modifying a noun, are the writer's bane. When used badly, the writing becomes trite with the use of too many adjectives. For example, in describing a woman, a writer putting down, "Jane was a beautiful woman, with classic features and a glowing skin," has used three adjectives and really said nothing that is original. I believe it was Mark Twain who wrote "when you catch an adjective, kill it." He also wrote, "as to the adjective, when in doubt, strike it out."

Twain is perfectly right when the adjective is not an unusual one. Often the adjective is used by second-rate writers because they don't have the power to express themselves in images. Because of the craze among publishers for best-sellers and blockbusters, a number of writers incapable of a beautiful phrase or sentence, make millions and are wined and dined by editors. Their writing is strictly pedestrian. They tell a story filled with plotlines and subplots. Their characters are wooden and interchangeable, merely names. The depth of the characters is paper thin. The language is banal. After reading one of these novels, it's hard to remember a single line, because no single line is worth remembering. They get away with this because the reading public for the most part, is ignorant of fine writing. The publishers themselves, infatuated with sales figures, are always looking for the "pageturner" and "good read," two terms that make me gag.

Alas, this ignorance has always been evident. Dickens, great and popular as he was, was not the most read writer of his time. That honor went to someone else, whose name I can't recall now, a woman who had an immense following. The easiest way to see how bad work holds up is to look at best seller lists of a decade or two ago, and try and recognize the names on it. I'm talking about fiction now. Non-fiction, with all the feelgood books, is even worse.

When you write seriously, your audience will be limited, but still can number in the millions, if you touch enough people. The classics endure, and are reprinted and read over and over. Salinger's The Catcher in the Rye has endured as a truthful book about adolescence. The Great Gatsby and The Sun Also Rises, as well as Faulkner's novels are read by succeeding generations. Jane Austen's wonderful works continually enjoy a huge readership, as do Dickens, Dostoievski, Kafka and Tolstoy. Great work will endure.

Not all of these writers had enormous talent for language, but those that did have thrilled me over and over again. Above all, I respect magic; and magic to me in writing means the talent to write at a level I couldn't ever imagine. I could of course understand the language, but how it was conceived, well, that was another story. In all my workshops, at a certain point, I'd read the following:

> "Ánd this is how I see the East.
> I have seen its secret places
> and looked into its very soul;
> but now I see it always from a small boat,
> a high outline of mountains, blue and afar
> in the morning, like faint mist at noon;
> a jagged wall of purple at sunset.
>
> I have the feel of the oar in my hand,
> the vision of a scorching blue sea in my eyes.
> And I see a bay, a wide bay
> smooth as glass and polished like ice,
> shimmering in the dark. A red light
> burns far off upon the gloom of the land,
> and the night is soft and warm.
>
> We drag at the oars with aching arms,
> and suddenly a puff of wind, a puff
> faint and tepid and laden with strange

odors of blossoms, of aromatic wood,
comes out of the still night- the first
sigh of the East on my face. That I can
never forget. It was impalpable and enslaving,
like a charm, like a whispered promise
of mysterious delight."

I had the lines written out this way, and would pass the copies around to the students before reading it aloud. They all were impressed with the imagery, but several thought it unfair that I would be showing them an example of poetry while they were writing short stories and novels. However, this isn't really poetry; it is an excerpt from Joseph Conrad's magnificent short story, "Youth." This writing is magical as far as I'm concerned, not only because of its beauty, but because of who wrote it. Joseph Conrad was born in Poland and English was his third language!

It is this graceful writing which will always knock me out, and which, in my estimation, separates the great writers of this world from the pedestrian plodders. Conrad's work is well worth studying. It was Hemingway who wrote that if he could bring back Conrad to life by getting rid of T.S. Eliot, he'd head to London with a meatgrinder. But alas, his death, like all others, was final. On his tombstone, Conrad had two lines of Edmund Spenser's poetry carved into the stone.

"Sleep after toyle, port after stormie seas,
Ease after warre, death after life, does greatly please."

One great writer honoring another with immortal lines of poetry.

The best way to study language, as I have repeated over and over again, is to study the best prose writers, and the finest poets. We are blessed in that Shakespeare wrote in English, our native tongue. He has influenced all other Western cultures, and is universally regarded as the greatest poet and dramatist who ever put pen to paper. And yet in my classes, very few of my students had read him except in required courses in college or high school. "He's old fashioned," they'd tell me. "He's hard to read." "It's a different antiquated language."

Their remarks are way out of line. Shakespeare is as fresh today as ever, and is still capable of astonishing and inspiring readers. Writers have everything to gain reading and studying Shakespeare. I think of lines as I write these words; Falstaff stating that "we all owe God one death."

Or the Duke of Illyria at the beginning of "Twelfth Night" reciting these lines:

> "If music be the food of love, play on;
> Give me excess of it, that, surfeiting
> The appetite may sicken and so die."

Or Richard II, awaiting death, saying "I wasted time and now doth time waste me." Or Romeo, throwing away the line, "he jests at scars that never felt a wound." I could devote a whole book to the lines of Shakespeare that have thrilled and excited me, inspired and delighted my soul.

To improve your imagery and language, read the greatest poets. Read Spenser and Marlowe, Marvell and Keats, Auden and Yeats, Dylan Thomas and T.S. Eliot. The list can go on and on. Study the imagery of the poets, and learn to incorporate this kind of beauty in your own work.

Above all, write simply. This is the most difficult form of writing and the most rewarding. The simplest writing can be the most powerful. Just re-examine the examples in the previous section. "We all owe God one death," or "I wasted time and now doth time waste me." The simplicity and truth of these sentences give them added power.

Weak writers try and baffle their readers with complexities, because they're incapable of writing simple declarative sentences. Hemingway, when he first started out, had a goal of writing a simple declarative sentence. He also learned from Gertrude Stein that repetition of words begets powerful images.

9. Repeating Words for Effect

There is a famous line from Gertrude Stein, an expatriate writer and art collector who lived in Paris with Alice B. Toklas. The statement is this: "A rose is a rose is a rose." Most people, upon hearing it, think it is nonsense. But what Gertrude Stein was saying is this–if you repeat a word such as "rose" the repetition gives it more power to affect the reader.

Here are two examples of this. The first is the famous beginning of A Farewell to Arms, by Ernest Hemingway.

"In the late summer of that year we lived in a house in a village that looked across the river and the plain to the mountains. In the bed of the river there were pebbles and boulders, dry and white in the sun, and the water was clear and swiftly moving and blue in the channels. Troops went by the house and down the road and the dust they raised powdered the leaves of the trees. The trunks of the trees too were dusty and the leaves fell early that year and we saw the troops marching along the road and the dust rising and leaves, stirred by the breeze, falling and the soldiers marching and afterward the road bare and white except for the leaves."

Note the repetition of words, the pebbles "dry and white in the sun," the road "bare and white," and the leaves, powdered and fallen and on the road. Rereading this I am once more aware of how easy it is to try and imitate Hemingway's style. It is clear writing, as clear as the pebbles and boulders in the stream. Many writers in the late 1920s and 1930s were imitators of his work, and even their imitations got published.

The next excerpt is from the short story, "A Painful Case," by James Joyce. It is from his collection of short stories, Dubliners, perhaps the finest collection of stories in the English language.

"...He gnawed the rectitude of his life; he felt that he had been outcast from life's feast. One human being had seemed to love him and he had denied her life and happiness; he had sentenced her to ignominy, a death of shame... No one wanted him; he was outcast from life's feast. He turned his eyes to the gray gleaming river, winding along towards Dublin. Beyond the river he saw a goods train winding out of Kingsbridge Station, like a worm with a fiery head winding through the darkness obstinately and laboriously. It passed slowly out of sight..."

In this excerpt, the river and the train wind along, one heading towards Dublin and the other away from the city. Joyce also alludes to the train as a worm "winding through the darkness." And then there is the repetition of the line "he was outcast from life's feast." As sad a line as has ever been written. We all, in moments of despair, may feel like that. The repetition of that phrase haunts the story and adds power to its final effect.

Although repetition can be effective, use it sparingly. And don't repeat words because you don't know any synonyms which can replace the repeated word.

10. A Few Words About Style

A writer's style can be defined as a combination of distinctive features of literary expression. This is a rough definition at best. Some writers, particularly Hemingway, have a distinctive style that is almost instantly recognized. The same holds true for Faulkner, during the period of The Sound and the Fury and As I Lay Dying. A writer Faulkner greatly admired, but who is little read today, Thomas Wolfe, had a distinctively recognizable style. This is the Thomas Wolfe of Look Homeward, Angel and The Web and the Rock, not the contemporary Tom Wolfe of The Right Stuff.

A number of foreign writers, such as Dostoievski, Mann and Chekhov have distinctive styles, but this may be as a result of their translators, who get into a particular prose rhythm, such as Constance Garnett, who translated much of Dostoievski.

Style shouldn't be ironbound, but should fit the subject.

One type of story or novel may lend itself to a particular style, but the writer may then move on, and change his style dramatically. William Faulkner's first published novel, Soldier's Pay, was written in a more ordinary style than his later, powerful works. Jack Kerouac's first published novel, The Town and the City, gave no hint of the later On The Road.

In my own writing career, my style has changed depending on the subject matter. A writer must be flexible in this regard and not keep writing in the same style just because he or she achieved some success with that style, if it doesn't suit the next work. One's writing style should accomodate the subject matter, not the other way around.

11. Humor

Life is, as we all know, a serious endeavor, and many writers are driven to be authors because of the way that life has damaged them. But there is always the comic side of life, and a writer without the ability to convey humor in his or her work is not dealing with the full spectrum of what life offers.

Shakespeare wrote comedies as well as tragedies, but even in his darkest tragedies, he allowed humor to shine through. Often, the humor dealt with common men rather than the exalted personages who inhabited the various courts he wrote about. In "Hamlet" for example, not only is Hamlet extremely witty, but in the scene with the gravedigger who has buried Yorick, Shakespeare allows the gravedigger to be earthy and humorous. It is not only effective, but it is a break from the dark world of Claudius's court in Elsinore. The same is true in MacBeth, where a drunken gatekeeper shows the audience that there is a world beyond the one where MacBeth and his wife plot murders. This intrusion of humor is refreshing and carries out its purpose.

The poet and philospher, George Santayana wrote fittingly in one of his poems:

"As in the midst of battle there is room for thoughts of love

And in foul sin for mirth..."

When a writer creates his world, even though that world is full of darkness and despair, humor should break up the mood, otherwise the reader is buried in the despair and may lose interest. This humor must be indigenous to the situation and not imposed just because there's an empty place that can be filled with humor. All of us have experienced humor in our lives, sometimes in the most incongruous situations, so why not incorporate it into our work? It's as much a part of life as sorrow or despair.

Sometimes, when life reaches an absurd level that we can't cope with, all that's left to our sanity is humor. The writer must recognize this and deal with it. The humor need not be blatant; it can be subtle. It can develop from any type of situation, or it can be as a result of witty dialogue. Mark Twain's power as a writer resulted from his humor even in a dark work like Huckleberry Finn.

Writing a humorous novel is a horse of another color completely. Perhaps humor is the most difficult genre to write in, and requires a certain talent in that direction. If you don't have the ear or talent for humor, avoid writing a book that you consider humorous. It can fail as dramatically as telling a joke to an audience, where the response is dead silence.

When writing a humorous scene, don't make the mistake of having the characters laugh and have a good time. When I see this in a novel, I am generally uneasy, even in a work like Hemingway's The Sun Also Rises, where his characters, in a witty moment, all laugh in a scene in a cafe.

The job of the writer is to make his readers, not his characters, laugh, when writing humor. When we watch something silly like the Three Stooges, we laugh. They never laugh. They're too busy copying with their absurd situations.

When we deal with absurdity, we should think of Joe Orton's advice. Orton was the playwright who wrote "Loot" and "What the Butler Saw," among his hit comedies. He was also the subject of John Lahr's book Prick Up Your Ears.

Orton stated that when you write about an absurd situation, write it as if it were real. Don't press for humor.

In "Loot," Truscott of the Yard arrives to investigate a crime. He announces that he solved the most baffling crime in the history of Scotland Yard. Asked about it, the inspector announces that it is the limbless girl's murder.

But who would want to kill a girl without arms and legs, a character asks. No, Truscott corrects him, it was the limbless girl who committed the murder. How was this possible? The inspector refuses to divulge the particulars of the crime, for "we don't want a carbon copy murder on our hands."

The whole thing is one absurdity after another, yet Orton plays it straight. It is one of the funniest scenes in modern theatre, with everyone discussing the limbless girl's murder seriously.

Writing humor is often turning pain into laughter. As someone said once, "it is tragedy when it happens to you, but comedy when it happens to someone else." Even the pain of depression leading to a possible suicide can be made humorous. It depends on the tack the writer takes. For example, suppose a character calls "suicide prevention," and tells about his depression and anxiety.

The person answering the phone, instead of being sympathetic, is a stickler for grammar. The conversation might go like this:

"Is this suicide prevention?"

"It is."

"God I'm so depressed. I'm laying on this bed, thinking..."

"Lying."

"What?"

"Lying. One lies on a bed, not lays on one."

"Anyway, I'm so depressed. I got nothing to live for anymore."

"Got?"

"Huh?"

"You mean, you have nothing to live for anymore."

"What did I say?"

"Got..."

And so forth. I fondly recall a scene written by Woody Allen, where a Mafioso is trying to connect with another wiseguy, but the operator keeps interrupting, and he never can make the connection. Allen reports that as a result of the wiretap of this conversation the Mafioso received a long prison sentence. The whole conversation was a series of "uhs" marked by operator interruptions. This kind of absurdity can be very funny.

Another way to show a humorous situation is for the readers or viewers to know something that the character doesn't. Suppose, in a film, we set up this situation. A gorilla has escaped from the zoo and goes into our hero's apartment. He rummages around for something to eat, and not quite knowing how to open the refrigerator, he goes into the bedroom. The ape is quite tired and curls up in the closet to go to sleep.

The hero comes home. We watch him hum as he pours himself a glass of wine, which he takes into the bedroom. He takes off his jacket, looks at himself in the mirror, makes a phone call and leaves a message on his girlfriend's machine. He goes to the closet but just as he is about to open the door, the phone rings. This kind of scene can be milked for laughs, for the audience knows what the character is ignorant of and is on tenterhooks as it awaits the emergence of the gorilla or its discovery by the hero.

On the other hand, in a different scenario, suppose that, instead of an ape, an escaped axe murderer has hidden in the closet and fallen asleep. A young woman comes home from work, and does the usual things; drinks a glass of wine, takes off her jacket, sits down and combs her hair, and so forth. Instead of comedy, we have a heightened sense of suspense, and the feeling of dread in this scene can be overwhelming.

There are many ways to express humor. Satire, in which human vice or folly is attacked through irony, derision or wit is one way. Irony, or the use of words to express something different from and often opposite to their deliberate meaning, is another. Sarcasm is caustic wit intended to wound or ridicule another person.

It is worthwhile to study the wit of a writer like Oscar Wilde, and, though he hasn't written a novel, I would suggest reading Fear and Loathing In Las Vegas, by Hunter Thompson, one of the funniest books ever written.

12. Sentimentality

To be sentimental is to be affectedly or extravagantly emotional, all major faults in a writer. It is interesting to know the synonyms associated with sentiment–they are mawkish, sloppy, maudlin and bathetic, among others. If any of those words are applied to your work you're in a world of trouble.

There is a big difference between emotion and sentimentality. Human beings have a range of emotion, and those emotions are the meat of the writer in creating dramatic scenes and in the interaction of characters. When a writer becomes sentimental, he moves away from true emotion to a place where he is trying to affect an emotion, particulary in a reader, by artificial means.

When a student reads something like the following to me my antennae rise. It is what Hemingway calls his "shit-detector."

"It was all over. He would never come back, never hold her in his arms again. Her great love was over. She sat on the bed, tears rolling down her eyes in profusion. How sad her life would be from now on. As she thought of the lonely years ahead, more tears flowed, staining her blouse."

Gag time, folks. We all have felt loss in our lives, whether it be a love or a parent or friend. If we want to state this loss, we must do it with emotional truth, not bathe the character in glop. We fail the reader in doing this.

My best advice is this: when you write about a charged emotional situation, write it as simply as possible, and show just what is happening, without exaggerating the emotion to the point of sentimentality.

Just presenting the scene is enough to touch the reader's emotions. There is power in simplicity and showing a situation truthfully has implied power. Let's assume we're dealing with a mother dying in a hospital. Her eldest son goes to her room:

"When he arrived at her bedside, he saw his mother, her head on two pillows stacked one above the other, an oxygen mask over her face. She looked smaller than he had ever seen her before. It was as if he were looking at a doll. There was a chair by the bed and he sat down. His mother's hands were above the blankets, both hands limp, heavily veined and full of age spots. He took one of the hands into his and held it. The hand was surprisingly cool. He sat there, watching her face and holding the cool hand.

The nurse who had called him at the hotel had told him it was a matter of time, an hour at the most. He sat there, listening to his mother's labored breathing under the mask. He became aware of his own breathing, and sitting there, he thought of mortality. His mortality, his mother's, the link between them of life and death, of birth and life. His mother's breathing became more labored. He got up and went out of the room and called in a nurse. She came and looked down at his mother, and took one of the limp hands of the old woman and tested its pulse.

"She's at peace," said the nurse. "She's going in peace. She feels no pain."

The nurse stayed in the room. He stood there, looking down at his mother. The breathing became more labored, then there was a gasp, and it was all over. He stood helplessly.

"She's gone," said the nurse. "She went peacefully."

The man took a deep breath. Then another deep breath. He felt his face grow numb. The nurse, glancing at him, asked if he wanted a tranquilizer. She was much younger than he was, a tall slim woman with deepset brown eyes. She was young enough to be his daughter. He shook his head.

"You should wait outside," she said. "There are things we

have to do."

"I understand."

"It's best if you wait in the corridor."

He nodded.

"You're all right, aren't you?" she asked.

"Yes."

"Come," she said, "let's go outside. You need to sit down. You're awfully pale. I'll take care of your mother later."

He let himself be taken away. He walked with the nurse holding his arm loosely. In the hallway, he became aware of the noise and the movement of people. Orderlies and nurses walked back and forth, doctors hurried to elevators. A television set was on in one corner of the room, and a group of people sat before it, watching a quiz show. The nurse let go of his arm, and walked over to a doctor, who looked up and then nodded his head.

Then the doctor and nurse walked past him to his mother's room. He wanted to go in and see her one more time, but it was better that the hospital staff handle whatever had to be done. He himself had calls to make, to his younger brother in Wilmington, to his sister in Chapel Hill.

The man stood in the corridor and took another deep breath, and rubbed one side of his face. It was still numb. He felt faint; he needed air. On the television screen, a young woman, no older than the nurse who had been in the room, had won a prize. She screeched with delight.

The man walked past the viewers into a long hallway. He knew that a door led out to the street at the end of that hallway. He walked slowly, breathing deeply. When he reached the outside door, he stood and breathed in the night air. It was misty out, and the night air was damp. He felt the mist on his face. Looking up, he could see the moon, shrouded in that same mist. A light rain began to fall."

How easily one can fall into sentimentality, especially in a scene involving the death of a mother before her son's eyes. I have reread the scene carefully. I have tried to make it as simple as I could. Of course, other writers would have dealt with it differently.

In the end, I had the man go outside and feel the night air upon his flesh, and see the moon shrouded in mist. When I reread the scene, I thought of Chekhov, who often, at the end of a story, brings the reader to natural phenomena. I think particularly of his story, "The Murder." We ourselves in life, when things get difficult, find solace in the night air, or in sunshine, or in the woods. It is our heritage as human beings to be comfortable in those environments, and the writer should not forget this.

A good exercise for students would be to write an episode charged with emotion, and to do it as simply as possible, so that no false emotion or sentimentality intrudes. Write it carefully. I'm sure you'll find, as I did in the above scene, that I constantly had to rewrite it to avoid the false emotions and avoid the bathos such a scene could easily engender.

Above all, avoid sentimentality. It sometimes is easy to get carried away with emotion, especially when writing about a true incident in one's life, where there was great sorrow or sadness. Therefore, it is wise to write about events that have occurred in the past, that you have thought out and come to grips with. Writing about events as they occur may place you in the trap of being whipsawed by emotion.

There is another danger, besides the trap of sentimentality that may result when you write about events as they are happening. Suppose you write about a present-day love affair. The affair may go well, then turn sour. Then get stronger. Your writing will reflect all this, and since you can't put any distance between your emotions and the events causing the emotions, you and the reader will be going on roller coaster rides.

I have found that it is difficult for me not only to write about recent events, but about a city I am presently residing in. Looking back, only my first novel dealt with the place I lived in. I wrote about Los Angeles in San Francisco, New York in Las Vegas, Las Vegas in Los Angeles, and so forth. This is not a hard and fast rule, but I always feel that distance, both in space and time, give the writer a better perspective on his work.

13. Ending the Novel

Just as the beginning is important in writing a novel, so is the ending. It is the final paragraph, even the final line, that we come away with, that haunts us after we have been involved with characters and narrative that have held and moved us for hundreds of pages.

The untalented writer often gives us a rousing finish; the fine writer a dying fall. The work is played out; it is over. As William Makepeace Thackery so aptly writes at the end of his magnificent novel, Vanity Fair:

"Come, children, let us shut up the box and the puppets, for our play is played out."

Some writers have wonderful endings to their novels and stories. Thomas Mann immediately comes to mind. In Felix Krull (the short story, not the novel) the protagonist's father has just shot himself, and the boy, Felix, rushes to his father's room and sees his father dead of a mortal wound. Here's how Mann ends the story:

"I stood beside the earthly husk of my progenitor, now growing cold, with my hand over my eyes, and paid him the abundant tribute of my tears."

The end of Death In Venice, perhaps the finest novella ever written, goes like this:

"Some minutes passed before anyone hastened to the aid of the elderly man sitting there collapsed in his chair. They bore him to his room. And before nightfall a shocked and respectful world received the news of his decease."

It is writing like this that won Mann the Nobel Prize for literature in 1929. Look at endings of novels written by the masters. Look particularly, if you want American examples, at The Great Gatsby, in which Fitzgerald is at his most poetic. And look at the dying fall of Hemingway's The Sun Also Rises, with its evocative "Yes," I said "isn't it pretty to think so," spoken by Jake Barnes to Lady Brett Ashley, summing up what might have been if he hadn't received that awful war wound.

The ending can be haunting, as in George Orwell's 1984, where Winston Smith is broken as an individual. Orwell writes as the last line: "He loved Big Brother."

There is the famous "Yes." spoken by Molly Bloom at the end of Ulysses, an affirmation of the sensual life, and then there is the "Yes?" tentatively spoken by Alexander Portnoy at the end of Philip Roth's Portnoy's Complaint.

When completing a novel, try and make the last lines memorable but in keeping with the tone of the novel. They should leave the reader emotionally moved and should be devoid of both sentimentality and artificiality.

14. Titles

By the time you finish your novel, you'll probably have thought of a title for the work. Or you may not be able to come up with a title. If the latter is true, there's no harm in sending off the novel without a title. You simply write "Untitled Novel" on the front page. It's not going to make that much difference to an agent or editor. If they like the writing and either decide to represent you or publish the novel, they'll be happy to work with you to create an apt title.

How important is the right title? I really don't know. A title, I believe, can sometimes help a book, but in the end, it's the content that counts. You can have a title "Dancing Naked with the President's Wife," and that will certainly draw attention, but if the book is lackluster, no one will buy it. It may get a little publicity because of the title, but you want more than fifteen minutes of fame.

After all, a title can only say so much, and often it says nothing about the contents of the book. Hemingway used The Sun Also Rises because it is part of a quote from the bible that personally meant a great deal to him. That novel is usually called a work of the lost generation, and perhaps "The Lost

Generation" would have been more apt.

My first novel was called Rapt In Glory. The title is meaningless as far as the story goes, for what does it have to do with three men robbing a drugstore in Brooklyn? But that phrase had moved me tremendously when I first saw it in the American War Cemetery outside of Florence.

If you come up with a title for your novel, it may be vetoed by the publisher. Unless you have a great deal of clout or you're wedded to it at the cost of not being published, the editor will generally have his way. I have fought editors on two of my titles, Nightmare of the Dark, and Sweet Land of Liberty. Today I'm satisfied with the latter but not with the first title.

When I was discussing the first title, I thought it should have the word "escape" in it. There had been a novel called Escape published some years before, so that title was out. Titles can't be copywrighted, but still you don't want to have the same title as a recent novel. Readers will get mixed up, and no publisher wants to promote a book that may inadvertently promote a different novel published by another house.

When the review of the novel came out in the Sunday New York Times, there was a subtitle to the review. The reviewer wrote "Escape From Hell," and I thought, yes, that should have been the title. But of course, by that time, it was too late.

My best advice is this–don't worry too much about the title, and don't be afraid not to have a title when you submit the work to an agent or a publisher. Or you could simply put down a title that might interest you and write under it "working title." That gives the agent or publisher the leeway to think of their own title for the work, without feeling that your title, which they might not like, is etched in stone.

X

THE GENRE NOVEL

Novels fall into several categories, or genres. There is the historical novel, the romance novel, science-fiction, the mystery novel, the detective novel, the social commentary novel, and so on and so forth.

In this work, I am not dealing with the various genres. My suggestion is to learn the craft of writing, and then all of your work will have power, no matter what category it falls into. When we think of historical novels, for example, we think of potboilers and popular trashy work for the most part, and yet Tolstoi's War and Peace is an historical novel, dealing with events that occurred at least a half a century before he wrote the book. And War and Peace is not only the great Russian novel, but perhaps the greatest novel ever written.

A detective novel like Dashiell Hammet's The Maltese Falcon is certainly head and shoulders above the pedestrian run of detecive fiction. A novel that may be considered social commentary is John Steinbeck's Grapes of Wrath. It is this work, along with Of Mice and Men, that won him the Nobel Prize for literature. Another novel falling into the same genre is Theodore Dreiser's An American Tragedy, a powerful work indeed. Dreiser was up for a Nobel Prize one year but lost to Sinclair Lewis, author of Main Street and Arrowsmith. I don't know who reads Lewis's novels these days, but An American Tragedy, as I have written before, and Dreiser's other great novel, Sister Carrie, live on.

Three friends of mine, K.W. Jeter, Tim Powers and Jim Blaylock, are all writers of science-fiction and/or horror novels. While I have not that much interest in that genre, I respect their work, for they know their craft, and their work could stand, without the science fiction or horror aspect, as powerful novels in their own right.

If you don't get your craft down, if you don't read the very best, you will have problems no matter what genre you decide to write in. It is important to read other categories of fiction even if you only want to write romances or mysteries. Learn your craft. There are definite rules to follow in the craft of writing. As T.S. Eliot wrote, "It's not wise to violate the rules until you know how to observe them."

So many young writers want to just get started, get that story down or write the novel, without any idea of what they are doing. Then they rush out to show their work to friends, who tell them, "wow, this is great stuff, man." And then they send it out and are stunned by the rejections. How could they be rejected when their friends loved the stories or the novel? Unfortunately, their friends aren't in a position to publish the work, or represent them as agents.

In Hollywood, when I was dealing with agents and producers, there was one phrase I winced at. The agent or producer would say, "I love it." That was the kiss of death. I had a friend who came out to Los Angeles with his screenplay and started showing it around. He called me one morning all excited.

"I showed it to ... and he loved it. He couldn't stop raving about it."

"That's good," I said. I didn't have the heart to tell him he was in trouble.

"Hey, Ed, you don't sound that excited by the news."

"Let's see what happens."

He thought I was a "down" person for not jumping with joy, but I've heard "I love it" several times, all with the same results. Sure enough, he called me, his voice mournful.

"I can't understand it," he said, "they loved it and now they messengered it back to me, without a comment. And they won't return my calls."

What I want to hear in Hollywood is the producer saying "I hate the goddamn script; it's utter crap, but DeNiro and Costner want to do it, so the hell with my opinion."

As I said before, don't bother with what your friends think about your writing. They're not going to publish it, so their opinion means nothing. In fact, their opinion can be destructive. If they love it, you find yourself euphoric, only to be let down by real professionals. If your friends hate it, then you might be discouraged and not bother to send it out. Either way you lose.

As a writer, be patient. Write carefully and do the best you can do. Patience! Don't rush to finish something so you can send it out. Don't let it out of your hands until you've done everything you can do with the work. Only then, when you're satisfied that no more can be added or subtracted, send it out.

We have discussed the rules of writing, which of course aren't ironclad. Rules are made to be broken. Artists have imagination, and aren't bound by strict rules. The rules we've put down deal with the craft of fiction. They must be studied, then once you've mastered them, move the work into art. And if you write in any particular genre, you may have to observe the rules that govern that category of fiction.

In any genre you write in, read the best that has been done in that field. How do you know what the best is? In any field, there are recognized masters. If you're writing science-fiction, for example, you'll find that Philip Dick, Isaac Asimov, Ray Bradbury and Arthur C. Clarke, to name a few writers, are respected authors in that genre. Go to the local library and ask a librarian to help you select the best work. If he or she can't do this, try another library. I don't count much on bookstore employees' opinions as a rule, though some may be knowledgeable.

In detective fiction, you'll come across Dashiell Hammet

and Raymond Chandler, as well as Conan Doyle, the creator of Sherlock Holmes, just to name a few. In the historical novel, Margaret Mitchell's Gone with the Wind should certainly be read. In mysteries, there are perhaps a dozen fine masters, such as Dorothy Sayers and Georges Simenon. Again, ask the librarian, or look on the bookshelves. Take a few books and sit down and look at them as though you were a professional writer. Is the writing original? Does the protagonist engage your attention? Are you immediately intrigued and then swept along with the story?

With the romantic novel genre, don't bother with the Harlequin Romances and stuff of that ilk. Read Jane Austen's novels, such as Sense and Sensibility, Emma, Mansfield Park and Pride and Prejudice. She is a much sunnier writer than the Brontes, Emily and Charlotte, whose works might be categorized as Gothic Romances. Emily Bronte's most famous work is Wuthering Heights, and Charlotte's is Jane Eyre.

Read the best, be patient with your work, create characters that live, touch the reader's emotions, and you will be successful as a writer, no matter what genre you decide to write in.

XI

HOW LONG SHOULD THE NOVEL BE

A question I was often asked was: "how long should the novel be?" Or "how big a novel do publishers want?" There is one simple answer to the first query, and it is this. Your novel should be as long as it has to be. When there is nothing more to write, the novel is finished. You can't put a page or word count on a novel; it must run its course.

As to the second query, the publishers may give you all kinds of answers, but they themselves don't know the answer to that question. Editors complain to me of the price of paper which make books so expensive these days. They talk of publishing shorter novels, but they are constantly searching for the blockbuster of 900 pages that their readership will gobble up.

Forget about editors when you work on your novel. Forget about publishers and forget about agents. Trust in yourself. You are the most important person in this group; you are the creative individual. If you have a story to tell and it requires 1,000 pages, so be it. If your story can be finished in 200 manuscript pages, then that is the size of your complete novel.

Just what constitutes a novel? This is another hard question. I would say offhand that the manuscript should run at least 150 pages, or 37,500 words. Some run less. A novelist like Philip Roth can get an extremely small book, no more than an extended short story, such as The Breast published as a novel. That's because he's Philip Roth and the publishers will cater to him.

More often, a work about that size in manuscript form will be considered a novella and will, if published, be accompanied by a group of short stories. That was the case with Roth's first work, Goodbye Columbus, a novella brought out with several short stories in one volume. Mann's Death In Venice came out in the same fashion, accompanied by a number of short stories, all small masterpieces. Both novellas represent very fine work. Goodbye Columbus, I consider Roth's finest work.

If your work is less than 150 pages, and you haven't been published before, your work is in a sort of no man's land. A publisher will be loath to publish this small a novel by itself, and may require the addition of several short stories. However, if the stories haven't been published previously, he or she might be reluctant to take on the book. It all depends on the publisher, and you stand a better chance in this regard with a small, rather than a major, publishing house.

Another question that comes up among beginning writers deals with the number of manuscript pages that become book pages. Just what is that ratio? For example, if you wrote a novel that's 250 manuscript pages long, how many book pages does that represent?

Before I answer that question, I'll deal with methods of writing novels. Before the advent of the computer, writers basically guessed the number of words their manuscripts added up to. They figured that each line had approximately ten words, and each page was twenty-five lines long, for a total of 250 words per page. If they wrote a 300 page manuscript, their approximate word count would be figured as 75,000.

With computers, it is easy to know the exact word count, since most programs have a "word count" feature. You no longer have to approximate; the word count is exact.

I looked at a number of books before writing this section, and found that the number of lines in books varied from book to book, from hardcover to paperback. Some were 39 lines, some 43, and some even 47 lines long per page.

If we use a round number, say, 40, as the average number

of book lines, then there will be approximately 400 words per page. If the average manuscript is 25 lines long and consists of approximately 250 words, then for every 16 pages of manuscript, there will be 10 book pages. Thus a 320 page manuscript will end up as 200 book pages.

Should we deal with words, rather than pages, we reach similar ratios. Suppose we wrote 80,000 words. Then we have a 200 page book. Use these ratios to guide yourself. If a writer comes to me and tells me that the exact word count of his novel is 94,000 words, I could then tell him that the book pages will be approximately 235 pages. I simply divide 94,000 by 400 to arrive at this answer.

Note that I use the word "approximately." Each publisher is unique, and there is no set word count or line number for the industry as a whole. But using this formula will give you a good idea of the number of pages to expect in a book, knowing either your total manuscript pages or your exact word count.

XII

DEDICATION AND PATIENCE

There are a lot of talented individuals out there, a great many people who want to be writers. Some have enormous talent and yet they'll never be published, never have their name on the spine of a book. Why not? Because writing is a jealous mistress and requires all of your attention. To quote Tonio Kroger in the short story by the same name, written by Thomas Mann,

"There he stood, suffering embarrassment for the mistake of thinking that one may pluck a single leaf off the laurel tree of art, without paying for it with his life."

The serious writer must be dedicated to his art. Writing is not a pastime or a hobby, not if one wants to exalt himself or herself. This doesn't mean that writing automatically becomes your full-time job. This may be impossible. As a beginning or would-be writer, you probably have another job or profession. You have to earn a living and support yourself, and perhaps, a family as well.

What I mean by attention is the engagement of the self, the constant searching inward to open oneself up, to express true feelings, to examine one's very soul. This is quite difficult but not impossible. As I wrote before we are all capable of murder and we are all saints, and the full spectrum of the human condition runs between these two extremes.

In addition to this, a writer must have patience. Patience to rewrite, to examine, to criticize his or her own work objectively. Patience to stay with the work and not show it to friends or relatives for a cheap pat on the back which means nothing, and generally is destructive. Don't write so you can say you're a "writer" when at a party. The next question is invariably, "oh, what do you write," followed by "have you been published." As you either hem and haw or worse, lie about what you've done, your self-image sinks into the ground.

When I lived in San Francisco in the 1970s, I attended a number of parties, and when people asked what I did for a living, I answered "I'm a writer." That's what I did for a living.

The next question was "I mean, what do you really do for a living?" Practically everyone who could read a book called himself or herself a writer in the city by the Bay. Writers were people who kept journals or wrote three lines of a short story, or had worked for five years on an outline of a novel.

After a while, when people asked what I did for a living, I simply said "I work at a desk." This satisfied the questioners, and no further questions were asked. They had met a typist or clerk and he was no threat to them.

In Los Angeles, I found a whole new set of questions. The first would be "what do you do for a living?"

"I'm a writer."

"You write for TV?"

"No."

"What do you write, like detective stories or sci-fi?"

"No."

"Oh, you write for a newspaper?"

That would be one general line of questions. Instead of asking, what do you write, and waiting for an answer, they jumped to assumptions without a moment's hesitation. One question I never ask is "what do you do for a living?" To me, that's a way of categorizing an individual. What difference does it make what a person does for a living? If you can't sense the worth of a person without knowing what he or she does for a living, then you're blindfolding your feelings.

After a while I denied being a writer to avoid these nonsensical assumptions and questions. When I was teaching at UCLA and USC I'd simply say I taught. "Taught what?"

"English." That stopped all questions.

At parties, people approached me and said, "hey, I hear you're a writer," and then, without waiting for a reply, told me they had a great story that I should write for them as a novel. Or that the story of their life was ripe material for a novel. I would listen patiently for a minute or two and then slide out from under the conversation with some excuse. If their story was so interesting, why didn't they write it? What did they want from me?

At a gathering of teachers at UCLA, a middle-aged man approached and regaled me with his success as a writer, telling me that in the late 1960s his novel was 10th on the best-seller list of the LA Times. He went on and on, then out of words, asked if I did any writing.

I nodded.

"Been published?"

"Well, you know how it is."

He gave me a withering glance and moved on. Imagine, I had taken up his valuable time and wasn't even a published writer. Of course my answer wasn't in the negative, but I have no interest in competing with people like this, throwing out credential after credential to keep up with them. I found that, when I started bragging about my writing career, I was in a bad state. And so I'd abruptly shut my mouth. Anyone that has to brag about his or her success to make an impression is in the throes of desperate insecurity.

Let's get back to patience and dedication. When writing a novel, you're in for the long haul. There are thousands of writers who start novels and never complete them each year. Just completing a novel is an accomplishment. It calls for dedication, which to my mind, is more important than talent. Talent is a dime a dozen, but only a few will stay for the long haul and tough it out in order to complete a novel.

Writing a novel shouldn't be a chore; it should be a joy. The process is as important as the finished product, for writing a novel is not only an accomplishment, but a learning experience. You learn the art and craft of writing, a fine art, and you learn a great deal about yourself in the process. If you write truthfully, it is better than any form of therapy, for you will dig deep inside yourself as few individuals have.

Writing a novel is not a simple task; it is rather daunting. When you first begin, and write a scene or two, you'll have completed a few pages of work, which seems like nothing at all compared to a finished novel. But the pages add up day by day if you continue working. Then one day, you'll be surprised to see upwards of two hundred manuscript pages in front of you. The work has taken form and is substantial.

How often should you work on the novel? I would suggest every day, once you get started. This isn't a hard and fast rule, for it depends on what is going on in your life. You may be working full-time, you may have a family to not only support but spend time with. But if that novel is burning inside you, it will become the most important thing in your life, and you will count the hours till you can get to the typewriter or computer to work on it.

Some writers spend hours each day and others much less time. Still others don't work every single day, but sporadically. I don't recommend the latter course. I find that the novel is always with me, day and night. It is something I think about before falling asleep, and if I get up during the night, I think about the work again. In the morning, when I awaken, it is with me. It accompanies me everywhere. It cries to be worked on and moved towards completion.

Finishing the novel is the great adventure. There will be times when you'll be stuck at some point. Stop writing, stand back from the work, go into your unconscious mind, open yourself up and then go on. Perservere. You are on one of the great adventures of life; don't give up. Dedicate yourself to your work, and the work will reward you.

After you finish a novel, it is time to take a break. It is difficult to go from one high to another, to finish one major work and then, without pause, to start another. The well has to be filled up again. Take it easy for awhile; otherwise you'll be putting too much pressure on yourself. I think of Tennessee Williams writing for hours every day of his life. After a while, he just wore himself out, and his later work deteriorated.

There is a rhythm to writing as there is to life. We can't be up twenty-four hours a day, day after day. We must sleep. We must rest. We work and then we relax. This is a basic precept of living. The same holds true for writing. We can't go on without stopping or pausing. We must refresh ourselves. Writing is difficult enough, the act of putting words on blank pages can drain anyone's energy. If you are able to accomplish a complete novel, then take a well-deserved rest before you undertake another.

XII

THE SHORT STORY

1. An Overview

At the very outset, in examining the art and craft of fiction, I discussed how to begin either a short story or a novel, and showed that the same principles governed each form. I concentrated on the novel, because I assumed that it was the dream of every fiction writer to write and publish a novel. However, some writers have no interest in the novel and concentrate instead on short stories. This doesn't make their work lesser, only different.

Two examples come to mind. First, there is Anton Chekhov, whose work I admire above all others, and who I feel closest to as a writer. The second is Raymond Carver, an American writer, who, in his relatively short writing career, produced a series of wonderful volumes of short stories.

Some writers turn out both short stories and novels with equal skill. Hemingway as well as Joyce Carol Oates, Franz Kafka, Thomas Mann and James Joyce mastered both forms. J.D. Salinger certainly belongs with this group.

Some writers I feel, and this is only a personal opinion, are better short story writers than novelists. I would include Isaac Bashevis Singer, a Nobel laureate in literature, and Ann Beattie, in this category. Also John Cheever, John Updike, Nelson Algren and William Saroyan. The Irish writer, William Trevor, should also be mentioned. Some writers are marvellous novelists but have not equalled their best work when writing short stories. I think immediately of Graham Greene, a brilliant English writer who certainly deserved the Nobel Prize. Though some of F. Scott Fitzgerald's short stories are constantly anthologized, I feel that his reputation will ultimately rest on The Great Gatsby and his longer works, including his unfinished novel, The Last Tycoon.

The short story has one basic limitation, and that is size. Otherwise there are no hard and fast rules as to its content and style. Innovative writers have stretched its limitations, and the best way to learn to write a short story is to read the best work by the best writers. Certainly the authors I have mentioned above will give you a good start.

Unlike the novel, the short story needs no broad landscape. The ground covered by the writer is tighter and the view is generally narrow. We don't need a climactic ending; an illumination will do. By illumination, I mean an insight by a character, which, though small, can be significant. A protagonist can see something he or she overlooked in his or her character; a flaw that has held them back or made them outcasts. Or a character can see into the heart of another person, and come to an understanding that has eluded him before.

I can give example after example. The important thing is that something happens, however small; that a change is realized, that an illumination of the human spirit is accomplished. It doesn't have to be upbeat; it can be the opposite, it can be full of horror as well. There are really no limitations except in the imagination of the writer.

A skilled short story writer, despite the smaller form, can show a world as full as any novel. A good example of this is James Joyce's "The Dead," which has a magnificent view of the world of Dublin society in the form of a dinner party. A whole world is contained in this story.

Study the great writers of this form. To my mind, the best collection of short stories in the English language is James Joyce's Dubliners. Joyce was one of the giants of Twentieth

Century literature, and should be read by any writer who considers doing serious work. The best short stories in any language in my estimation are the later ones by Anton Chekhov. There are many anthologies of his work available in paperback, and these should be part of the library of any writer. The Collected Stories of William Trevor are highly recommended. He is a true master of this form.

In the short story, we look for the same things we cherish in a fine novel; language and imagery, characters that live and breathe, a narrative drive and an evocative situation that engages our emotions.

2. The Short Story Market

It is easier to write a short story than to write a novel. The very size of each makes this obvious. There is a larger market for the short story, with magazines such as The New Yorker, Playboy and Esquire paying fairly substantial sums upon acceptance. Other well-known magazines such as Atlantic Monthly, Commentary, Good Housekeeping, Harper's Magazine, McCall's, Mademoiselle and Redbook regularly publish short stories.

In addition to these periodicals, there are literally hundreds of smaller magazines, many of them college literary journals, that publish short stories. The market is out there. Unfortunately, the pay for stories is often small and in many cases the writer has to be satisfied with free copies or a subscription to the magazine as payment. It is very difficult to make a living being a short story writer.

The only way to make money is to either be regularly published in magazines like The New Yorker or to have a collection of your stories come out as a book. This is rather difficult, however. Unless you are a Raymond Carver, Ann Beattie, John Cheever, John Updike, Tillie Olsen, Margaret Atwood, Mavis Gallant or Alice Adams, to name a number of well-known and respected short story writers, publishers are leery of putting out a collection of short stories. They're generally money losers, and even if successful, make precious little money over the advances.

As a beginning or unpublished writer, you might first want to hone your craft with the short story. A novel may take a year or more to complete, while you can write a short story in a couple of sittings. It is a good feeling to complete work of any size, and you don't need an agent to send out stories to magazines.

3. Submissions

At the outset, I wouldn't bother with The New Yorker or other large circulation magazines. For one thing, your chances of getting published are almost nil. These magazines generally take work from writers with national or international reputations, and even if they like your story, the fact that you have no name in letters will work against you. Of course, some unknowns do get published by major magazines. The odds against this happening, however, are astronomical. Therefore, starting out, I would suggest going into the other market, the literary and small magazine market.

How do you find a list of these smaller periodicals? It's fairly simple. Each year there are the O.Henry Awards for best short stories, published as Prize Stories, by Doubleday. In the back of the book are a list of periodicals that were consulted for the awards, together with their addresses.

In addition to this annual work, there is Best American Short Stories, published by Houghton Mifflin Company, which not only has a list of magazines, with their addresses, but also has the name of the editor-in-chief of each periodical, giving you a personal name to send your story to.

When deciding to send out a short story, don't bother with a query letter first. By query letter, I mean a letter telling something about the short story and asking an editor if he or she would be interested in receiving the story. How would an editor know? He or she has no idea of your talent or the worth of the story. Send out the story directly. It will probably be read and a decision will be made whether to reject or publish it.

At this point I want to interject a story I told every class of students at UCLA. At that time, Wayne Gretsky was playing hockey for the LA Kings, and by any standard, Gretsky was a brilliant player. One evening, at home, I was flipping through the channels and there was Gretsky being interviewed by a journalist. The journalist asked "Wayne, why did you take that last shot at goal? It was a crazy shot and I didn't think it had a chance of going in."

Gretsky answered with words of wisdom. "Because every shot you don't take at goal won't go in. I took the shot and it went in."

I would tell my classes about the Gretsky interview, then add. "There is one sure thing about writing. One absolute. Every story you don't send out won't get published. You can be sure of that. And of course, every story you don't write, won't be sent out." To be a writer, you must write. Simple as that. And having written a short story you're contented with, send it out.

The worst thing that is going to happen is a rejection. That's it. There's not going to be a knock at the door, with some hoodlum holding a baseball bat, asking if you sent a short story to a literary magazine. Your knees won't be broken; you'll simply be rejected. And if you can't take rejection, don't bother writing.

Always enclose a stamped, self-addressed envelope if you want to get the story back, assuming it's rejected. If you don't do this, then they'll reject the story and you'll never hear from the magazine's editors or get your story returned. Postage is expensive and many of these magazines operate on shoestring budgets, and they're not going to put out postage on your behalf.

If your funds are limited, you might not want the manuscript back. Then enclose a simple, stamped envelope with your name and return address, so, if they reject the manuscript, you'll get the rejection, not the short story. It may be cheaper to keep copying stories than to pay for return postage, but that's up to you.

In the old days, before the advent of Xerox machines, you could send out a story to one magazine, unless you were retyping original copies of the story. If you copied it or sent a carbon, the editor would know and automatically reject it. Today, it's difficult to tell what is original and what is not, and with the printers attached to computers, all work is original.

I would therefore suggest that you send a story to a number of magazines at once. Many of them take weeks and sometimes even months to respond. Why not put time on your side? The question invariably comes up, as it often did in my workshops, "what if two magazines decide to accept your story?"

Well, that's not the worst situation to be in. Suppose that magazine A accepts your story, and a week later you find that magazine B accepted the story as well. What do you do? You act in your best interest. Magazines, editors, agents and publishers act in their best interests, so why shouldn't you, the creative writer, do the same?

Since there is a rather long time period between acceptance and publication of even a story, you decide which magazine either pays more or is more prestigious. And you allow that acceptance to hold. To the other magazine's editor you simply write a letter thanking him or her for the acceptance, telling the editor that you inadvertently sent the story to a couple of magazines and magazine A already accepted it. But you'll give magazine B first shot at your next story.

Will that turn them off? Not likely. The fact that other magazines are accepting your work will only whet their appetite for future stories. Success breeds success. Editors want to publish writers who have already had some success with their work.

I have previously described the letter one should send out to an editor, but I'll repeat myself here, because I feel it's rather important. Before going into the letter, I would warn against praising your work or denigrating your work by writing, for example, "it still needs work, but I feel I can work with an editor in improving it." The editor you send this missive to will think, "yeah, but not this editor, jerk."

Praising your work has the same effect. You're telling the editor how wonderful you are, and trying to make the editor guilty about rejecting "the best work I've done." The editor doesn't need a guilt trip; he needs good work for the next issue of the magazine. With that phrase in your submission letter, expect a rejection.

The submission letter should be as follows:

"Dear ...

I'm enclosing a short story, entitled ... which consists of approximately . . . words, along with a stamped, self-addressed envelope.

I would be interested in your feelings concerning the work.

Thanking you, I remain,

Sincerely,"

Today computers can give you an exact word count, so if you know this, put it in. Otherwise calculate about 250 words per page, double-spaced. You must send out the work double-spaced.

In the above letter I left out one important thing. If you have been published before, then put in that information, such as:

"I've had stories previously published in:"

And list the magazines or periodicals. If you've had books published, list them also. Today, you can format letters on computers to list all the credentials, with just the name of the editor and/or magazine to be filled in. The more credentials the better, but still, it all depends on the work you are presently submitting. That is the most important criterion.

If you are writing a number of short stories and sending them out, keep records and make files for each story, either on paper or on the computer. You don't want to waste time and postage sending out a story to an editor who has already rejected it. He'll think you're a complete amateur.

Finally, don't worry about rejections. Every famous writer has been rejected. F. Scott Fitzgerald, before he hit it big, papered his walls with rejection slips and letters. At the beginning you may get form rejection slips. They're the worst to get, because the editor has no real interest in the present, and probably, future work. But if your work touches a chord somewhere, you may get a personal rejection letter, telling you, in essence, "we won't publish this story, but would be interested in seeing other work." With a letter like that, you can send off other stories to this editor, reminding him, in your submission letter, that he asked for other stories from you.

Above all, don't be discouraged. If your work is continually rejected with printed slips, then it pays to put it aside and look it over again carefully. Perhaps the work isn't publishable; perhaps you're not doing your best. You must look at your work hard and carefully, and as objectively as you can.

When you do get an acceptance, then you know you're on your way. I had a student who received rejection after rejection. I had read his work and edited some of it after the rejections; basically his work needed cutting. His writing was strong, and I encouraged him to keep submitting his stories. Sooner or later, something good would happen. Then he received an acceptance from The Missouri Review. This opened the floodgates. At last count, he was approaching twenty published stories in magazines.

XIV

GETTING AN AGENT

1. Where to Find an Agent

The good news is that, in submitting short stories, you don't really need an agent. Editors will take a look at your work, especially those of small literary and college magazines. However, submitting a novel without an agent is entirely another matter.

It is practically impossible to send work to a major publishing house without representation. If you look at the annual Writer's Market, which lists most of the publishing houses, you'll see precious few that will look at unsolicited work. Some smaller houses may wish to see work by unpublished authors but the major houses aren't really interested. If you're a good enough writer, they figure, you've gotten yourself an agent to represent you. Without an agent, many houses won't even open the envelope containing your work but will simply send it back.

Well, then, how do you get an agent? There are many agents out there, all over the country. The best representation, I feel, is a New York agent, who is in the middle of things in the Big Apple, the publishing center of America.

But before we go further, the question arises–when should you seek representation? My feeling is this–if you're working on your first novel, be patient, and wait for its completion before contacting any agent. Make sure that you can finish your work. If you've not been published, it's better to show as much work as possible. A completed novel is better than a novel consisting of a few chapters. Editors and agents want to see what you can do, and they know, even if the first few chapters show fine work, there's no guarantee that the rest of the novel will live up to the same standard.

Therefore, with your first work, or if you've not been published before, wait to finish the work before going after an agent. This doesn't mean that you should send the agent the entire novel, but that you should be prepared to do this if the agent so wishes. You should send some sample chapters representing the beginning of the work. I would send at least 100 pages and a synopsis of the rest of the book, chapter by chapter. It doesn't have to be a complete outline of everything happening in each chapter, but should give the agent enough information to judge where the work is headed.

Writer's Market will list a number of agents willing to look at work by unpublished writers. Generally, these agents will name the work they have already represented. If an agent does only romances, don't send her or him a serious crime novel. Try and match your work to an agent's interests.

You can take a shot at some of the bigger New York agencies. To find them, simply get ahold of a New York Telephone Yellow Pages. When dealing with major agents, I wouldn't send material to them directly. I would write a query letter describing the novel you've completed, and asking their feelings about seeing some of your work. You can mention that you'd be happy to send 70-100 pages and a synopsis of the rest of the novel. Who knows? You may catch the interest of an agent, who will ask to see your work.

Networking is good for an unpublished writer. He or she may go to a writer's conference and meet literary agents there, or meet published writers who will be glad to suggest an agent if they feel his or her work is strong enough for publication. Be aware of what is going on in local universities and colleges. Often there will be a writer's conference of some sort. Go and meet agents and published writers in this way. Get some names and some recommendations. This is a good way to open doors.

Another way is to get short stories published, even in the smaller magazines. Agents are always on the lookout for fresh talent and some religiously read these periodicals, looking for a new exciting writer. The student who had published close to twenty stories that I mentioned in a previous section, had a major agent contact him after one of his stories was published.

If you can't get a New York agent but can get a smaller agency or even a one-man agency somewhere in America to represent you, take a shot with this agent. He or she will be able to submit your work to various publishing houses, and once it's there, it's up to an editor to take or reject the work. That's the important thing, to get your novel to an editor who can make some sort of decision about it. He or she may not be able to accept it alone, but may kick it upstairs to a more senior editor. Then you've got a good chance to get that novel published.

An agent usually takes ten or fifteen percent of all monies earned by the book as his or her commission. Fifteen percent is becoming the norm, and is what you should expect to pay as a commission. If you are accepted as a client, I would suggest not signing a contract with the agent, except for a short, limited period of six months to a year. Even a year might be much, but if the agent insists on this time period and you have confidence that he or she has faith in the novel, sign the contract.

It has been my experience that an agent will "love" your work until the rejection letters start coming in. While you may have faith in the work, the agent may quickly lose interest. He or she may feel they're wasting time and money sending out the novel after a number of rejections, and may just flat out lose faith in the novel and you as a writer. If this is the case, you don't want to be stuck on a three-year contract with someone who's shoved your manuscript into a drawer for the duration of the contract.

The best way to deal with the agent is by a handshake or an oral agreement. Tell him or her that you'll give them sufficient time to send out the manuscript to various publishers, and that you will stick by the agency during this time. If the agent says, "I need at least six months," you can agree verbally. The agent and you should have some sort of bond; don't deal with an agent you don't like, because in the end, you'll suffer. It's most important to keep your feelings open in this regard.

2. Advantages of a First Novel

It's difficult to get published if you've written a serious novel, rather than one strictly appealing to an audience of bestseller readers, who want "escape" in the form of trash. The odds against getting a first novel published are prohibitive, but not impossible. Publishers constantly publish books; that's what they're in business for.

In some ways, the first novel has a better shot than a second novel, written by a published author, which has gone nowhere. Suppose an editor is deciding between your novel, which he likes, and which is an unknown quantity as far as sales go. It may not get off the ground, or it may soar into the bestseller lists. Who knows? On the other hand, he has a second novel by an author whose sales for the first book were in the 3,000 book range. The editor may very well pick your work. The other author hasn't established a good track record; and the expectation for sales may be the same dismal 3,000 copies.

In this day and age, publishers don't carry novelists along, waiting for the big book. They want profits from the getgo. In this respect, a first novel has a better chance of being published if the editor feels it can appeal to a large number of readers, or at least make back the advance plus some profits for the house.

XV

THE BOOK CONTRACT AND ADVANCE

1. The Acceptance

You've written a fine novel and you've put your very soul into it. It's taken over a year to write. You've sacrificed time and family and friends to do this book. You've revised it carefully, often getting up in the middle of the night with fresh insight into a character or situation. Therefore, when you sent it to an agent, you knew in your heart that you'd done everything you could with the work.

The agent you send it to agrees. He wishes to represent you and your novel. You agree to his representation and he starts sending it out to publishers. It's rejected by the first five houses, but some of the rejection letters are encouraging. Editors like the work, but are afraid to take a chance with this serious novel, for reasons of money.

Then, one morning, sitting at work, you get a call from your agent. He tells you that X House has accepted your novel. You sit up straight; are you hearing right? It's true, your agent tells you, but there's one problem. They're offering $7,500 as an advance, and he feels that's not enough.

Immediately, you feel anxious. You want to scream at the agent, take the $7,500, don't blow the deal. Oh God, what if they change their mind? But the publisher won't reject the work for a few thousand dollars more, the agent assures you. He's going to try for $12,500 and will settle for ten grand.

"Are you sure," you say in a choked voice, "are you sure they won't reject it if you ask for more money?"

The agent assures you he knows what he is doing. You're not so sure, but it's out of your hands.

That's one of the advantages of having an agent. He can be calm and dispassionate about your work; he can ask for more money and turn the conversation into a business deal, no more and no less. You can't do this. If you faced the editor at the same publishing house alone, without representation, and she said, "we'll give you an advance of $1,000, but we'll publish the book," you'd be grabbing for the pen to sign the contract. You might have even signed if you were told there'd be no advance, but your novel will be published. You want to see your name on the cover and on the spine of the book. You want to be a published novelist. You want...you want...

After the call from your agent, you're a nervous wreck. Sometimes you have confidence in him, and sometimes, usually in the middle of the night, you wake up, tempted to call him at his home and beg him to take the $7,500 and not jeopardize the deal. It's three in the morning and you lift the receiver, then some kind of sanity prevails. You don't make the call.

A week later, the agent calls again. Oh God, he's blown the deal, you think, when you hear his voice. He doesn't seem to be overjoyed; his affect is flat. You say hello and wait for the bad news.

"I told them $7,500 was out of the question; I asked for $12,500," he says.

"Yes?" You can hardly recognize your own voice.

"They hemmed and hawed; hell, they've made a mint with a couple of their big books, so I pressed on. Well, we made a deal. You're going to get $10,500."

You don't know what to say.

"I expect the contracts after the weekend. As soon as I get them, I'll send them to you to sign by priority mail. I could Fedex them, but there's no real hurry. The book won't be coming out for several months."

You agree that priority mail will be fast enough. You say goodbye, thank him and put down the phone. Your shirt is sticking to you. Jesus, you think, if someone saw me now, Mr. Cool, just a bundle of nerves. A total wreck.

But soon you're whistling a happy tune. Your novel is going to be published, and what's more, the crazy publisher is going to give you money to make your dream come true. They actually pay you to publish your novel. That's the nuttiest thing about this book business.

2. The Book Contract

There's no need to hire a lawyer to look over a book contract, if you have an experienced agent. He or she can advise you properly. Most contracts are standard, with few differences from one to another.

Basically, this is what you're going to be looking for:

a. The size of the advance.

b. When the advance is going to be paid. Usually, half on signing of the contract and the other half upon a completed manuscript acceptable to the publisher. If the novel is already accepted, no problem here.

c. Royalties. The usual royalty arrangement is this; you get 10% of the cover price for the first 5,000 copies, 12 1/2% for the next 5,000 copies sold, and 15% thereafter for all sales. This is for hardcover books.

Expect different arrangements for paperback books. They may run from 6% to 8% for a set number of books, which may be 50,000 or more, and then it kicks up from 6% to 8% or 8% to 10%, which is a high percentage in the world of paperback novels. Many contracts call for a standard percentage, such as 6% or 8%, no matter how many books are sold.

The royalty arrangements aren't set in stone. If you're a writer of blockbusters, the publisher may start you off with 15% from the first hardcover book sold. But if you're a first-time author, expect the standard 10, 12 1/2 and 15% arrangement.

We mentioned the cover price. That's how royalties are determined. If the book is priced at $20, and you get 10%, you get $2 per book. This is so even if a major chain sells the book at a 40% discount for $12. You still get $2 per book, which is 10% of the cover price.

d. Copyright in your name.

e. When the book will be published; usually an outside date is inserted in the contract, with the publisher giving themselves nine months or one year or whatever leeway they're comfortable with.

f. 50% of paperback rights go to you, the other half to the publisher. So, if the paperback rights are sold for $60,000, you get $30,000. The same percentage is usual for book club rights.

g. 100% of movie rights to you. This is standard, which means if the book is sold to the movies for a million bucks, it's all yours, kid.

h. Should the book go out of print, you have reversionary rights to the work. Let's assume the book is published in March, 1997 and there is one printing only, of 10,000. The sales end up being 8,575, and there is no second printing.

The book is eventually remaindered; that is, the extra unsold copies are reduced drastically in price and given to remainder houses or large bookstore chains to be sold for $3.95 instead of the original $19.95. The editor should notify you of the remaindering of the book, and offer to sell you copies at a greatly reduced price, perhaps $1 or $2 per book.

Now enter reversionary rights. If you notify the company in writing that you wish them to reprint the book, and they don't agree to do so, after six months, the rights to the book revert to you. In essence, you own the book again and can do what you want with it.

Normally, with a book out of print, a simple letter asking for the reversionary rights will be enough. Unless the publisher has other plans for the book, you'll get your rights back by letter.

i. You should get ten free copies of the book on publication.

There will be other clauses in the standard contract, covering all sorts of eventualities, but again, if you have an experienced agent, there will be no problem in signing the contract and being protected as an author.

As the publishing world moves into the electronic age, there will be other possible rights that can be negotiated, such as putting the book on audio tape, CD Roms of the work, and so forth. Many of these rights are negotiable. Because of these complications, I strongly suggest that you join The Author's Guild.

3. The Author's Guild

The Author's Guild is an organization exclusively devoted to writers and their interests. They have fought for authors on many fronts, such as enhanced copyright protection by Congress, and more liberal contracts by publishers. It is the oldest and largest association of published authors in the United States.

It is an organization well worth joining. In addition to a bulletin issued several times a year giving information on members making news, news about publishers, legal matters concerning authors, a bulletin board for members, it offers membership assistance in both legal and professional matters. They are especially helpful with information concerning book contracts.

The eligibility requirements are as follows: Any author may join the Guild who has had a book published by an established American publisher within the last seven years; has had three works of fiction or nonfiction published by a periodical of general circulation within the past 18 months; or, in the opinion of the Membership Committee, is entitled to a membership due to his or her professional standing. Any author who has a contract with a publisher for a work not yet published may join the Guild as an Associate Member. The first year's dues are $90.

The Author's Guild is located at 330 West 42nd Street, 29th floor, New York, NY 10036.

4. Vanity Presses

A vanity press is a publishing house that charges an author to publish his book. In other words, the writer bears all the expense in the publication process. This can add up to significant money, often in the thousands of dollars for a limited run of 1,000 or 2,000 copies.

If your work is rejected, and you can't seem to get a publisher for your novel, the vanity press route may sound seductive. After all, you'll have a book with your name on the cover as author. However, our best advice is this–don't use a vanity press. There are several good reasons for my advice.

First of all, you're paying to have a book published. This is strictly an amateurish move, telling the world that you don't have the talent to get a publisher to accept your novel. Anyone who sees a vanity press novel knows it is inferior work, otherwise the author wouldn't have to pay to get the novel printed.

Secondly, suppose you get 2,000 copies of your novel printed by a vanity press. What are you going to do with the copies? A number of these presses, as part of the inducement to use them, announce that they will help with the distribution of the novel. Now, distributing a novel or any published book is key to its success. Established publishers (not vanity presses) have resources for distribution, either through their own salesmen, or companies like Ingram or Baker and Taylor. What a vanity press will do is simply send out some copies to chains, asking them to purchase the novel.

No book chain will do this. Their most difficult sell is a novel that isn't a bestseller. Certainly they won't handle a novel that is published by a vanity press. So, forget about distribution. You can stuff the books in your garage and sell a couple to friends and relatives, and that's about it. And pay off the loan you took to publish the book.

Thirdly, you won't get reviewed. No newspaper or magazine is going to review a vanity press novel. Why not? For one thing, suppose they review it. Where is the public going to find the book? In your living room, stacked against a wall? If the book isn't out in the marketplace, it won't be reviewed.

Finally, by selling out to a vanity press, you're giving up being a writer of serious work. It's better to have an unpublished manuscript in the closet than have a book no one wants to read in print. Showing it to family or friends might impress the few who don't read anyway, and wouldn't know the difference between a self-published book and a microwave oven.

If you can't get your novel published, it may be that it just isn't good enough, or you haven't given it your best shot. Or that the publishing world doesn't recognize your talent. That's a possibility. If your work is good enough, someone somewhere will recognize your skill and power as a writer. A publishing house might not want to publish this particular novel but would be interested in seeing future work.

There may come a point where the novel has been rejected by a dozen publishers and the agent feels its useless to send it out to any more houses. Then you have to make a decision, whether to seek another agent or take back the novel. But whatever decision you make, it shouldn't include publishing the novel at your own expense.

When people tell me about all the garbage that's out in the bookstores, I tell them that it's the best the publishers get. Even though your writing may be better than that which is being published today, you must realize that the writing and publishing world is a subjective one, and sometimes good work just doesn't get published. Don't give up. Keep writing. If you're good enough, you'll break through eventually.

XVI

SOME FINAL THOUGHTS

Throughout this work, I've tried to give practical advice to would-be and beginning writers, from the viewpoint of a writer who has been in the trenches. In my dealings with editors, agents and publishers, I learned a great deal about the publishing business, and more importantly, about myself.

To be a writer is more than being someone who puts words on blank sheets. It is an attitude, a way of looking at the world and at yourself, that will set you apart from those who will never share the joy and yes, the agony of completing a work, whether it be a short story or novel.

I have, in this work, tried to share my feelings about the profession. I have tried to show that to be a writer is to open yourself up to all human experiences, to understand, and not to judge, to wonder and not to moralize. If you are on a crusade, then write tracts or run for office. If you are interested in the human spirit, in the feelings that we all share, then write fiction.

Do the very best you can. I repeat this advice. Write the truth as you best know it. Create characters that live and breathe, put them in situations where they move and at times astonish the reader and yourself. If you do all this, if you also have a talent, then to my mind you're a success whether or not you get published. If you strive and fail, and do the best you can do, who can not but admire you for the effort. The process of writing is the joy of writing; finishing the novel is the capstone of your work, and getting published but the icing on the cake.

Authors Discussed in this Book

(Bold letters indicate author is quoted)

Mann, Thomas
Marlowe, Christopher
McCullers, Carson
Melville, Herman
Mitchell, Margaret
Nabokov, Vladimir
Oates, Joyce Carol
O'Connor, Flannery
Olsen, Tillie
Orton, Joe
Orwell, George
Porter, Katherine Ann
Powers, Tim
Proust, Marcel
Remarque, Erich Maria
Roth, Philip
Salas, Floyd
Salinger, J.D.
Saroyan, William
Santayana, George
Sayers, Dorothy
Shakespeare, William
Sheldon, Sidney

Silberstang, Edwin
Simenon, Georges
Sinclair, Upton
Spenser, Edmund
Stein, Gertrude
Steinbeck, John
Stendhal (Marie Henri Beyle)
Talese, Gay
Thackery, William Makepeace
Thomas, Dylan
Thompson, Hunter
Thoreau, Henry
Tolstoi, Leo
Trevor, William
Turgenev, Ivan
Twain, Mark
Updike, John
Uston, Ken
Williams, Tennessee
Wilner, Herbert
Wolfe, Thomas
Wolfe, Tom
Yeats, William Butler